TROILUS AND CRESSIDA

The RSC Shakespeare

Edited by Jonathan Bate and Eric Rasmussen

Chief Associate Editors: Héloïse Sénéchal and Jan Sewell

Associate Editors: Trey Jansen, Eleanor Lowe, Lucy Munro,
Dee Anna Phares

Troilus and Cressida

Textual editing: Eric Rasmussen

Introduction and Shakespeare's Career in the Theater: Jonathan Bate

Commentary: Christopher Campbell and Héloïse Sénéchal

Scene-by-Scene Analysis: Esme Miskimmin

In Performance: Jan Sewell (RSC stagings) and Peter Kirwan (overview)

The Director's Cut (interviews by Jonathan Bate and Kevin Wright):
Michael Boyd and Trevor Nunn

The RSC Shakespeare

William Shakespeare

TROILUS AND CRESSIDA

Edited by Jonathan Bate and Eric Rasmussen

Introduction by Jonathan Bate

The Modern Library
New York

2010 Modern Library Paperback Edition

Copyright © 2007, 2010 by The Royal Shakespeare Company

Published in the United States by Modern Library, an imprint of
The Random House Publishing Group, a division of
Random House, Inc., New York.

The version of *Troilus and Cressida* and the corresponding footnotes
that appear in this volume were originally published in *William Shakespeare:
Complete Works,* edited by Jonathan Bate and Eric Rasmussen, published
in 2007 by Modern Library, an imprint of The Random House
Publishing Group, a division of Random House, Inc.

ISBN 978-0-8129-6931-3

Printed in the United States of America

www.modernlibrary.com

2 4 6 8 9 7 5 3 1

CONTENTS

INTRODUCTION

TRAGICAL-COMICAL-HISTORICAL?

Troilus and Cressida perhaps reveals more of Shakespeare's mature mind at work than any of the other plays. It is highly intelligent, rich in rhetorical complexity and linguistic invention, mentally rigorous, morally skeptical, sexually charged, full of dangerous intellectual and political energy, markedly unpleasant. Most characteristically of all, it is impossible to characterize generically, being at once comedy, tragedy, history, and satire.

It was written toward the end of Shakespeare's great run of comedies. In the First Folio of his collected plays, for reasons of licensing and as a result of printing problems, *Troilus and Cressida* was a last-minute addition. It arrived so belatedly that it is absent from the contents list, and indeed some early copies were published without it. The editors managed to squeeze it in between the histories and the tragedies, which is a fitting place: it is a tragedy in that the Trojan War, the subject of Homer's *Iliad*, was Western tragedy's foundational theme, but it had been published independently in Quarto format in 1609 as *The Famous History of Troilus and Cresseid*, a title emphasizing a medieval romance accretion to the classical epic tale. A prefatory epistle in some copies of the Quarto performs a delicate balancing act, acknowledging that the play is "passing full of the palm comical," but emphasizing its serious literary content and praising Shakespeare's works for being "so framed to the life that they serve for the most common commentaries of all the actions of our lives."

The critical reception of the play has long been bedeviled by the difficulty of establishing its genre. The early nineteenth-century German poet Heinrich Heine remarked that it was neither comedy nor tragedy in the usual sense and that it accordingly could not be judged by received standards of criticism. At the end of the nineteenth century, a new designation provided a way out of the generic impasse: "problem play." The term arose in response to the innovative drama that emerged at that time as part of a wider movement toward realism in the arts. It was first used with respect to plays by dramatists such as Henrik Ibsen that approached contentious social issues via debates between the characters on stage, each of whom stood for a particular point of view. Whether the subject was the confinement of women in marriage (*A Doll's House*, 1879), the visitation of the sexual sins of the father upon the son (*Ghosts*, 1882), or the strong idealist pitched against petit bourgeois self-interest (*An Enemy of the People*, 1882), Ibsen was master of the drama of social problems. In the British theater, George Bernard Shaw followed in his wake. So it was that in *Shakespeare and His Predecessors* (1896), the critic F. S. Boas suggested that a group of Shakespeare's middle-period works had characteristics similar to those of the Ibsenesque problem play. His prime examples were *Troilus and Cressida* together with the contemporaneously written bitter comedies (later sometimes called "dark" comedies), *All's Well That Ends Well* and *Measure for Measure*: "All these dramas introduce us into highly artificial societies, whose civilization is ripe unto rottenness . . . throughout these plays we move along dim untrodden paths, and at the close our feeling is neither of simple joy nor pain; we are excited, fascinated, perplexed, for the issues raised preclude a completely satisfactory outcome."

"In such unpopular plays as *All's Well*, *Measure for Measure* and *Troilus and Cressida*, we find [Shakespeare] ready and willing to start at the twentieth century if only the seventeenth century would let him": this is Shaw in the "Preface, Mainly about Myself" in his *Plays Unpleasant*, a collection of three of his dramas about social hypocrisy and the corrupting effect of money, first published in 1898. The best of those plays is about prostitution (*Mrs Warren's Profession*), while the "problem" at the center of *All's Well* and *Measure for Measure* turns on a "bed trick" in which a man thinks he is sleeping with one woman when it is really another. In short, then, to say that *Troilus and Cressida* was a "problem" play was to say—as one couldn't spell out specifically in the late Victorian era—that it was a play about sex.

Critics in the first half of the twentieth century remained somewhat coy about admitting this. There was much talk of how the play was filled with cynicism and loathing. Thus Mark van Doren, an urbane American critic, writing in 1939:

> The style of *Troilus and Cressida* is loud, brassy, and abandoned. The world which Chaucer has left so tenderly intact explodes as if a mine had been touched off beneath it, while a host of characters, conceived partly in doubt and partly in disgust, rave at the tops of their never modulated voices. All of them are angry, all of them are distrustful and mendacious; and the tone of each is hardened to rasping by some unmotivated irritation.[1]

All true, but is the "irritation" really unmotivated? After all, the Trojan War itself was motivated by the abduction (seduction? rape?) of Helen by Paris. Helen is the traditional embodiment of sex on legs. She provokes desire, pride, possessiveness, jealousy, disgust, bitterness, the sense of affronted honor: exactly the complex of emotions that runs through the play. In *Romeo and Juliet* the romantic lovers are pitted against the world around them. The love of Troilus and Cressida, by contrast, may have its romantic moments, but the play is utterly realistic about how their relationship does not escape the cruelty, irrationality, sordidness, selfishness, and pain that is everywhere else on the battlefield of Troy.

Some scholars have wrongly inferred from certain phrases in the Quarto preface (which is reproduced at the beginning of our textual notes) that the play was written solely for private performance, perhaps for a sophisticated audience of student lawyers at the Inns of Court, who would have appreciated its vein of formal debate and rhetorical elaboration. But the language of Pandarus, with its direct addresses to "tongue-tied maidens," "sisters of the door-hold trade," and "Winchester geese" (meaning Southwark prostitutes), implies the social and sexual mix of the Globe audience, not the male exclusivity of the Inns of Court. There is no reason to doubt that the play was, in the words of the title page of other copies of the Quarto, "acted by the King's Majesties Servants at the Globe." The suggestion that *Troilus* is somehow too intellectual for the public playhouse, that it was written for elite "private" taste, is mere condescension. Plenty of other Globe plays by Shakespeare and his contemporaries stretch the intellectual sinews while simultaneously appealing to the humor of the privy and the bedroom. At the same time, there is no doubt that the sensibility expressed in the play bears a resemblance to that of such lawyer-dramatists as John Marston, who were educated in the Inns of Court and came to prominence in the theater world in the first years of the seventeenth century:

> A pattern of *misrule* prevails—political as well as personal, parodies of authority in mock-courts and governments . . . Linguistic misrule, including double entendres, scatology, and scurrility, also recurs, along with paradox and mock-encomia . . . *Mock-rhetoric* . . . is heard . . . As rhetorical order seems inverted, forms of reason are stood on their head . . . *Mock-chivalry* occurs . . . *Social manners* are reflected parodically . . . *Academic emphases* recur . . . *Law references*, as well as mock-legalisms, recur.[2]

Despairing of whether to call it history, comedy, or tragedy, many twentieth-century critics, with some justification, regarded *Troilus and Cressida* as a satire, very much in the mode of writers such as Marston. The military plot concerning Achilles, Agamemnon, Ajax, Hector, and the rest is derived primarily from Homer and his descendants, most notably George Chapman's 1598 translation of seven books of *The Iliad* into elevated English verse. The love plot concerning Troilus and Cressida, the efforts of Pandarus to bring them together, and the infidelity of Cressida in the Greek camp, is derived primarily from Chaucer's *Troilus and Criseyde*. The handling of each plot is equally cynical. In its love plot the play is an anti-romance, while in its martial plot it is an anti-epic. In his anti-heroic representation of the exemplary heroes of the Trojan War, Shakespeare undermines both the style and the attitudes of Chapman's recent translation of Homer. The prologue speaks in high Chapmanesque style of "princes orgulous," "crownets regal," "strong immures," and "warlike freightage," but the action begins with Troilus saying "I'll unarm again" and going on to describe himself as "weaker than a woman's tear . . . Less valiant than the virgin in the night." The admission of a "feminine" language strips all glamour from the male code of war. But then the code of love is submitted to a similar pummeling: Pandarus compares the art of love to breadmaking, with its progression from grinding to bolting to kneading to leavening to cooling. Troilus idealizes his love in courtly language, but at the same time compares his desire to a wound, speaking of "the open ulcer of my heart."

Scabs, pus, and running sores ooze through the play, while the foul-mouthed Thersites proves to be the truest commentator on the war. In the second scene we are given a first account of Hector, traditionally the most noble of heroes. Here, however, he is reported to be wrathful, chiding his devoted wife Andromache and striking his armorer. An honorable man should respect his wife and servants: the honor of Hector is thus questioned from the start. There is a clear progression from the reported striking of the armorer to Hector's ignominious end, in which he is killed because of an act of vanity: he has unarmed himself in order to put on the alluring golden armor of a slain warrior. Our first image of Ajax, another magnificent hero in Homer, is yet one more debunking. "They say he is a very man *per se,* / And stands alone," says Alexander: this sounds like the glorious self-sufficiency of the epic hero. "So do all men / Unless they are drunk, sick, or have no legs," replies Cressida: "stands alone" is taken literally and thus reduced to ignobility. And, sure enough, Ajax does prove to be a singularly unheroic blockhead. As for the great Achilles, he has withdrawn from the battle and is camping around in his tent with his gay lover, Patroclus, acting out parodies of the inflated mannerisms of the other Greek generals.

"WHAT'S AUGHT BUT AS 'TIS VALUED?"

Again and again, *Troilus and Cressida* reveals the discrepancy between the polished surface that is projected by a value system, whether the heroic code of war or the idea of courtly love, and the tawdry reality beneath. At a philosophical level, the effect of this is deeply troubling: it is to question whether there can be such a thing as an absolute moral value.

In a purposeful anachronism during the debate about whether or not the war is worth fighting, Trojan man of action Hector appeals to the Greek thinker who was regarded in Shakespeare's time as the father of moral philosophy: having begun by commending the argumentative powers of his brothers Troilus and Paris, Hector adds that they have reasoned "superficially, not much / Unlike young men, whom Aristotle thought / Unfit to hear moral philosophy." To the modern ear, the language is typically dense and frustrating. Why can't Hector say "like young men," we wonder, instead of "not much" / brief pause for the end of the verse line / "Unlike young men"? Trust Shakespeare to prefer "not unlike" to mere "like." The flow of argument through the play is like a serpentine river, twisting and turning with double negatives, retractions, qualifications, hypothetical cases, generalizations exploded by particular instances. The modern equivalent is the tortured language of legal opinions and government regulations, which is perhaps why the play is sometimes considered to have been a showpiece for lawyers. But we need to remember that rhetoric—the construction of elaborate edifices of argument that are expounded *pro* and *contra* with both words and sentence structures arranged in highly complex ways—was the absolute staple of each long day's work in the Elizabethan grammar school classroom. Anyone in Shakespeare's original audience with a few years' formal education would have had their ears tuned to the mode of speaking that characterizes the formal debates in the respective council scenes of the Trojans and Greeks. And for some in the audience who lacked a formal education—women among them—the theater was an alternative classroom, a place to learn the art of manipulating words without the burden of having to do so in Latin.

Motivating the expansion of the grammar school network in sixteenth-century England was the educational revolution known to scholars as "humanism." The purpose of study was not only to achieve a command of the linguistic arts, but also to be inspired to virtue by the example of the ancient heroes: to learn integrity from Hector, fortitude from Andromache, courage from Achilles, leadership from Agamemnon, strength from Ajax, wisdom from Ulysses, and so forth. It is this moral dimension that the play systematically strips away. The mythic heroes are resolutely anti-heroic. The idea that manliness can be proved in battle is subverted by the voice of Thersites. Thus when Menelaus and Paris, great rivals in Helen's love, meet in single combat: "The cuckold and the cuckold-maker are at it. / Now, bull! Now, dog!" Here, "at it" suggests sexual congress as well as fighting, while "bull" and "dog" reduce the grandeur of the plain of Troy to the baying confines of the baiting ring (on London's Bankside, theater and bearbaiting shared the same arenas). As Thersites lances martial values, so the leering Pandarus reduces love to sex: coming to Troilus and Cressida after they have spent the night together for the first time, he addresses his niece as if she were synonymous with her sexual parts, battered and chafed by the repeated assaults of Troilus' member ("How go maidenheads? . . . Ah, poor *chipochia*! Hast not slept tonight? Would he not—a naughty man— let it sleep?"). Hector quotes Aristotle as saying that "young men" are shallow in the art of moral philosophy. The play seems to reply that young men will be young men: they will squabble and sulk, they will argue for the sake of it and swear till the air is blue, they thrive on anger and violence. And old men are no better: they are petulant and manipulative, prurient and self-interested. As for women, Andromache makes but a fleeting appearance, Cassandra is no more than the voice of doom, Helen is not so much the most beautiful woman in the world as one half of a comic double act with Pandarus, and Cressida knows that her only means of survival is to use her sexuality.

Moral philosophy is not a fixed point of reference. It is itself interrogated and found wanting. Hector attempts to distinguish between the dangers of actions based on emotion ("the hot passion of distempered blood") and the propriety of those based on reason ("a free determination / 'Twixt right and wrong"). But in the case of the Trojan War, right and wrong cannot be judged objectively: "What's aught but as 'tis valued?" asks Troilus. Hector tries to maintain the case that value exists above "particular will," but the play as a whole—with its constant counterpointing of Trojan and Greek, battlefield and bedroom, high rhetoric and low bawdyness—proposes that all moral judgments are relative. It is Ulysses who makes this point most eloquently: a man or an action can only be judged "by reflection, / As when his virtues shining upon others / Heat them and they retort that heat again / To the first giver." This argument is articulated as part of a cunning scheme to persuade Achilles to switch back from the role of Patroclus' effeminate lover to the Greek army's most masculine warrior: the image of the bullish Ajax being presented as top soldier will retort on Achilles and make him strive to regain his military preeminence.

Ulysses' speech about the need for society to maintain a strict hierarchical order or "degree" is part of the same strategy. He argues that one of the causes of the untuning of degree in the Greek camp is that their exemplary warrior Achilles is sulking in his tent when he should be in the appropriate place for an exemplary warrior, namely on the battlefield. But the method he proposes by which Achilles is to be restored to his proper place is itself a disruption of degree. Hector has issued a challenge to single combat. Degree should dictate that Hector's equal on the Greek side, Achilles, is put forward, but Ulysses proposes Ajax instead, thus snubbing Achilles and provoking him into rejoining the army. Ulysses then achieves his end by rigging an election. Even in the midst of a rhetorically powerful vision of the chaos that ensues when the moral and social order are not upheld, Ulysses lets slip his knowledge of the relativity of value. "Take but degree away,"

> And the rude son should strike his father dead:
> Force should be right, or rather, right and wrong,
> Between whose endless jar justice resides,
> Should lose their names, and so should justice too.
> Then everything includes itself in power,
> Power into will, will into appetite,
> And appetite, an universal wolf,
> So doubly seconded with will and power,
> Must make perforce an universal prey,
> And last eat up himself. . . .

In the very act of warning that "right and wrong" will "lose their names" if "degree" is not observed, Ulysses adds parenthetically that justice resides not inherently on the side of right, as one would expect it to, but rather in the "endless jar" between right and wrong.

The play as a whole is a demonstration that order, moral and social, is not a predetermined value system answerable to a harmonious cosmic design, but rather a process, an endless debate and negotiation of terms, in which reason and judgment cannot be separated from appetite and will.

So it is that two kinds of absolute statement are juxtaposed against each other. On the one hand, aspirations to truth and fixity: "True swains in love shall in the world to come / Approve their truths by Troilus . . . As truth's authentic author to be cited, / 'As true as Troilus' shall crown up the verse." And on the other, cynical reductions to the lowest common denominator of the body: "Here is such patchery, such juggling and such knavery! All the argument is a cuckold and a whore, a good quarrel to draw emulations, factions and bleed to death upon. Now, the dry serpigo on the subject, and war and lechery confound all!"

"Hector is dead, there is no more to say": that is how a tragedy ought to end. But having said that line, Troilus says "Stay yet." Shakespeare just won't stop arguing with himself. If there is a victor in these endless jars, it is the voice of the cynical commentators, Thersites and Pandarus. The latter gets the last word, addressing the theater audience in a broken sonnet that is a symptom of this play's fragmented world.

Troilus disintegrates because of the incompatibility between his mental image of Cressida and what he sees of her in the Greek camp when she has become Diomedes' mistress: "This is and is not Cressid." The sight causes him to believe that the whole rationality of the world has collapsed and "The bonds of heaven are slipped, dissolved, and loosed." He has not, however, seen Cressida brutally manhandled and kissed, treated like a piece of meat, on her arrival in the camp. Shakespeare's point in bringing Troilus to "madness of discourse" is not to make a moral judgment about Cressida—you can't help feeling that he admires her improvisational skills and the way in which she maintains linguistic dignity even as her body is taken by another man—but rather to strip away the illusion that bodily beauty and strength are signs of inner grace and greatness. The symbolic figure that comes closest to the rotten core of the play is that knight in sumptuous armor who is pursued by Hector. He is so fair without, but what does Hector find within? A "Most putrefied core," a decaying human body.

THE CRITICS DEBATE

A play of debate, *Troilus and Cressida* has stimulated exceptionally lively literary critical debate in the age of professionalized Shakespeare studies.

The sense of a collapsed moral order, a world in ruins, gave the play special force in the wake of the First World War, which was when it first truly established its place in the theatrical repertoire, and again in the Second World War. In a book called *The Frontiers of Drama*, its preface dated January 1945, the critic Una Ellis-Fermor wrote apropos of *Troilus* that "our actual experience of disintegration and disruption, so unlike that of any age between, has thrown fresh light upon the nature and foundations of what we call civilization; prospects once mercifully rare are now common and familiar, and much that has not, in the interval, been generally forced upon the imagination, now lies upon the common road."

It was also during the Second World War that E. M. W. Tillyard published his influential *The Elizabethan World Picture* (1942), in which Ulysses' oration on "degree" was held up as the epitome of the "order" that Shakespeare advocated or at least craved. It is obvious from the perspective of historical distance that Tillyard's belief in the Elizabethans' nostalgia for a more settled medieval world order was his own yearning for the stability that had been destroyed by Nazi ideology and the war. Modern critics are accordingly brusque in their dismissal of Tillyard's reading of Ulysses' speech as a Shakespearean prescription for society:

Ulysses' great oration on order is no better than Agamemnon's and Nestor's pompous, bumbling efforts to speak as kings . . . the *topoi* in *Troilus and Cressida* call attention to the fundamental commonplaceness of Ulysses' mind—*this* is the wily Ulysses, who spent ten years outwitting his enemies, human, divine, monstrous, and natural, here reduced to a version of

Gloucester or Polonius, mouthing the unexamined platitudes of a doctrine of order which the play itself constantly subverts.[3]

The word "subversion" is everywhere in modern criticism of the play. Thersites has taken center stage:

> Thersites is a malevolent force, a type of primal hatred and pride, and what Shakespeare has done is to take the conventional character of the satirist and strip away his pretensions to being a moral healer and intensify his basic loathing of all mankind. In Thersites we are very close to those basic drives and outlook which give rise to satire, and which in this case are not redirected by any extraneous moral considerations or glossed over by any pretension to justice and honesty.[4]

The idea that the play subverts all prior moral certainties has meant that modern critics have been rather more sympathetic to the character of Cressida than their predecessors were. In a pioneering lecture, the Cambridge critic A. P. Rossiter suggested that

> Cressida is *not* simply a little harlot; and, though admittedly "designing," is too frail to stick to her design. Her passion is quite genuine . . . so is her grief at her separation from Troilus. Only nothing is deep rooted in her . . . Thersites has the last word on her; but she is only the feminine of the rest of them. They *all* fancy or pretend they are being or doing one thing, whereas they are shown up as something quite different: something which egoism, or lack of moral insight, prevents their recognizing.[5]

Around the same time, her strength of character was praised in Polish critic Jan Kott's influential book, *Shakespeare Our Contemporary*:

> Cressida is one of the most amazing Shakespearian characters . . . She is cynical, or rather would-be cynical . . . She is bitter and ironic. She is passionate, afraid of her passion and

ashamed to admit it. She is even more afraid of feelings. She distrusts herself. She is our contemporary because of this self-distrust, reserve, and need of self-analysis. She defends herself by irony.[6]

The play as a whole is "our contemporary," it has frequently been argued, because of its relentless exposure of the relativity of all values:

> The association of fame and glory and the like with the rape of Helen, and the attempt to make that rape seem more glamorous by persisting in fighting for it, is recognized by Hector to be pure illusion . . . The Trojans choose the illusion of fame and glory, knowing it to be an illusion, and knowing that Helen herself is not the real motive for fighting.[7]

Masculine reputation is reduced to mere "opinion":

> Words such as "worthy," "glory," "fame," "merit," "esteem," "estimate," "estimation," "value," "cost," "honour" are everywhere. And "opinion" occurs ten times, far more than in any other Shakespeare play. It is commonplace . . . that reputation, honor, fame, and all the rest depend on opinion. Opinion is what people say. In the matter of reputation, it is what other people say about you. One cannot have fame or glory by one's own inward knowledge; it has to come from the mouths of others, not from within.[8]

With the breakdown of hierarchy that is the subject of this play, the consequences predicted by Ulysses . . . are exactly fulfilled: the traditional bonds that once defined human relations are replaced by "appetite . . . will and power" . . . Proper relationship is destroyed, and the ethics of the marketplace . . . govern men's and women's dealings with one another . . . The disturbance of the hierarchical order leaves the individual not autonomous and free, but bound to definition by relation of a different, more destructive sort. Deprived of the legitimate sanctions of hierarchy, the individual must create his or her own value, an appearance to please the beholding eye, in what is essentially a selling of the self.[9]

A related aspect of the play that has especially appealed to modern criticism has been its literary self-consciousness. Not only received moral values, but also received myths, stories, and literary characterizations are called into question:

> The play also persistently calls attention to its intertextuality, its anachronicity, its dependence upon a prodigious literary and rhetorical legacy. Within Shakespeare's dramatization of familiar legend, a vast encyclopedia of citation is embedded. The myth, the Matter of Troy, the classical topos, the set piece, the commonplace, the cliché, the name that has become a concept; references to books, texts, representations, figures of rhetoric—all these are on display as though to insist on the text's derivative status.[10]

The ironic retelling of a familiar story undermines the preconceptions created by cultural tradition. Whereas previous versions of the Troy legend turned the story to ethical account, Shakespeare declined to do so. In his thoroughgoing work of *demythologizing*, the classical heroes fail to live up to their literary and historic identities:

> The whole play carries an element of general parody in relation to the grand Homeric legend of the Trojan war, as the heroes of that are displayed in the fumbling and insecure postures of Shakespeare's characters . . . Shakespeare also . . . establishes and exploits a dislocation of character from role, and a discontinuity between speech and action in, for example, the presentation of Ajax, or of Troilus, whose grand rhetoric as lover is comically exploded by the matter-of-fact practicality of Pandarus.[11]

Whereas classical culture had idealized male bonds and male bodies, Shakespeare's play diminishes and sexualizes them:

What we see as Achilles stalks Hector, what we hear as he speaks, is a violent parody of a lover's blazon [in which the body is itemized] . . . Seen in the terms that Achilles himself provides, the slaughter of Hector becomes an act of sexual consummation, a homosexual gang rape that Achilles and his Myrmidons carry out on their unarmed victim . . . Thersites derides this coupling of two males, not in moral terms, however, but in political terms. He sees it all as a matter of one man's power over another. A "varlet" is primarily a social, not a moral, inferior. Patroclus deserves insults, not because he is morally wrong, but because he willingly accepts an unmanly, passive role: he is Achilles' "masculine whore."[12]

The evolution of critical responses to the play is clearly seen in changing attitudes to the two camps. For G. Wilson Knight, writing in the 1930s,

The Trojan party stands for human beauty and worth, the Greek party for the bestial and stupid elements of man, the barren stagnancy of intellect divorced from action, and the criticism which exposes these things with jeers. The atmospheres of the two opposing camps are thus strongly contrasted, and the handing over of Cressida to the Greeks . . . has thus a symbolic suggestion . . . Among [the Trojans] we find love and honour of parents, humour, conviviality, patriotism: all which are lacking among the Greeks. The Trojans remain firm in their mutual support. Their cause is worthy, if only because they believe in it. They speak glittering words of honour, generosity, bravery, love. Here is a strange and happy contrast with the shadowed world of the Greek camp, where all seems stagnant, decadent, paralysed. Troy is a world breathing the air of medieval, storied romance; the Greek camp exists on that of Renaissance satire and disillusion.[13]

Jan Kott in the 1960s retains the neat opposition, but suggests that the idealizing, "medieval" values of the Trojans are regarded as outdated:

The Greeks are down-to-earth, heavy and brutal. They know that the war is being fought over a cuckold and a hussy, and they do not have to make themselves believe that they die for the sake of loyalty and honour. They are part of another, new world . . . The Trojans insist on their ridiculous absolutes and a medieval code of combat. They are anachronistic.[14]

By the 1990s, the sharp distinction has collapsed altogether. Indeed, Greek language is seen to be Trojan and Trojan to be Greek:

The Greek camp, taking its identity from Homer, is an all-male world dominated by an ethic of honor and combat; the Trojan camp, inspired by Chaucer and other romance writers, is a courtly world devoted to an ethic of chivalric love. This geo-graphical division, which almost suggests a gender distinction between the male/Greek and female/Trojan, effects a curious dislocation of rhetoric: imagery of battle shapes the experience of love in the Trojan camp; imagery of love and courtship col-ors the depiction of combat and male rivalry in the Greek camp.[15]

The play works out in the Trojan scenes the arbitrariness and hollowness of the two most valued aristocratic codes of the Elizabethan court, romance and chivalry. Even Hector, who is the least satirized, most heroic character in the play, succumbs to the corrosive dynamics of the drama when, quite against his careful Aristotelian ethical argument, he advocates keeping Helen and continuing the war. The elaborate chivalry of the Trojan interactions with the Greeks seems simply ridiculous in the face of the war's material death and destruction.[16]

Wherever there is war and debate about the rights and wrongs of going to war, *Troilus and Cressida* will be a living play. Sadly, that means it will go on living as long as human society.

Shakespeare endures through history. He illuminates later times as well as his own. He helps us to understand the human condition. But he cannot do this without a good text of the plays. Without editions there would be no Shakespeare. That is why every twenty years or so throughout the last three centuries there has been a major new edition of his complete works. One aspect of editing is the process of keeping the texts up to date—modernizing the spelling, punctuation, and typography (though not, of course, the actual words), providing explanatory notes in the light of changing educational practices (a generation ago, most of Shakespeare's classical and biblical allusions could be assumed to be generally understood, but now they can't).

Because Shakespeare did not personally oversee the publication of his plays, editors also have to make decisions about the relative authority of the early printed editions. Half of the sum of his plays only appeared posthumously, in the elaborately produced First Folio text of 1623, the original "Complete Works" prepared for the press by Shakespeare's fellow actors, the people who knew the plays better than anyone else. The other half had appeared in print in his lifetime, in the more compact and cheaper form of "Quarto" editions, some of which reproduced good quality texts, others of which were to a greater or lesser degree garbled and error-strewn. In the case of a few plays there are hundreds of differences between the Quarto and Folio editions, some of them far from trivial. *Troilus and Cressida* comes into the latter category. Editors accordingly have to decide whether to base their text on the Quarto, the Folio, or some combination of the two.

If you look at printers' handbooks from the age of Shakespeare, you quickly discover that one of the first rules was that, whenever possible, compositors were recommended to set their type from existing printed books rather than manuscripts. This was the age before mechanical typesetting, where each individual letter had to be picked out by hand from the compositor's case and placed on a stick (upside down and back to front) before being laid on the press. It was an age of murky rushlight and of manuscripts written in a secretary hand that had dozens of different, hard-to-decipher forms. Printers' lives were a lot easier when they were reprinting existing books rather than struggling with handwritten copy. Easily the quickest way to have created the First Folio would have been simply to reprint those eighteen plays that had already appeared in Quarto and only work from manuscript on the other eighteen.

But that is not what happened. Whenever Quartos were used, playhouse "promptbooks" were also consulted and stage directions copied in from them. And in the case of several major plays where a reasonably well-printed Quarto was available, *Troilus* notable among them, the Folio printers were instructed to work from an alternative, playhouse-derived manuscript. This meant that the whole process of producing the first complete Shakespeare took months, even years, longer than it might have done. But for the men overseeing the project, John Hemings and Henry Condell, friends and fellow actors who had been remembered in Shakespeare's will, the additional labor and cost were worth the effort for the sake of producing an edition that was close to the practice of the theater. They wanted all the plays in print so that people could, as they wrote in their prefatory address to the reader, "read him and again and again," but they also wanted "the great variety of readers" to work from texts that were close to the theater-life for which Shakespeare originally intended them. For this reason, the *RSC Shakespeare*, in both *Complete Works* and individual volumes, uses the Folio as its base text wherever possible. Significant Quarto variants are, however, noted in the textual notes, and a handful of Quarto-only passages are appended after the textual notes.

The following notes highlight various aspects of the editorial process and indicate conventions used in the text of this edition:

Lists of Parts are supplied in the First Folio for only six plays, not including *Troilus and Cressida*, so the list here is editorially supplied. Capitals indicate that part of the name used for speech headings in the script (thus "PRIAM, King of Troy").

Locations are provided by the Folio for only two plays, of which *Troilus and Cressida* is not one. Eighteenth-century editors, working in an age of elaborately realistic stage sets, were the first to provide detailed locations ("***another part of the Greek camp***"). Given that Shakespeare wrote for a bare stage and often an imprecise sense of place, we have relegated locations to the explanatory notes at the foot of the page, where they are given at the beginning of each scene where the imaginary location is different from the one before. In the case of *Troilus and Cressida*, the action is set in either the city of Troy or the camp of the besieging Greek army or the battlefields between the two.

Act and Scene Divisions were provided in the Folio in a much more thoroughgoing way than in the Quartos. Sometimes, however, they were erroneous or omitted; corrections and additions supplied by editorial tradition are indicated by square brackets. Five-act division is based on a classical model, and act breaks provided the opportunity to replace the candles in the indoor Blackfriars playhouse which the King's Men used after 1608, but Shakespeare did not necessarily think in terms of a five-part structure of dramatic composition. The Folio convention is that a scene ends when the stage is empty. Nowadays, partly under the influence of film, we tend to consider a scene to be a dramatic unit that ends with either a change of imaginary location or a significant passage of time within the narrative. Shakespeare's fluidity of composition accords well with this convention, so in addition to act and scene numbers we provide a ***running scene*** count in the right margin at the beginning of each new scene, in the typeface used for editorial directions. Where there is a scene break caused by a momentarily bare stage, but the location does not change and extra time does not pass, we use the convention ***running scene continues***. There is inevitably a degree of editorial judgment in making such calls, but the system is very valuable in suggesting the pace of the plays.

Speakers' Names are often inconsistent in Folio. We have regularized speech headings, but retained an element of deliberate inconsistency in entry directions, in order to give the flavor of Folio.

Verse is indicated by lines that do not run to the right margin and by capitalization of each line. The Folio printers sometimes set verse as prose, and vice versa (either out of misunderstanding or for reasons of space). We have silently corrected in such cases, although in some instances there is ambiguity, in which case we have leaned toward the preservation of Folio layout. Folio sometimes uses contraction ("turnd" rather than "turned") to indicate whether or not the final "-ed" of a past participle is sounded, an area where there is variation for the sake of the five-beat iambic pentameter rhythm. We use the convention of a grave accent to indicate sounding (thus "turnèd" would be two syllables), but would urge actors not to overstress. In cases where one speaker ends with a verse half line and the next begins with the other half of the pentameter, editors since the late eighteenth century have indented the second line. We have abandoned this convention, since the Folio does not use it, nor did actors' cues in the Shakespearean theater. An exception is made when the second speaker actively interrupts or completes the first speaker's sentence.

Spelling is modernized, but older forms are very occasionally maintained where necessary for rhythm or aural effect.

Punctuation in Shakespeare's time was as much rhetorical as grammatical. "Colon" was originally a term for a unit of thought in an argument. The semicolon was a new unit of punctuation (some of the Quartos lack them altogether). We have modernized punctuation throughout, but have given more weight to Folio punctuation than many editors, since, though not Shakespearean, it reflects the usage of his period. In particular, we have used the colon far more than many editors: it is exceptionally useful as a way of indicating how many Shakespearean speeches unfold clause by clause in a developing argument that gives the illusion of enacting the process of thinking in the moment. We have also kept in mind the origin of punctuation in classical times as a way of assisting the actor and orator: the comma suggests the briefest of pauses for breath, the colon a middling one, and a full stop or period a longer pause. Semicolons, by contrast, belong to an era of punctuation that was only just coming in during Shakespeare's time and that is coming to an end now: we have accordingly only used them where they occur in our copy texts (and not always then). Dashes are sometimes used for parenthetical interjections where the Folio has brackets. They are also used for interruptions and changes in train of thought. Where a change of addressee occurs within a speech, we have used a dash preceded by a period (or occasionally another form of punctuation). Often the identity of the respective addressees is obvious from the context. When it is not, this has been indicated in a marginal stage direction.

Entrances and Exits are fairly thorough in Folio, which has accordingly been followed as faithfully as possible. Where characters are omitted or corrections are necessary, this is indicated by square brackets (e.g. "[*and Attendants*]"). *Exit* is sometimes silently normalized to *Exeunt* and *Manet* anglicized to "remains." We trust Folio positioning of entrances and exits to a greater degree than most editors.

Editorial Stage Directions such as stage business, asides, indications of addressee and of characters' position on the gallery stage are only used sparingly in Folio. Other editions mingle directions of this kind with original Folio and Quarto directions, sometimes marking them by means of square brackets. We have sought to distinguish what could be described as *directorial* interventions of this kind from Folio-style directions (either original or supplied) by placing them in the right margin in a different typeface. There is a degree of subjectivity about which directions are of which kind, but the procedure is intended as a reminder to the reader and the actor that Shakespearean stage directions are often dependent upon editorial inference alone and are not set in stone. We also depart from editorial tradition in sometimes admitting uncertainty and thus printing permissive stage directions, such as an **Aside?** (often a line may be equally effective as an aside or as a direct address—it is for each production or reading to make its own decision) or a **may exit** or a piece of business placed between arrows to indicate that it may occur at various different moments within a scene.

Line Numbers in the left margin are editorial, for reference and to key the explanatory and textual notes.

Explanatory Notes at the foot of each page explain allusions and gloss obsolete and difficult words, confusing phraseology, occasional major textual cruces, and so on. Particular attention is given to non-standard usage, bawdy innuendo, and technical terms (e.g. legal and military language). Where more than one sense is given, commas indicate shades of related meaning, slashes alternative or double meanings.

Textual Notes at the end of the play indicate major departures from the Folio. They take the following form: the reading of our text is given in bold and its source given after an equals sign, "Q" signifies a reading from the First Quarto of 1609, "F" a reading from the First Folio of 1623, with "F2" indicating a correction that derives from the Second Folio of 1632, "F3" a correction introduced in the Third Folio of 1664, "F4" from the Fourth Folio of 1685, and "Ed" one that derives from the subsequent editorial tradition. The rejected Folio ("F") reading is then given. Thus for Act 1 Scene 2 line 216: "**1.2.216 note** = Q. F = not." This means that the Quarto reading "note" has been preferred to Folio's "not" in Pandarus' line "Mark him, note him," since we judge that "not him" is likely a printer's error in the Folio (though it could conceivably be argued that Cressida is looking at another warrior and Pandarus is saying "mark him [Troilus], not him [the other one]").

KEY FACTS

MAJOR PARTS: (*with percentage of lines/number of speeches/scenes on stage*) Troilus (15%/131/13), Ulysses (14%/80/7), Pandarus (11%/153/8), Cressida (8%/152/6), Thersites (8%/90/7), Achilles (6%/74/9), Hector (6%/57/7), Agamemnon (6%/52/7), Nestor (5%/38/6), Aeneas (4%/44/8), Diomedes (3%/54/11), Paris (3%/27/5), Ajax (2%/55/8), Patroclus (2%/37/5).

LINGUISTIC MEDIUM: 70% verse, 30% prose.

DATE: 1601–02. Registered for publication 7 February 1603 ("as yt is acted by my lo: Chamberlens Men"). Not mentioned by Meres in 1598; influenced by Chapman's Homer translation of the same year. The armed prologue (Folio only) seems to parody that of Ben Jonson's *Poetaster* (performed summer 1601). There are apparent allusions to the play in *Thomas Lord Cromwell* (Chamberlain's Men, registered for publication in August 1602) and Thomas Middleton's *The Family of Love* (?1602–03).

SOURCES: Chaucer's *Troilus and Criseyde* (perhaps in Speght's 1598 edition) for the love plot; George Chapman's translation of seven books of Homer's *Iliad* (1598) and William Caxton's *Recuyell of the Historyes of Troye* (1474, the first printed book in English) for the war. Perhaps also John Lydgate's *Troy Book* (1513) and Robert Henryson's *The Testament of Cresseid* (1532).

TEXT: Quarto, 1609, in two separate states: one with title page *The Historie of Troylus and Cresseida. As it was acted by the Kings Maiesties seruants at the Globe. Written by William Shakespeare*, the other with title page omitting reference to the stage (*The Famous Historie of Troylus and Cresseid. Excellently expressing the beginning of their loues, with the conceited wooing of Pandarus Prince of Licia. Written by William*

Shakespeare) and a prefatory epistle that makes claims for the readerly as opposed to the theatrical text. The nature of the printer's copy for both the Quarto and Folio's *The Tragedie of Troylus and Cressida* is fiercely debated by scholars, as is the relationship between the texts. The original intention of the Folio editors was to print *Troilus* after *Romeo and Juliet*, using the Quarto as copy text (a few early copies of the Folio survive with a canceled last page of *Romeo* and first page of *Troilus*). But printing was broken off after three pages, perhaps due to a copyright dispute, and *Troilus* was eventually squeezed in between the Histories and Tragedies (after the setting of the "Catalogue" of plays in the Folio's preliminary matter). When printing was resumed, a manuscript that had many differences from the Quarto text was used, though the influence of Quarto can still be strongly detected. Some scholars suppose that Folio was printed from an annotated Quarto, but this does not square with the superiority of many individual Quarto readings: why annotate a sound reading in a printed text with an alteration that makes less good sense? It is therefore probable that an independent scribal copy, perhaps based on the theater promptbook, and perhaps reflecting playhouse revision, also lies behind the Folio. In accordance with our editorial policy, we follow Folio where it is viable, but, in light of the demonstrable presence of Quarto in the editing or printing of the Folio, we adopt Quarto readings where Folio cannot be defended.

On two occasions the text includes passages that seem to be authorial "first thoughts" intended for deletion. Most modern editors relegate such lines to an appendix. Our fidelity to Folio means that we have not done so, though we have indicated the lines in question by enclosing them within double solidi (// //): they should almost certainly be cut in performance, but are of great interest in apparently revealing Shakespeare in the process of composition.

TROILUS
AND CRESSIDA

LIST OF PARTS

PROLOGUE, in armour

Trojans

PRIAM, King of Troy

HECTOR

DEIPHOBUS

HELENUS, a priest

PARIS ⎬ his sons

TROILUS

MARGARELON, a bastard

CASSANDRA, Priam's daughter, a prophetess

ANDROMACHE, wife of Hector

HELEN, wife of Paris, previously wife of Menelaus

PANDARUS, a lord

CRESSIDA, his niece

CALCHAS, her father who has joined the Greeks

ALEXANDER, her servant

AENEAS ⎬ military

ANTENOR ⎬ commanders

BOY, servant to Troilus

Greeks

AGAMEMNON, Commander-in-Chief

MENELAUS, his brother

ULYSSES

NESTOR

ACHILLES

PATROCLUS, his friend

AJAX

DIOMEDES

THERSITES

MYRMIDONS, Achilles' soldiers

Servants, Attendants

The Prologue

[Enter the Prologue, in armour]

In Troy there lies the scene. From isles of Greece
The princes orgulous, their high blood chafed,
Have to the port of Athens sent their ships
Fraught with the ministers and instruments
5   Of cruel war: sixty and nine, that wore
Their crownets regal, from th'Athenian bay
Put forth toward Phrygia, and their vow is made
To ransack Troy, within whose strong immures
The ravished Helen, Menelaus' queen,
10   With wanton Paris sleeps, and that's the quarrel.
To Tenedos they come,
And the deep-drawing barks do there disgorge
Their warlike fraughtage: now on Dardan plains
The fresh and yet unbruisèd Greeks do pitch
15   Their brave pavilions: Priam's six-gated city,
Dardan, and Tymbria, Helias, Chetas, Troien,
And Antenorides, with massy staples
And corresponsive and fulfilling bolts,
Stir up the sons of Troy.
20   Now expectation, tickling skittish spirits,
On one and other side, Trojan and Greek,
Sets all on hazard. And hither am I come,
A prologue armed, but not in confidence
Of author's pen or actor's voice, but suited

The Prologue   2 orgulous proud, haughty   **high** noble/proud   **chafed** heated, roused
4 Fraught laden   **ministers** agents, i.e. soldiers   **instruments** weapons   **6 crownets**
coronets, small crowns   **7 Phrygia** region of Asia Minor (now Turkey), location of Troy
8 immures walls   **9 ravished** abducted/raped   **10 wanton** lustful/willful, uncontrolled
11 Tenedos island near Troy   **12 deep-drawing barks** heavily laden ships lying low in the
water   **disgorge** empty out (literally "vomit up")   **13 fraughtage** cargo   **Dardan** Trojan
(from Dardanus, son of Zeus and the great ancestor of the Trojan rulers)   **15 brave pavilions**
splendid tents (**brave** plays on the sense of "boastful, insolent")   **16 Dardan . . . Antenorides**
the names of the six gates of Troy   **17 massy . . . bolts** massive metal hoops and the
correspondingly sized bolts that fit into them   **20 tickling** toying with/vexing, provoking
skittish lively, readily roused   **22 on hazard** at risk   **23 armed** equipped with weapons/
wearing armor/prepared   **in confidence Of** overconfident about   **24 suited . . . argument**
costumed to suit the theme

25 In like conditions as our argument,
To tell you, fair beholders, that our play
Leaps o'er the vaunt and firstlings of those broils,
Beginning in the middle, starting thence away
To what may be digested in a play.
30 Like or find fault, do as your pleasures are:
Now good or bad, 'tis but the chance of war.   [*Exit*]

Act 1 Scene 1   *running scene 1*

Enter Pandarus and Troilus

TROILUS   Call here my varlet, I'll unarm again:
Why should I war without the walls of Troy
That find such cruel battle here within?
Each Trojan that is master of his heart,
5 Let him to field: Troilus, alas, hath none.
PANDARUS   Will this gear ne'er be mended?
TROILUS   The Greeks are strong and skilful to their strength,
Fierce to their skill and to their fierceness valiant,
But I am weaker than a woman's tear,
10 Tamer than sleep, fonder than ignorance,
Less valiant than the virgin in the night,
And skilless as unpractised infancy.
PANDARUS   Well, I have told you enough of this: for my part, I'll
not meddle nor make no further. He that will have a cake out
15 of the wheat must needs tarry the grinding.
TROILUS   Have I not tarried?

---

25 argument plot/quarrel   **27 vaunt and firstlings** beginnings (**vaunt** plays on sense of
"boast")   **broils** battles, turmoil   **28 in the middle** a translation of the Latin *in medias res*; the
Roman writer Horace advised the aspiring epic poet to go straight to the heart of a story
29 digested understood/condensed within   **1.1** *Location: Troy* *Pandarus* his name
came to signify the function of a "pander" or go-between   **1 varlet** personal servant   **unarm**
disarm, remove armor   **2 without** outside   **5 field** the battlefield   **none** i.e. no heart to be
master of, no urge to fight   **6 gear** business (perhaps with connotations of "sexual organs")
7 to in addition to/in proportion to   **10 Tamer** more docile/more dull, spiritless   **fonder** more
foolish   **12 skilless** ignorant, unaware   **unpractised** inexperienced/guileless   **14 meddle
nor make** interfere, get involved (perhaps suggestive; both words could mean "have sex")
15 tarry await   **grinding** plays on the sense of "sexual intercourse"

	PANDARUS	Ay, the grinding, but you must tarry the bolting.
	TROILUS	Have I not tarried?
	PANDARUS	Ay, the bolting, but you must tarry the leav'ning.
20	TROILUS	Still have I tarried.

PANDARUS   Ay, to the leavening, but here's yet in the word
'hereafter' the kneading, the making of the cake, the heating
of the oven and the baking; nay, you must stay the cooling
too, or you may chance to burn your lips.

25   TROILUS   Patience herself, what goddess e'er she be,
Doth lesser blench at suff'rance than I do.
At Priam's royal table do I sit;
And when fair Cressid comes into my thoughts —
So, traitor, when she comes? When is she thence?

30   PANDARUS   Well, she looked yesternight fairer than ever I saw
her look, or any woman else.

TROILUS   I was about to tell thee — when my heart,
As wedgèd with a sigh, would rive in twain,
Lest Hector or my father should perceive me —
35   I have, as when the sun doth light a-scorn,
Buried this sigh in wrinkle of a smile:
But sorrow, that is couched in seeming gladness
Is like that mirth fate turns to sudden sadness.

PANDARUS   An her hair were not somewhat darker than
40   Helen's — well, go to — there were no more comparison
between the women. But, for my part, she is my kinswoman:
I would not, as they term it, praise her, but I would somebody

---

17 bolting sifting of flour (plays on the slang sense of "bolt," i.e. "penis")   **19 leav'ning**
fermenting of the dough with leaven   **22 making of** plays on the sense of "having sex with"
heating . . . oven plays on the sense of "sexual arousal of the woman" (**oven** was a slang term
for "vagina")   **23 stay** wait for   **cooling** of the cake/of lust   **24 burn your lips** also
suggestive of the effects of venereal disease   **26 Doth . . . suff'rance** flinches less at suffering
suff'rance suffering/patient endurance   **29 traitor** i.e. to love (Troilus berates himself for
suggesting that he might sometimes forget Cressida)   **thence** out of my thoughts
33 wedgèd split with a wedge (possibly plays on the slang sense of "wedge," i.e. penis)   **would**
seemed about to/wanted to   **rive in twain** split in two   **35 a-scorn** in scorn, mockingly
(Troilus compares his feigned jollity to the falsely cheerful glare of the sun)   **37 couched**
concealed/expressed   **39 An** if   **40 go to** expression of dismissive impatience   **were** would
be   **42 would** wish

had heard her talk yesterday, as I did. I will not dispraise your
sister Cassandra's wit, but—

45 TROILUS   O Pandarus! I tell thee, Pandarus —
When I do tell thee, there my hopes lie drowned,
Reply not in how many fathoms deep
They lie indrenched. I tell thee I am mad
In Cressid's love. Thou answer'st she is fair,
50 Pour'st in the open ulcer of my heart
Her eyes, her hair, her cheek, her gait, her voice,
Handlest in thy discourse, O, that her hand
In whose comparison all whites are ink
Writing their own reproach, to whose soft seizure
55 The cygnet's down is harsh and spirit of sense
Hard as the palm of ploughman: this thou tell'st me —
As true thou tell'st me — when I say I love her,
But, saying thus, instead of oil and balm,
Thou lay'st in every gash that love hath given me
60 The knife that made it.

PANDARUS   I speak no more than truth.

TROILUS   Thou dost not speak so much.

PANDARUS   Faith, I'll not meddle in't. Let her be as she is: if she
be fair, 'tis the better for her: an she be not, she has the
65 mends in her own hands.

TROILUS   Good Pandarus, how now, Pandarus?

PANDARUS   I have had my labour for my travail: ill-thought on
of her and ill-thought on of you: gone between and between,
but small thanks for my labour.

70 TROILUS   What, art thou angry, Pandarus? What, with me?

---

43 dispraise disparage   **44 wit** intelligence   **47 fathoms** a measure of depth; a fathom is
about six feet   **48 indrenched** drowned, submerged   **49 In Cressid's love** for love of Cressida
52 Handlest you handle (anticipates **hand**)   **that her hand** that hand of hers   **53 In whose
comparison** in comparison to which   **54 to** compared to   **soft seizure** gentle grasp
55 cygnet baby swan   **spirit of sense** i.e. the most delicate touch (literally, the invisible
essence thought to transmit sensation to the mind)   **58 oil and balm** soothing, healing
ointments (both words may play on the sense of "semen"; i.e. only sexual climax will heal
Troilus's lovesickness)   **59 gash** wound (may play on the sense of "vagina")   **65 mends**
remedy (i.e. she can use cosmetics; possibly also suggestive of masturbation)   **67 I . . . travail**
nothing but effort has been the reward for my pains (**travail** plays on the sense of "travel,"
alluding to Pandarus' role as a go-between)   **on of** of by

PANDARUS   Because she's kin to me, therefore she's not so fair as Helen: an she were not kin to me, she would be as fair on Friday as Helen is on Sunday. But what care I? I care not an she were a blackamoor: 'tis all one to me.

75   TROILUS   Say I she is not fair?

PANDARUS   I do not care whether you do or no. She's a fool to stay behind her father: let her to the Greeks, and so I'll tell her the next time I see her. For my part, I'll meddle nor make no more i'th'matter.

80   TROILUS   Pandarus—

PANDARUS   Not I.

TROILUS   Sweet Pandarus—

PANDARUS   Pray you speak no more to me: I will leave all as I found it, and there an end.   *Exit Pandarus*

Sound alarum

85   TROILUS   Peace, you ungracious clamours, peace, rude sounds!
Fools on both sides! Helen must needs be fair
When with your blood you daily paint her thus.
I cannot fight upon this argument:
It is too starved a subject for my sword.
90   But Pandarus — O gods, how do you plague me!
I cannot come to Cressid but by Pandar,
And he's as tetchy to be wooed to woo
As she is stubborn, chaste, against all suit.
Tell me, Apollo, for thy Daphne's love,
95   What Cressid is, what Pandar, and what we?
Her bed is India: there she lies, a pearl.

---

72 an . . . Sunday i.e. if she were not my relative, I would say that she is as beautiful in the plain clothes appropriate to a fasting day as Helen is in her Sunday best   **74 blackamoor** black African   **75 fair** beautiful/fair-complexioned   **77 behind her father** since her father's departure   **let her** let her go/rent her out   *alarum* call to battle (usually trumpets or drums)   **85 ungracious** inconsiderate, unmannerly   **rude** harsh/uncivilized   **87 paint** i.e. as if with cosmetics, rouge   **88 upon this argument** for this cause   **89 starved** meager, insubstantial   **92 tetchy** irritable, peevish   **wooed to woo** entreated to court (Cressida)   **93 suit** courtship   **94 Apollo** Greek sun god   **Daphne** wood nymph pursued by Apollo; she evaded him by praying to the river god Peneus for deliverance and was thereupon turned into a laurel tree   **95 we** I   **96 India** East/West Indies (thought of as regions of great wealth)

Between our Ilium and where she resides,
Let it be called the wild and wand'ring flood,
Ourself the merchant, and this sailing Pandar
100   Our doubtful hope, our convoy and our bark.

Alarum. Enter Aeneas

AENEAS   How now, Prince Troilus? Wherefore not afield?

TROILUS   Because not there: this woman's answer sorts,
For womanish it is to be from thence.
What news, Aeneas, from the field today?

105 AENEAS   That Paris is returnèd home and hurt.

TROILUS   By whom, Aeneas?

AENEAS   Troilus, by Menelaus.

TROILUS   Let Paris bleed, 'tis but a scar to scorn:
Paris is gored with Menelaus' horn.   *Alarum*

110 AENEAS   Hark, what good sport is out of town today!

TROILUS   Better at home, if 'would I might' were 'may'.
But to the sport abroad: are you bound thither?

AENEAS   In all swift haste.

TROILUS   Come, go we then together.   *Exeunt*

[Act 1 Scene 2]

                                                      running scene 2

Enter Cressida and her Man [Alexander]

CRESSIDA   Who were those went by?

ALEXANDER   Queen Hecuba and Helen.

CRESSIDA   And whither go they?

ALEXANDER   Up to the eastern tower,
5   Whose height commands as subject all the vale,

97 Ilium Troy/the royal palace of Troy   98 flood sea   99 merchant trader/merchant ship
sailing possible pun on "selling"   100 convoy escort   bark small vessel (used to escort a
larger merchant ship)   101 Wherefore not afield? Why are you not on the battlefield?
102 Because not there i.e. "just because"   woman's answer alludes to the proverb "because
is woman's reason"   sorts is fitting   108 scar to scorn wound so slight it deserves nothing
but scorn/wound given in return for Paris' scornful behavior to Menelaus   109 horn
imagined growth on the head of a cuckold (man with an unfaithful wife; Paris has stolen
Menelaus' wife, Helen)   110 sport action, entertainment (in his reply, Troilus shifts the sense
to "sexual amusement")   out of town i.e. outside Troy's walls   112 abroad in the outside
world   1.2   5 commands as subject dominates, overlooks

To see the battle. Hector, whose patience
Is as a virtue fixed, today was moved:
He chides Andromache and struck his armourer,
And, like as there were husbandry in war,
10   Before the sun rose he was harnessed light,
And to the field goes he, where every flower
Did as a prophet weep what it foresaw
In Hector's wrath.

CRESSIDA   What was his cause of anger?

15   ALEXANDER   The noise goes, this: there is among the Greeks
A lord of Trojan blood, nephew to Hector:
They call him Ajax.

CRESSIDA   Good, and what of him?

ALEXANDER   They say he is a very man *per se*, and stands alone.

20   CRESSIDA   So do all men, unless they are drunk, sick, or have
no legs.

ALEXANDER   This man, lady, hath robbed many beasts of their
particular additions: he is as valiant as the lion, churlish as
the bear, slow as the elephant: a man into whom nature hath
25   so crowded humours that his valour is crushed into folly, his
folly sauced with discretion. There is no man hath a virtue
that he hath not a glimpse of, nor any man an attaint but he
carries some stain of it: he is melancholy without cause, and
merry against the hair: he hath the joints of everything, but
30   everything so out of joint that he is a gouty Briareus, many
hands and no use, or purblinded Argus, all eyes and no sight.

---

7 fixed steadfast   **moved** roused, angry (plays on the literal sense to provide antithesis with
fixed)   9 like as as if   **husbandry** careful management (rising early for work); plays on being
a "husband"   **10 harnessed light** dressed in light armor/armored quickly   **15 noise** rumor,
report   **16 nephew** cousin   **18 Good** very well   **19 *per se*** in himself/in a class of his own
(Latin)   **stands alone** is peerless (Cressida's response plays on the literal sense, and on the
sexual sense of "is erect")   **20 drunk . . . legs** i.e. cannot stand up/are impotent
23 particular additions distinctive characteristics, essential attributes   **churlish** violent/
ungracious   **24 slow** ponderous, slow-moving   **25 humours** contradictory moods,
temperamental characteristics   **27 glimpse** trace, small part   **attaint** fault, stain
29 against the hair contrary to the prevailing mood, perversely   **joints** parts, components
30 gouty diseased, with swollen deformed joints   **Briareus** legendary monster with a hundred
hands and fifty heads   **31 purblinded** blind   **Argus** legendary monster with a hundred eyes

CRESSIDA   But how should this man, that makes me smile make Hector angry?

ALEXANDER   They say he yesterday coped Hector in the battle
35   and struck him down, the disdain and shame whereof hath ever since kept Hector fasting and waking.

Enter Pandarus

CRESSIDA   Who comes here?

ALEXANDER   Madam, your uncle Pandarus.

CRESSIDA   Hector's a gallant man.

40   ALEXANDER   As may be in the world, lady.

PANDARUS   What's that? What's that?

CRESSIDA   Good morrow, uncle Pandarus.

PANDARUS   Good morrow, cousin Cressid. What do you talk of?— Good morrow, Alexander.— How do you, cousin?
45   When were you at Ilium?

CRESSIDA   This morning, uncle.

PANDARUS   What were you talking of when I came? Was Hector armed and gone ere ye came to Ilium? Helen was not up, was she?

50   CRESSIDA   Hector was gone, but Helen was not up.

PANDARUS   E'en so; Hector was stirring early.

CRESSIDA   That were we talking of, and of his anger.

PANDARUS   Was he angry?

CRESSIDA   So he says here.

55   PANDARUS   True, he was so; I know the cause too: he'll lay about him today, I can tell them that, and there's Troilus will not come far behind him: let them take heed of Troilus, I can tell them that too.

CRESSIDA   What, is he angry too?

60   PANDARUS   Who, Troilus? Troilus is the better man of the two.

CRESSIDA   O Jupiter, there's no comparison.

PANDARUS   What, not between Troilus and Hector? Do you know a man if you see him?

---

34 coped grappled, fought with   **35 disdain** anger, wounded pride   **whereof** of which
36 waking sleepless   **48 ere** before   **55 lay about him** strike out/fight hard   **61 Jupiter**
Roman supreme god   **63 know a man** recognize a proper man (Cressida affects to understand
merely "recognize a person"; **know** may play on the sense of "have sex with")

CRESSIDA	Ay, if I ever saw him before and knew him.
65 PANDARUS	Well, I say Troilus is Troilus.
CRESSIDA	Then you say as I say, for I am sure he is not Hector.
PANDARUS	No, nor Hector is not Troilus in some degrees.
CRESSIDA	'Tis just to each of them: he is himself.
PANDARUS	Himself? Alas, poor Troilus, I would he were.
70 CRESSIDA	So he is.
PANDARUS	Condition, I had gone barefoot to India.
CRESSIDA	He is not Hector.
PANDARUS	Himself? No, he's not himself: would a were himself! Well, the gods are above, time must friend or end. Well, Troilus, well. I would my heart were in her body. No, Hector is not a better man than Troilus.
CRESSIDA	Excuse me.
PANDARUS	He is elder.
CRESSIDA	Pardon me, pardon me.
80 PANDARUS	Th'other's not come to't; you shall tell me another tale, when th'other's come to't. Hector shall not have his wit this year.
CRESSIDA	He shall not need it if he have his own.
PANDARUS	Nor his qualities.
85 CRESSIDA	No matter.
PANDARUS	Nor his beauty.
CRESSIDA	'Twould not become him: his own's better.
PANDARUS	You have no judgement, niece; Helen herself swore th'other day that Troilus for a brown favour — for so 'tis, I must confess — not brown neither—
CRESSIDA	No, but brown.
PANDARUS	'Faith, to say truth, brown and not brown.

---

67 **in some degrees** in some respects/by a long distance   68 **just** fair/accurate
71 **Condition . . . India** i.e. Troilus is as likely to recover his true self as I am to walk barefoot to
India   **Condition** on the condition that   73 **a** he   74 **time . . . end** i.e. time will tell   **friend**
befriend   77 **Excuse me** expression of polite disbelief or disagreement, like **Pardon me**
80 **Th'other's . . . to't** i.e. Troilus is not as fully mature (**come to't** may have connotations of
being sexually active)   **tell . . . tale** i.e. change your tune (**tale** may pun on "tail," i.e. "penis")
81 **have his wit** be able to compete with Troilus' intelligence   87 **become** suit   89 **a brown
favour** someone with a dark complexion (considered less attractive)   91 **No, but brown**
Cressida mocks Pandarus' quibbling distinctions

CRESSIDA   To say the truth, true and not true.

PANDARUS   She praised his complexion above Paris.

95 CRESSIDA   Why, Paris hath colour enough.

PANDARUS   So he has.

CRESSIDA   Then Troilus should have too much: if she praised him above, his complexion is higher than his: he having colour enough, and the other higher, is too flaming a praise for a good complexion. I had as lief Helen's golden tongue had commended Troilus for a copper nose.

PANDARUS   I swear to you, I think Helen loves him better than Paris.

CRESSIDA   Then she's a merry Greek indeed.

105 PANDARUS   Nay, I am sure she does. She came to him th'other day into the compassed window — and, you know, he has not past three or four hairs on his chin—

CRESSIDA   Indeed, a tapster's arithmetic may soon bring his particulars therein to a total.

110 PANDARUS   Why, he is very young, and yet will he within three pound lift as much as his brother Hector.

CRESSIDA   Is he so young a man and so old a lifter?

PANDARUS   But to prove to you that Helen loves him, she came and puts me her white hand to his cloven chin—

115 CRESSIDA   Juno have mercy! How came it cloven?

PANDARUS   Why, you know 'tis dimpled. I think his smiling becomes him better than any man in all Phrygia.

CRESSIDA   O, he smiles valiantly.

PANDARUS   Does he not?

120 CRESSIDA   O yes, an 'twere a cloud in autumn.

---

97 should i.e. must therefore   **98 his . . . his** i.e. Troilus' . . . Paris'   **99 flaming** extravagant, high-flown/brightly colored, flushed   **100 as lief** rather, just as soon   **101 copper** red (from drinking; conceivably suggests the metal noses occasionally worn by those who had lost their real noses to syphilis)   **104 merry Greek** jolly person/one of loose morals   **106 compassed** curved, rounded   **108 tapster's arithmetic** i.e. simple calculation   **tapster** barman, tavern keeper   **109 particulars** individual details, particular features   **112 old** experienced   **lifter** weightlifter/thief (possibly also plays on the sense of "one who has sex")   **114 cloven** dimpled (Cressida plays on the literal sense of "split apart")   **115 Juno** queen of the Roman gods, wife of Jupiter   **120 an . . . autumn** i.e. as if he were a dark cloud or a cloud through which the sun is vainly trying to shine

PANDARUS Why, go to, then. But to prove to you that Helen loves Troilus—

CRESSIDA Troilus will stand to the proof, if you'll prove it so.

PANDARUS Troilus? Why, he esteems her no more than I esteem
125 an addle egg.

CRESSIDA If you love an addle egg as well as you love an idle head, you would eat chickens i'th'shell.

PANDARUS I cannot choose but laugh to think how she tickled his chin. Indeed, she has a marvellous white hand, I must
130 needs confess—

CRESSIDA Without the rack.

PANDARUS And she takes upon her to spy a white hair on his chin.

CRESSIDA Alas, poor chin. Many a wart is richer.

135 PANDARUS But there was such laughing! Queen Hecuba laughed that her eyes ran o'er.

CRESSIDA With millstones.

PANDARUS And Cassandra laughed.

CRESSIDA But there was more temperate fire under the pot of
140 her eyes: did her eyes run o'er too?

PANDARUS And Hector laughed.

CRESSIDA At what was all this laughing?

PANDARUS Marry, at the white hair that Helen spied on Troilus' chin.

145 CRESSIDA An't had been a green hair, I should have laughed too.

PANDARUS They laughed not so much at the hair as at his pretty answer.

CRESSIDA What was his answer?

---

123 stand . . . proof stand up to the test (plays on the sense of "be erect for sex") **125 addle** rotten/partly hatched (the sense Cressida picks up on in her reply) **126 If . . . i'th'shell** perhaps alludes to the proverb "as good be an addled egg as an idle bird" (**addle** puns on **idle**) **129 marvellous** marvelously **130 confess** admit (Cressida plays on the idea of confession after torture) **131 rack** torture instrument that stretched the limbs **134 richer** i.e. has more hairs than Troilus' youthful chin **136 that** so much that **ran o'er** watered **137 millstones** proverbially the hard-hearted weep millstones **139 pot** cooking pot **143 Marry** by the Virgin Mary **145 green** plays on the sense of "youthful, inexperienced" **148 pretty** artful, clever

150 PANDARUS Quoth she, 'Here's but two and fifty hairs on your chin, and one of them is white.'

CRESSIDA This is her question.

PANDARUS That's true, make no question of that. 'Two and fifty hairs,' quoth he, 'and one white: that white hair is my father, 155 and all the rest are his sons.' 'Jupiter!' quoth she, 'Which of these hairs is Paris, my husband?' 'The forked one,' quoth he, 'pluck't out, and give it him.' But there was such laughing, and Helen so blushed, and Paris so chafed, and all the rest so laughed, that it passed.

160 CRESSIDA So let it now, for it has been a great while going by.

PANDARUS Well, cousin. I told you a thing yesterday: think on't.

CRESSIDA So I do.

PANDARUS I'll be sworn 'tis true, he will weep you, an 'twere a man born in April.   *Sound a retreat*

165 CRESSIDA And I'll spring up in his tears, an 'twere a nettle against May.

PANDARUS Hark, they are coming from the field: shall we stand up here and see them as they pass toward Ilium? Good niece, do, sweet niece Cressida.

170 CRESSIDA At your pleasure.

PANDARUS Here, here, here's an excellent place, here we may see most bravely. I'll tell you them all by their names as they pass by, but mark Troilus above the rest.

Enter Aeneas [and passes over the stage]

CRESSIDA Speak not so loud.

175 PANDARUS That's Aeneas. Is not that a brave man? He's one of the flowers of Troy, I can tell you. But mark Troilus: you shall see anon.

CRESSIDA Who's that?

---

154 hairs puns on "heirs"   **155 all . . . sons** traditionally, Priam had fifty sons; perhaps the forked hair counts as two   **156 forked** split (alludes to the cuckold's horns that supposedly grew from the head of a man with an unfaithful wife)   **158 so chafed** was so irritated **159 it passed** the occasion surpassed all description   **160 So . . . now** i.e. let it pass, be forgotten   **going by** i.e. in the telling   **163 weep . . . April** i.e. weep like one born in the month of showers   **165 spring** grow (plays on the sense of the season itself)   **an . . . May** as if I were a nettle anticipating the arrival of May (plays on the notion of "nettling," i.e. irritating Troilus) **172 bravely** splendidly   **173 mark** note, observe   **175 brave** splendid/bold   **177 anon** shortly

Enter Antenor [and passes over the stage]

PANDARUS   That's Antenor. He has a shrewd wit, I can tell you,
180   and he's a man good enough: he's one o'th'soundest
judgement in Troy whosoever, and a proper man of person.
When comes Troilus? I'll show you Troilus anon: if he see
me, you shall see him nod at me.

CRESSIDA   Will he give you the nod?

185   PANDARUS   You shall see.

CRESSIDA   If he do, the rich shall have more.

Enter Hector [and passes over the stage]

PANDARUS   That's Hector, that, that, look you, that there's a
fellow! Go thy way, Hector! There's a brave man, niece. O
brave Hector! Look how he looks! There's a countenance. Is't
190   not a brave man?

CRESSIDA   O brave man!

PANDARUS   Is a not? It does a man's heart good. Look you what
hacks are on his helmet. Look you yonder, do you see? Look
you there? There's no jesting, there's laying on, take't off
195   who will, as they say. There be hacks!

CRESSIDA   Be those with swords?

Enter Paris [and passes over the stage]

PANDARUS   Swords, anything, he cares not: an the devil come to
him, it's all one. By God's lid, it does one's heart good. Yonder
comes Paris, yonder comes Paris. Look ye yonder, niece. Is't
200   not a gallant man too, is't not? Why, this is brave now. Who
said he came hurt home today? He's not hurt. Why, this will
do Helen's heart good now, ha? Would I could see Troilus
now. You shall see Troilus anon.

CRESSIDA   Who's that?

---

179 shrewd sharp   **180 one o'th'soundest judgement** one of those with the greatest wisdom,
discretion   **181 whosoever** out of anyone   **proper . . . person** fine example of a man
184 give . . . nod acknowledge you with a nod of the head/call you a fool (**nod**)   **186 the . . .
more** i.e. your foolishness will increase further   **188 Go thy way** expression of well-wishing
189 countenance (fine) face/demeanor/appearance   **192 a** he   **193 hacks** dents, gashes
194 jesting make believe/playing   **laying on** (evidence of) vigorous attack   **take't . . . will**
whatever anyone says to the contrary (plays on the antithesis between "lay on" and "take off")
196 with swords dents made with swords   **198 God's lid** God's eyelid (a common oath)

Enter Helenus [and passes over the stage]

205 PANDARUS   That's Helenus. I marvel where Troilus is. That's
Helenus, I think he went not forth today: that's Helenus.

CRESSIDA   Can Helenus fight, uncle?

PANDARUS   Helenus? No. Yes, he'll fight indifferent well. I
marvel where Troilus is. Hark, do you not hear the people
210 cry 'Troilus'? Helenus is a priest.

CRESSIDA   What sneaking fellow comes yonder?

Enter Troilus [and passes over the stage]

PANDARUS   Where? Yonder? That's Deiphobus. 'Tis Troilus!
There's a man, niece!—
Hem! Brave Troilus, the prince of chivalry!

215 CRESSIDA   Peace, for shame, peace!

PANDARUS   Mark him, note him. O brave Troilus! Look well
upon him, niece. Look you how his sword is bloodied, and his
helm more hacked than Hector's, and how he looks, and
how he goes. O admirable youth! He ne'er saw three and
220 twenty. Go thy way, Troilus, go thy way! Had I a sister were a
grace, or a daughter a goddess, he should take his choice. O
admirable man! Paris? Paris is dirt to him, and I warrant
Helen, to change, would give money to boot.

Enter Common Soldiers [and pass over the stage]

CRESSIDA   Here come more.

225 PANDARUS   Asses, fools, dolts. Chaff and bran, chaff and bran;
porridge after meat. I could live and die i'th'eyes of Troilus.
Ne'er look, ne'er look. The eagles are gone: crows and daws,
crows and daws! I had rather be such a man as Troilus than
Agamemnon and all Greece.

---

205 marvel wonder   **206 he** i.e. Troilus   **forth** out (to fight)   **208 indifferent** moderately
211 sneaking creeping/shifty   **214 Hem!** Pandarus either tries to catch Troilus's attention,
coughs awkwardly to cover his error or tries to prompt Cressida's agreement   **218 helm**
helmet   **219 goes** walks, bears himself   **ne'er . . . twenty** is not yet twenty-three
221 grace in Greek mythology, one of the three goddesses of grace and beauty   **222 to**
compared to   **warrant** am sure   **223 change** exchange (one man for the other)   **to boot** in
addition   **225 Chaff and bran** husks, i.e. useless things   **226 porridge after meat** a vegetable
soup after the main course (both terms could also refer to sexual organs or their possessors)
227 daws jackdaws (proverbially foolish birds)

230 CRESSIDA   There is among the Greeks Achilles, a better man
than Troilus.

PANDARUS   Achilles? A drayman, a porter, a very camel.

CRESSIDA   Well, well.

PANDARUS   'Well, well'? Why, have you any discretion? Have
235 you any eyes? Do you know what a man is? Is not birth,
beauty, good shape, discourse, manhood, learning, gentleness,
virtue, youth, liberality, and so forth, the spice and salt that
seasons a man?

CRESSIDA   Ay, a minced man, and then to be baked with no
240 date in the pie, for then the man's date's out.

PANDARUS   You are such another woman! One knows not at
what ward you lie.

CRESSIDA   Upon my back, to defend my belly; upon my wit, to
defend my wiles; upon my secrecy, to defend mine honesty;
245 my mask, to defend my beauty, and you, to defend all these:
and at all these wards I lie at, at a thousand watches.

PANDARUS   Say one of your watches.

CRESSIDA   Nay, I'll watch you for that, and that's one of the
chiefest of them too: if I cannot ward what I would not have
250 hit, I can watch you for telling how I took the blow, unless it
swell past hiding, and then it's past watching.

---

232 **drayman** cart-driver   **camel** i.e. misshapen, lumbering   234 **discretion** good
judgment   235 **birth** noble ancestry   236 **discourse** conversational skill/sound
understanding   **gentleness** good breeding, courtesy   237 **liberality** generosity
239 **minced** cut into small pieces for cooking/dainty, effeminate, pretentious   **no . . . pie** i.e.
with a crucial ingredient lacking/with an impotent penis (no use to the vaginal **pie**)
240 **the . . . out** he is out of date, no good   241 **You . . . woman!** What a woman you are!
at . . . lie which defensive position you assume (fencing term; plays on the notion of sexual
positions, which Cressida picks up on in her reply)   243 **belly** stomach/womb/vagina   **wit**
may play on a sense of "genitals"   244 **wiles** tricks   **secrecy** ability to keep secrets (such as
a love affair or pregnancy)/sexual organs   **honesty** integrity/virtue/chastity   245 **mask**
worn to shield the complexion from the sun and retain a fashionable pallor   246 **wards**
defensive positions/designated guard stations   **watches** vigilant observances/periods of the
night during which a guard was kept (plays on "watch and ward," i.e. to keep guard)
247 **watches** wakeful periods of the night (also suggestive of secretive sexual activity, perhaps
with more than one man)   248 **watch** be wary of   249 **them** i.e. things I have to guard
against   **ward** defend   250 **hit** struck/penetrated sexually   **watch . . . telling** be on guard
to prevent you revealing   251 **swell** become infected/swell with pregnancy   **past watching**
too late to safeguard against

Enter [Troilus'] Boy

PANDARUS   You are such another!

BOY   Sir, my lord would instantly speak with you.

PANDARUS   Where?

255   BOY   At your own house.

PANDARUS   Good boy, tell him I come.   [*Exit Boy*]
        I doubt he be hurt. Fare ye well, good niece.

CRESSIDA   Adieu, uncle.

PANDARUS   I'll be with you, niece, by and by.

260   CRESSIDA   To bring, uncle?

PANDARUS   Ay, a token from Troilus.

CRESSIDA   By the same token, you are a bawd.   *Exit Pandarus*
        Words, vows, gifts, tears, and love's full sacrifice,
        He offers in another's enterprise,
265   But more in Troilus thousand-fold I see
        Than in the glass of Pandar's praise may be;
        Yet hold I off. Women are angels, wooing:
        Things won are done, joy's soul lies in the doing.
        That she beloved knows nought that knows not this:
270   Men prize the thing ungained more than it is:
        That she was never yet that ever knew
        Love got so sweet as when desire did sue.
        Therefore this maxim out of love I teach:
        'Achievement is command; ungained, beseech.'
275   That though my heart's contents firm love doth bear,
        Nothing of that shall from mine eyes appear.

                            Exit [with Alexander]

Boy servant   252 You . . . another! What a woman you are!   257 doubt fear   259 by and
by soon   260 To bring i.e. are you going to bring something   261 token lover's gift,
keepsake   262 By . . . token on that basis   bawd procurer, pimp   264 in . . . enterprise on
behalf of another   266 glass mirror, reflection   267 wooing while being wooed
268 done finished with (plays on the sense of "sexually conquered")   269 she woman who
is   270 Men . . . is men value what they have not got more than its worth   271 That . . .
sue never was there a woman for whom love was as sweet after she had been won as when
she was still being wooed   273 out of drawn from   274 'Achievement . . . beseech'
"Winning a woman's love gives a man control; if she has not been won, he must continue
entreating her"   275 That so that   though . . . bear i.e. although my heart loves surely,
steadily

[Act 1 Scene 3]   *running scene 3*

> *Sennet. Enter Agamemnon, Nestor, Ulysses, Diomedes, Menelaus,*
> *with others*

AGAMEMNON   Princes,
What grief hath set the jaundice on your cheeks?
The ample proposition that hope makes
In all designs begun on earth below
5   Fails in the promised largeness: checks and disasters
Grow in the veins of actions highest reared,
As knots, by the conflux of meeting sap,
Infect the sound pine and diverts his grain
Ṭortive and errant from his course of growth.
10   Nor, princes, is it matter new to us
That we come short of our suppose so far
That after seven years' siege yet Troy walls stand,
Sith every action that hath gone before,
Whereof we have record, trial did draw
15   Bias and thwart, not answering the aim
And that unbodied figure of the thought
That gave't surmisèd shape. Why then, you princes,
Do you with cheeks abashed behold our works
And think them shame, which are indeed nought else
20   But the protractive trials of great Jove
To find persistive constancy in men,
The fineness of which metal is not found
In fortune's love? For then the bold and coward,

1.3   *Location: the Greek camp, not far from Troy   Sennet* trumpet call signaling a
procession   **2 grief** grievance, displeasure   **jaundice** i.e. yellowness (suggestive of jealousy
and disease)   **3 proposition** offer, proposal   **makes . . . below** gives to all enterprises begun
here on earth   **5 in . . . largeness** to fulfill its promise   **checks** obstacles   **6 veins** i.e. vessels
in a plant for carrying **sap   actions highest reared** the most ambitious military endeavors
7 by . . . sap at the point where flowing streams of sap meet   **8 sound pine** healthy pine tree
grain i.e. the grain of the wood   **9 Tortive and errant** twisted and straying   **11 suppose**
expectation/intention   **13 Sith . . . thwart** since every previous recorded military action went
wrong   **15 not . . . shape** not falling out in accordance with the original plan   **18 works**
deeds, endeavors   **20 protractive** protracted, drawn-out   **Jove** Jupiter, Roman king of the
gods   **21 persistive** persistent, enduring   **22 metal** strong substance (plays on "mettle," i.e.
courage, character)   **23 In fortune's love** during the good times

The wise and fool, the artist and unread,
25 The hard and soft seem all affined and kin.
But in the wind and tempest of her frown,
Distinction with a loud and powerful fan,
Puffing at all, winnows the light away;
And what hath mass or matter by itself
30 Lies rich in virtue and unminglèd.
NESTOR   With due observance of thy godly seat,
Great Agamemnon, Nestor shall apply
Thy latest words. In the reproof of chance
'Lies the true proof of men: the sea being smooth,
35 How many shallow bauble boats dare sail
Upon her patient breast, making their way
With those of nobler bulk!
But let the ruffian Boreas once enrage
The gentle Thetis, and anon behold
40 The strong-ribbed bark through liquid mountains cut,
Bounding between the two moist elements,
Like Perseus' horse: where's then the saucy boat
Whose weak untimbered sides but even now
Co-rivalled greatness? Either to harbour fled,
45 Or made a toast for Neptune. Even so
Doth valour's show and valour's worth divide
In storms of fortune; for in her ray and brightness
The herd hath more annoyance by the breeze
Than by the tiger, but when the splitting wind

---

24 **artist** scholar   25 **affined** related (continues aural play on **find, fineness**)   26 **her** i.e.
fortune's   27 **Distinction** the practice of distinguishing between things   28 **winnows**
separates and blows away (as the lighter chaff is separated from the wheat by the **wind**)
29 **matter** substance, worth   30 **virtue** worth, value   31 **observance of** respect for   **seat**
throne, i.e. authority   32 **apply** interpret   33 **reproof** rebuffing, rebuking, defiance
34 **proof** test (puns on **reproof**)   35 **bauble** toy-like   38 **Boreas** Greek god of the north wind
39 **Thetis** sea nymph, mother of Achilles (here represents the sea)   40 **bark** ship   **liquid
mountains** i.e. waves   41 **two moist elements** i.e. air and water   42 **Perseus' horse** Pegasus,
the winged horse of Greek mythology that sprang from Medusa's blood when Perseus
beheaded her; technically, he belonged to Bellerophon   **saucy** insolent   43 **untimbered**
unsound, lacking a strong wooden frame   **even . . . greatness** only a moment ago
accompanied and competed with greater ships   45 **toast** sop, piece of bread soaked in wine
Neptune Roman god of the seas   **Even so** in just such a way   46 **show** outward appearance
47 **her** i.e. fortune's   48 **breeze** gadfly (which bites animals)/light wind

50   Makes flexible the knees of knotted oaks,
        And flies fled under shade, why, then the thing of courage,
        As roused with rage with rage doth sympathize,
        And with an accent tuned in selfsame key
        Retires to chiding fortune.
55 ULYSSES   Agamemnon,
        Thou great commander, nerve and bone of Greece,
        Heart of our numbers, soul and only spirit,
        In whom the tempers and the minds of all
        Should be shut up, hear what Ulysses speaks:
60   Besides the applause and approbation
        The which— most mighty for thy place and
            sway,—   *To Agamemnon*
        And thou most reverend for thy stretched-out life,— *To Nestor*
        I give to both your speeches, which were such
        As Agamemnon and the hand of Greece
65   Should hold up high in brass, and such again
        As venerable Nestor, hatched in silver,
        Should with a bond of air, strong as the axle-tree
        In which the heavens ride, knit all the Greeks' ears
        To his experienced tongue: yet let it please both,
70   Thou great, and wise, to hear Ulysses speak.
    AGAMEMNON   Speak, prince of Ithaca, and be't of less expect
        That matter needless, of importless burden,
        Divide thy lips than we are confident,
        When rank Thersites opes his mastic jaws,
75   We shall hear music, wit and oracle.

---

51 shade shelter   **52 sympathize** respond, be in accordance   **54 Retires** returns, reverts
56 nerve sinew, muscle   **57 numbers** i.e. army   **only** sole/preeminent, exceptional   **spirit**
vital power, essence of life   **58 tempers** temperaments   **59 shut up** incorporated, absorbed
61 The which which   **place and sway** position and authority   **62 reverend** worthy,
respected   **stretched-out** long-lasting   **64 and** i.e. who is   **65 in brass** engraved in brass,
i.e. as a model of eloquence   **66 hatched in silver** i.e. white-haired   **hatched** streaked,
inlaid/engraved   **67 air** i.e. his speech   **axle-tree . . . ride** axis on which the universe revolves
(the heavens were thought to revolve around the earth)   **68 knit** unite, tie   **70 great, and
wise** i.e. Agamemnon, and Nestor   **71 Ithaca** island west of Greece, home of Ulysses   **of less
expect** less likely   **72 importless burden** insignificant content   **74 rank** stinking/diseased/
lustful/coarse   **opes** opens   **mastic** gummy/rotten (possibly also relates to "mastix," a
scourge)

ULYSSES   Troy, yet upon his basis, had been down,
                And the great Hector's sword had lacked a master,
                But for these instances.
                The specialty of rule hath been neglected;
80   And look how many Grecian tents do stand
                Hollow upon this plain, so many hollow factions.
                When that the general is not like the hive
                To whom the foragers shall all repair,
                What honey is expected? Degree being vizarded,
85   Th'unworthiest shows as fairly in the mask.
                The heavens themselves, the planets and this centre
                Observe degree, priority and place,
                Insisture, course, proportion, season, form,
                Office and custom, in all line of order:
90   And therefore is the glorious planet Sol
                In noble eminence enthroned and sphered
                Amidst the other, whose med'cinable eye
                Corrects the ill aspects of planets evil,
                And posts, like the commandment of a king,
95   Sans check, to good and bad. But when the planets
                In evil mixture to disorder wander,
                What plagues and what portents, what mutiny,
                What raging of the sea, shaking of earth,
                Commotion in the winds, frights, changes, horrors,
100   Divert and crack, rend and deracinate
                The unity and married calm of states

---

76 yet . . . basis still standing on its foundations   **had** would have   **78 instances** factors,
reasons   **79 specialty of rule** rights and obligations of effective authority   **80 how** however
81 Hollow empty   **so . . . factions** there are just as many deceptive factions   **82 general**
military leader   **hive** beehive (i.e. the focal point, center of command)   **83 repair** return
84 Degree rank, hierarchy   **vizarded** masked, concealed   **85 shows as fairly** appears just as
attractive, as worthy   **86 this centre** i.e. the earth (which, according to the Ptolemaic model,
was the center of the universe)   **88 Insisture** regularity, constancy, steady continuance
89 Office particular function   **90 Sol** the sun (thought to be a **planet**)   **91 sphered**
contained within its sphere (each planet was thought to orbit within a hollow crystalline
sphere)   **92 other** i.e. other planets   **med'cinable** healing   **93 ill** sick, unwell/ominous,
causing misfortune   **aspects** planetary positions, directions of alignment   **94 posts** speeds
95 Sans check without pause   **96 mixture** conjunction   **to disorder wander** move into
unfavorable alignment   **100 deracinate** uproot   **101 married** harmonious, united

Quite from their fixure? O, when degree is shaked,
Which is the ladder to all high designs,
The enterprise is sick! How could communities,
105   Degrees in schools and brotherhoods in cities,
Peaceful commerce from dividable shores,
The primogenitive and due of birth,
Prerogative of age, crowns, sceptres, laurels,
But by degree, stand in authentic place?
110   Take but degree away, untune that string,
And, hark, what discord follows. Each thing meets
In mere oppugnancy. The bounded waters
Should lift their bosoms higher than the shores
And make a sop of all this solid globe:
115   Strength should be lord of imbecility,
And the rude son should strike his father dead:
Force should be right, or rather, right and wrong,
Between whose endless jar justice resides,
Should lose their names, and so should justice too.
120   Then everything includes itself in power,
Power into will, will into appetite,
And appetite, an universal wolf,
So doubly seconded with will and power,
Must make perforce an universal prey,
125   And last eat up himself. Great Agamemnon,
This chaos, when degree is suffocate,
Follows the choking.
And this neglection of degree is it

102 **Quite** completely   **fixure** fixed position   **degree** rank, hierarchy (plays on the sense of "ladder's rung")   103 **high designs** noble undertakings (**high** plays on its literal sense)
105 **Degrees in schools** academic ranks   **brotherhoods** guilds   106 **dividable shores** countries separated by sea   107 **primogenitive** primogeniture, the inheritance rights of an eldest son   109 **But** except, other than   **stand . . . place** remain in their legitimate positions
112 **mere oppugnancy** total conflict   **bounded** enclosed, contained (by their shores)
113 **Should** would   114 **make . . . globe** i.e. drown the world   **sop** piece of bread soaked in wine   115 **imbecility** physical weakness   116 **rude** violent, uncivilized   118 **jar** conflict, clash   119 **names** individual identities   120 **includes** subsumes, absorbs/concludes, terminates   121 **will** willfulness   **appetite** desire, greed   123 **seconded** supported, assisted
124 **make . . . prey** inevitably prey upon everything   126 **suffocate** suffocated   127 **choking** act of suffocating

That by a pace goes backward, in a purpose
130   It hath to climb. The general's disdained
By him one step below, he by the next,
That next by him beneath, so every step
Exampled by the first pace that is sick
Of his superior, grows to an envious fever
135   Of pale and bloodless emulation:
And 'tis this fever that keeps Troy on foot,
Not her own sinews. To end a tale of length,
Troy in our weakness lives, not in her strength.

NESTOR   Most wisely hath Ulysses here discovered
140   The fever whereof all our power is sick.

AGAMEMNON   The nature of the sickness found, Ulysses,
What is the remedy?

ULYSSES   The great Achilles, whom opinion crowns
The sinew and the forehand of our host,
145   Having his ear full of his airy fame,
Grows dainty of his worth, and in his tent
Lies mocking our designs: with him Patroclus
Upon a lazy bed the livelong day
Breaks scurril jests,
150   And with ridiculous and awkward action —
Which, slanderer, he imitation calls —
He pageants us. Sometime, great Agamemnon,
Thy topless deputation he puts on,
And, like a strutting player, whose conceit
155   Lies in his hamstring, and doth think it rich

---

129 by a pace step by step   **in . . . climb** when the intention had been to climb upward
133 Exampled given the example, shown a precedent   **the . . . superior** the morally corrupt
step taken previously by his superior   **135 emulation** rivalry/grudging envy   **136 on foot**
upstanding   **139 discovered** revealed   **140 power** army/strength/authority   **143 opinion**
public opinion/reputation   **144 forehand** foremost part, mainstay   **host** army   **145 airy**
widely acknowledged/insubstantial   **146 dainty of** particular, fastidious about
148 Upon . . . bed lazily upon a bed (transferred epithet)   **149 Breaks** cracks, makes
scurril scurrilous, vulgar   **150 ridiculous** comically derisory   **awkward** unfavorable,
perverse (also possibly "turned the wrong way, back foremost," suggesting a joke about anal
sex)   **152 pageants** impersonates, parodies   **153 topless deputation** supreme role   **puts
on** imitates   **154 conceit** intellect, wits   **155 hamstring** i.e. legs

To hear the wooden dialogue and sound
'Twixt his stretched footing and the scaffoldage,
Such to-be-pitied and o'er-wrested seeming
He acts thy greatness in: and when he speaks,
160   'Tis like a chime a-mending, with terms unsquared,
Which from the tongue of roaring Typhon dropped
Would seems hyperboles. At this fusty stuff
The large Achilles, on his pressed bed lolling,
From his deep chest laughs out a loud applause,
165   Cries 'Excellent! 'Tis Agamemnon just.
Now play me Nestor: hum and stroke thy beard,
As he being dressed to some oration.'
That's done, as near as the extremest ends
Of parallels, as like as Vulcan and his wife,
170   Yet god Achilles still cries, 'Excellent!
'Tis Nestor right. Now play him me, Patroclus,
Arming to answer in a night alarm.'
And then, forsooth, the faint defects of age
Must be the scene of mirth: to cough and spit,
175   And, with a palsy-fumbling on his gorget,
Shake in and out the rivet: and at this sport
Sir Valour dies; cries 'O, enough, Patroclus,
Or give me ribs of steel! I shall split all

156 wooden dull, lifeless, stupid/resounding on a wooden surface   **dialogue . . . scaffoldage**
echoing noise of his long strides over the stage platform   **158 to-be-pitied . . . seeming**
pitiable and overstrained appearance   **160 a-mending** in need of tuning   **terms unsquared**
ill-fitting words, clumsy expressions   **161 Typhon** giant monster of Greek mythology who
made war upon the gods and was associated with winds, earthquakes, and volcanoes
162 fusty moldy, stale (glances perhaps at "fustian," i.e. inflated, hyperbolic language)
163 large powerfully built (also suggesting self-importance and licentiousness)   **pressed**
weighed down (with his body)   **164 deep** large and resounding   **165 just** exactly   **166 me**
for me   **hum** murmur in displeasure or in thought/make a throat-clearing sound
167 dressed to prepared for, ready to begin   **168 as . . . parallels** i.e. unconvincingly
(parallel lines never meet)   **169 as . . . wife** Vulcan differs completely from his wife Venus: he
is the deformed Roman god of fire, she the beautiful goddess of love   **170 god** sarcastic
(perhaps nods to Achilles' near-immortal status in mythology; his mother was the sea nymph
Thetis who made him invulnerable, apart from his heel)   **171 me** for me   **172 answer in**
respond to   **173 forsooth** in truth   **faint** frail, feeble   **175 palsy-fumbling** fumbling
because his hand is shaking   **palsy** shaking fit, tremor, paralysis   **gorget** piece of armor
protecting the throat   **176 rivet** bolt for fastening armor   **sport** amusement   **177 Sir**
Valour sarcastic title for Achilles   **dies** i.e. dies laughing

In pleasure of my spleen.' And in this fashion,
180   All our abilities, gifts, natures, shapes,
Severals and generals of grace exact,
Achievements, plots, orders, preventions,
Excitements to the field, or speech for truce,
Success or loss, what is or is not, serves
185   As stuff for these two to make paradoxes.
NESTOR   And in the imitation of these twain —
Who, as Ulysses says, opinion crowns
With an imperial voice — many are infect.
Ajax is grown self-willed, and bears his head
190   In such a rein, in full as proud a place
As broad Achilles, and keeps his tent like him;
Makes factious feasts, rails on our state of war,
Bold as an oracle, and sets Thersites,
A slave whose gall coins slanders like a mint,
195   To match us in comparisons with dirt,
To weaken and discredit our exposure,
How rank soever rounded in with danger.
ULYSSES   They tax our policy, and call it cowardice,
Count wisdom as no member of the war,
200   Forestall prescience, and esteem no act
But that of hand: the still and mental parts,
That do contrive how many hands shall strike
When fitness calls them on, and know by measure
Of their observant toil the enemies' weight —

---

179 spleen thought to be the seat of laughter and strong emotion   **181 Severals . . . exact** accomplished virtues, both individual and universal   **182 preventions** defensive measures   **183 Excitements** exhortations, encouragement   **185 paradoxes** absurdities, statements contrary to received belief   **186 twain** two   **188 an imperial voice** absolute approval, a ruling vote   **infect** infected   **189 bears . . . rein** (like a horse) resists the reins, is skittish and willful (**rein** puns on "reign")   **190 in . . . place** just as proudly/with just such a proud sense of his own status   **191 broad** physically large/outspoken, unrestrained   **keeps** keeps to   **192 factious** divisive, faction-forming   **rails on** denounces, rants about   **194 slave** rogue, wretch/lackey   **gall** bitterness   **coins . . . mint** invents insults as fast as a mint coins money   **196 exposure** vulnerable situation   **197 How . . . danger** however abundantly we are surrounded by dangers   **198 tax our policy** criticize our strategy/condemn our diplomacy   **200 Forestall prescience** obstruct forward planning   **201 that of hand** physical combat/immediate action   **202 contrive** plan   **203 fitness** the right moment/a proper state of readiness   **know . . . weight** by careful observation judge the enemy's strength

205   Why, this hath not a finger's dignity.
      They call this bed-work, mapp'ry, closet-war,
      So that the ram that batters down the wall,
      For the great swing and rudeness of his poise,
      They place before his hand that made the engine,
210   Or those that with the fineness of their souls
      By reason guide his execution.
NESTOR   Let this be granted, and Achilles' horse
      Makes many Thetis' sons.   *Tucket*
AGAMEMNON   What trumpet? Look, Menelaus.
215 MENELAUS   From Troy.
      Enter Aeneas
AGAMEMNON   What would you 'fore our tent?
AENEAS   Is this great Agamemnon's tent, I pray you?
AGAMEMNON   Even this.
AENEAS   May one that is a herald and a prince
220   Do a fair message to his kingly ears?
AGAMEMNON   With surety stronger than Achilles' arm
      'Fore all the Greekish heads, which with one voice
      Call Agamemnon head and general.
AENEAS   Fair leave and large security. How may
225   A stranger to those most imperial looks
      Know them from eyes of other mortals?
AGAMEMNON   How?
AENEAS   Ay,
      I ask that I might waken reverence,
230   And on the cheek be ready with a blush
      Modest as morning when she coldly eyes

---

205 hath . . . dignity is not deemed worth a finger (in relation to the whole body)   **206 bed-work** armchair strategy, dreaming up of plans   **mapp'ry** map-making   **closet-war** i.e. war conducted from the study   **207 ram** battering ram   **208 For** due to   **rudeness . . . poise** brute force of its impact   **209 place . . . engine** value more highly than the man who designed it   **210 fineness . . . souls** subtlety of their intelligence   **211 his execution** the operation of the battering ram   **212 Let . . . sons** if this is the case then Achilles' horse is worth many an Achilles (son of **Thetis**)   *Tucket* personal trumpet call   **216 'fore** before   **220 fair** courteous   **221 surety** security   **arm** might, power   **222 'Fore . . . heads** foremost among or leading the Greek army   **224 leave** permission   **large** comprehensive/generous   **229 waken reverence** summon a respectful demeanor (in myself)   **231 coldly** with the chill of dawn/chastely, modestly

The youthful Phoebus.
Which is that god in office, guiding men?
Which is the high and mighty Agamemnon?

235   **AGAMEMNON**   This Trojan scorns us, or the men of Troy
Are ceremonious courtiers.

  AENEAS   Courtiers as free, as debonair, unarmed,
As bending angels: that's their fame in peace.
But when they would seem soldiers, they have galls,
240   Good arms, strong joints, true swords, and,
Jove's accord,
Nothing so full of heart. But peace, Aeneas,
Peace, Trojan, lay thy finger on thy lips.
The worthiness of praise distains his worth,
245   If that the praised himself bring the praise forth.
But what the repining enemy commends,
That breath fame blows, that praise, sole pure, transcends.

  AGAMEMNON   Sir, you of Troy, call you yourself Aeneas?

  AENEAS   Ay, Greek, that is my name.

250   **AGAMEMNON**   What's your affair I pray you?

  AENEAS   Sir, pardon, 'tis for Agamemnon's ears.

  AGAMEMNON   He hears nought privately that comes from Troy.

  AENEAS   Nor I from Troy come not to whisper him:
I bring a trumpet to awake his ear,
255   To set his sense on the attentive bent,
And then to speak.

  AGAMEMNON   Speak frankly as the wind:
It is not Agamemnon's sleeping hour,
That thou shalt know. Trojan, he is awake,
260   He tells thee so himself.

---

232 **Phoebus** Roman name for the sun god   237 **free** honorable, generous   **debonair**
gracious   **unarmed** i.e. during peacetime   238 **bending** bowing, reverential   **fame**
reputation   239 **galls** spirit to resent insult   241 **Jove's accord** with Jove's favor
242 **Nothing . . . heart** no one is so courageous   244 **distains his worth** sullies its value
245 **If . . . forth** if the subject of praise does the praising himself   246 **repining** begrudging,
discontented   **commends** compliments   247 **That . . . blows** fame broadcasts that praise
sole entirely/incomparably   254 **trumpet** trumpeter   255 **sense . . . bent** hearing in an
attentive direction   257 **frankly** freely

AENEAS   Trumpet, blow loud,
      Send thy brass voice through all these lazy tents,
      And every Greek of mettle, let him know
      What Troy means fairly shall be spoke aloud.

The trumpets sound

265   We have, great Agamemnon, here in Troy
      A prince called Hector — Priam is his father —
      Who in this dull and long-continued truce
      Is rusty grown. He bade me take a trumpet,
      And to this purpose speak: kings, princes, lords,
270   If there be one amongst the fair'st of Greece
      That holds his honour higher than his ease,
      That seeks his praise more than he fears his peril,
      That knows his valour, and knows not his fear,
      That loves his mistress more than in confession,
275   With truant vows to her own lips he loves,
      And dare avow her beauty and her worth
      In other arms than hers — to him this challenge.
      Hector, in view of Trojans and of Greeks,
      Shall make it good, or do his best to do it.
280   He hath a lady, wiser, fairer, truer,
      Than ever Greek did compass in his arms,
      And will tomorrow with his trumpet call
      Midway between your tents and walls of Troy,
      To rouse a Grecian that is true in love:
285   If any come, Hector shall honour him:
      If none, he'll say in Troy when he retires,
      The Grecian dames are sunburnt and not worth
      The splinter of a lance. Even so much.

---

263 mettle spirit (picks up on **brass** to play on the sense of "metal")　　**267 dull** lifeless, inactive　**270 fair'st** noblest, most honorable　　**271 ease** personal comfort　　**274 That . . . loves** who loves his lady more than can be demonstrated by mere words and potentially untrustworthy vows　　**277 In . . . hers** by taking up weapons rather than remaining in her embraces　**281 compass** embrace　　**282 will** come　　**284 rouse** challenge, stir up (with sexual connotations)　　**286 retires** returns　　**287 sunburnt** dark or tanned complexions were considered unattractive　　**288 splinter . . . lance** breaking a lance in combat (**lance** plays on the sense of "penis")　·　**Even so much** i.e. that is the sum of my message

AGAMEMNON   This shall be told our lovers, Lord Aeneas:
290   If none of them have soul in such a kind,
             We left them all at home. But we are soldiers,
             And may that soldier a mere recreant prove,
             That means not, hath not, or is not in love!
             If then one is, or hath, or means to be,
295   That one meets Hector: if none else, I'll be he.

NESTOR   Tell him of Nestor, one that was a man
             When Hector's grandsire sucked. He is old now,
             But if there be not in our Grecian mould
             One noble man that hath one spark of fire,
300   To answer for his love, tell him from me
             I'll hide my silver beard in a gold beaver
             And in my vantbrace put this withered brawn,
             And meeting him will tell him that my lady
             Was fairer than his grandam and as chaste
305   As may be in the world. His youth in flood,
             I'll pawn this truth with my three drops of blood.

AENEAS   Now heavens forbid such scarcity of youth!

ULYSSES   Amen.

AGAMEMNON   Fair Lord Aeneas, let me touch your hand:
310   To our pavilion shall I lead you first.
             Achilles shall have word of this intent,
             So shall each lord of Greece, from tent to tent.
             Yourself shall feast with us before you go
             And find the welcome of a noble foe.

                              Exeunt. Ulysses and Nestor remain

315 ULYSSES Nestor.

NESTOR   What says Ulysses?

ULYSSES   I have a young conception in my brain,
             Be you my time to bring it to some shape.

---

290 **soul** inner conviction, spirit   **kind** matter, business   292 **mere recreant** complete
coward   293 **not** not to be   **not** not been   297 **grandsire** grandfather   **sucked** i.e. was a
baby   301 **beaver** helmet's visor   302 **vantbrace** armor for the forearm   **brawn** muscle,
arm   304 **grandam** grandmother   305 **flood** full flow, vigorous health   306 **pawn** pledge
three . . . blood i.e. what little blood I have left   310 **pavilion** ceremonial tent   317 **conception**
plan/notion (with connotations of pregnancy)   318 **Be . . . shape** i.e. help me to develop and
give birth to this idea

	NESTOR	What is't?
320	ULYSSES	This 'tis:

Blunt wedges rive hard knots: the seeded pride
That hath to this maturity blown up
In rank Achilles must or now be cropped
Or, shedding, breed a nursery of like evil,
325 To overbulk us all.

NESTOR   Well, and how?

ULYSSES   This challenge that the gallant Hector sends,
However it is spread in general name,
Relates in purpose only to Achilles.

330 NESTOR   The purpose is perspicuous even as substance
Whose grossness little characters sum up:
And, in the publication, make no strain
But that Achilles, were his brain as barren
As banks of Libya — though, Apollo knows,
335 'Tis dry enough — will, with great speed of judgement,
Ay, with celerity, find Hector's purpose
Pointing on him.

ULYSSES   And wake him to the answer, think you?

NESTOR   Yes, 'tis most meet; who may you else oppose
340 That can from Hector bring his honour off,
If not Achilles? Though 't be a sportful combat,
Yet in this trial much opinion dwells,
For here the Trojans taste our dear'st repute
With their fin'st palate: and trust to me, Ulysses,

---

321 Blunt . . . knots blunt tools are needed to split tough knotty wood, i.e. Achilles must be stopped by decisive action   **seeded** planted/matured, overgrown   **322 blown up** become swollen/bloomed/become infected   **323 rank** puffed up/overabundantly growing/diseased **or** either   **324 shedding** spilling/scattering seed   **nursery** training ground/collection of young plants   **like** similar   **325 overbulk** outgrow, dominate   **327 gallant** fine, splendid/ brave   **328 spread . . . name** issued to everyone   **330 perspicuous . . . up** as obvious as wealth, whose enormity is revealed in little digits   **332 in . . . strain** when it is announced publicly, have no doubt   **334 banks of Libya** shores of the Libyan desert   **335 dry** barren, dull   **336 celerity** swiftness   **337 on** at   **338 wake . . . answer** will it rouse him to respond **339 meet** fitting   **oppose** put forward as an opponent   **340 from . . . off** acquit himself honorably against Hector   **341 sportful** recreational, not pursued to the death   **342 trial** contest, test of skill   **opinion** reputation   **343 taste . . . repute** sample our most precious reputation   **344 fin'st** refined, most discerning

345 Our imputation shall be oddly poised
In this wild action. For the success,
Although particular, shall give a scantling
Of good or bad unto the general,
And in such indexes, although small pricks
350 To their subsequent volumes, there is seen
The baby figure of the giant mass
Of things to come at large. It is supposed
He that meets Hector issues from our choice;
And choice, being mutual act of all our souls,
355 Makes merit her election, and doth boil,
As 'twere from forth us all, a man distilled
Out of our virtues; who miscarrying,
What heart from hence receives the conqu'ring part
To steel a strong opinion to themselves,
360 Which entertained, limbs are his instruments,
In no less working than are swords and bows
Directive by the limbs.

ULYSSES   Give pardon to my speech:
Therefore 'tis meet Achilles meet not Hector.
365 Let us, like merchants, show our foulest wares,
And think perchance they'll sell: if not,
The lustre of the better yet to show,
Shall show the better. Do not consent
That ever Hector and Achilles meet,

---

345 imputation reputation   **oddly poised** unbalanced, i.e. at great risk   **346 wild** reckless
success result, outcome   **347 particular** specific to the individual fighter   **scantling**
guideline, measure   **348 the general** everyone   **349 indexes** tables of contents/prefaces
pricks marks, indicators (plays on the sense of "penis")   **350 To** compared to   **subsequent**
volumes the following main portion of the book (with erectile connotations)   **351 baby**
figure i.e. microcosm (plays on the idea of conception)   **352 at large** in full (plays on the idea
of pregnancy)   **353 issues** results (plays on the sense of "is born")   **355 election** basis for
choice   **boil** distill by boiling   **356 distilled** extracted, refined   **357 miscarrying** should he
fail   **358 heart** spirit, encouragement   **hence** this (failure)   **part** side, i.e. the Trojans
359 steel . . . themselves strengthen their good opinion of themselves (**steel** plays on "steal")
360 Which . . . limbs which opinion being held, limbs become weapons no less effective than
the swords and bows controlled by those limbs   **364 meet** fitting   **meet** encounter in combat
365 foulest most unattractive   **366 perchance** perhaps

370   For both our honour and our shame in this
       Are dogged with two strange followers.
NESTOR   I see them not with my old eyes: what are they?
ULYSSES   What glory our Achilles shares from Hector,
       Were he not proud, we all should wear with him:
375   But he already is too insolent,
       And we were better parch in Afric sun
       Than in the pride and salt scorn of his eyes,
       Should he scape Hector fair. If he were foiled,
       Why then, we did our main opinion crush
380   In taint of our best man. No, make a lott'ry,
       And by device let blockish Ajax draw
       The sort to fight with Hector: among ourselves
       Give him allowance as the worthier man,
       For that will physic the great Myrmidon
385   Who broils in loud applause, and make him fall
       His crest that prouder than blue Iris bends.
       If the dull brainless Ajax come safe off,
       We'll dress him up in voices: if he fail,
       Yet go we under our opinion still
390   That we have better men. But, hit or miss,
       Our project's life this shape of sense assumes:
       Ajax employed plucks down Achilles' plumes.
NESTOR   Now, Ulysses,
       I begin to relish thy advice;
395   And I will give a taste of it forthwith

---

371 strange followers i.e. undesirable outcomes (regardless of whether Achilles wins or loses)
373 shares takes   **375 insolent** arrogant   **376 were . . . sun** would be better off shriveling
up under the African sun   **377 salt** bitter, stinging (perhaps, picking up on **parch**, with
connotations of "thirst-provoking, drying out")   **378 scape** escape   **fair** successfully
379 did . . . crush would destroy the chief part of our reputation   **380 taint** the dishonoring
381 device strategy, trick   **blockish** stupid   **382 sort** lot   **383 allowance** acknowledgment
384 physic dose with medicine, cure   **Myrmidon** i.e. Achilles (who led a band of Myrmidon
warriors from Thessaly)   **385 broils** basks, glows   **fall** lower, let fall   **386 crest** feathers on
his helmet (with connotations of the strutting cock's crest)   **Iris** i.e. the rainbow (of which
Iris, the messenger of the Greek gods, was goddess)   **bends** arches   **387 come safe off**
emerges successfully from the combat   **388 dress . . . voices** cover him with praise/we can
retain the general conviction   **389 Yet . . . opinion** we can maintain our reputation
391 Our . . . assumes the outcome of our plan comes down to this   **392 employed** used in
this way   **394 relish** taste, appreciate

To Agamemnon. Go we to him straight.
Two curs shall tame each other: pride alone
Must tarre the mastiffs on, as 'twere their bone.   *Exeunt*

[Act 2 Scene 1]

running scene 3 continues

Enter Ajax and Thersites

AJAX   Thersites!

THERSITES   Agamemnon, how if he had boils, full, all over,
generally?

AJAX   Thersites!

5 THERSITES   And those boils did run? Say so: did not the general
run? Were not that a botchy core?

AJAX   Dog!

THERSITES   Then there would come some matter from him: I see
none now.

10 AJAX   Thou bitch-wolf's son, canst thou not hear? Feel,
then.   *Strikes him*

THERSITES   The plague of Greece upon thee, thou mongrel beef-
witted lord!

AJAX   Speak then, you whinid'st leaven, speak. I will beat
15 thee into handsomeness.

THERSITES   I shall sooner rail thee into wit and holiness: but I
think thy horse will sooner con an oration than thou learn a
prayer without book. Thou canst strike, canst thou? A red
murrain o'thy jade's tricks!

---

396 straight straightaway   **397 curs** dogs   **398 tarre** incite, provoke   **2.1**   **2 how** what
full everywhere/big, swollen   **3 generally** everywhere (puns on Agamemnon's rank as
general)   **5 run** seep (sense then shifts to "run away")   **Say so** say it were so   **did** would
6 botchy core boil-covered body/flawed (i.e. cowardly) heart (**core** may pun on "corps," i.e.
"soldiers stationed on guard"; it can also mean "hardened mass in the center of a boil")
8 matter pus/significant subject matter, reason   **12 mongrel** alludes to Ajax's Greek/Trojan
ancestry; his mother Hesione was sister to King Priam, his father was the Greek Telamon
beef-witted thick-headed, brainless   **14 whinid'st** moldiest   **leaven** agent used to ferment
dough   **beat** plays on the idea of kneading dough   **15 handsomeness** graciousness,
courtesy (playing on the antithetical idea of a beating making Thersites more physically
handsome)   **16 rail** berate, rant   **wit** intelligence   **holiness** respectful piety   **17 con**
memorize   **18 red murrain** bloody plague (literally, disease affecting cattle and sheep)
19 jade's tricks worthless horse's bad habits/whore's acts (picks up on **strike** as "copulate")

20	AJAX	Toadstool, learn me the proclamation.
	THERSITES	Dost thou think I have no sense, thou strik'st me thus?
	AJAX	The proclamation!
	THERSITES	Thou art proclaimed a fool, I think.
25	AJAX	Do not, porcupine, do not; my fingers itch.
	THERSITES	I would thou didst itch from head to foot and I had the scratching of thee: I would make thee the loathsom'st scab in Greece.
	AJAX	I say, the proclamation!
30	THERSITES	Thou grumblest and railest every hour on Achilles, and thou art as full of envy at his greatness as Cerberus is at Proserpina's beauty, ay, that thou bark'st at him.
	AJAX	Mistress Thersites!
	THERSITES	Thou shouldst strike him.
35	AJAX	Cobloaf!
	THERSITES	He would pun thee into shivers with his fist, as a sailor breaks a biscuit.
	AJAX	You whoreson cur! *Beats him*
	THERSITES	Do, do.
40	AJAX	Thou stool for a witch!
	THERSITES	Ay, do, do, thou sodden-witted lord! Thou hast no more brain than I have in mine elbows: an asinico may tutor thee. Thou scurvy-valiant ass, thou art here but to thrash Trojans, and thou art bought and sold among those of any wit, like a barbarian slave. If thou use to beat me, I will begin
45		

20 **Toadstool** poisonous mushroom (plays on the sense of "toad's excrement") **learn me** inform me of 21 **sense** feeling 25 **porcupine** suggesting Thersites' prickly nature **itch** i.e. to beat you 28 **scab** crust covering a wound/rascal 30 **on** at 31 **Cerberus** three-headed guard dog of the classical underworld 32 **Proserpina** Roman goddess of the classical underworld 35 **Cobloaf** a small loaf of bread with a round head 36 **pun** pound **shivers** splinters, pieces 37 **sailor . . . biscuit** ships' biscuits were proverbially dry and brittle 38 **whoreson cur** bastard dog **whoreson** son of a whore (a common term of abuse) 40 **stool** stool/seat containing a toilet/ducking-stool 41 **sodden-witted** stupid/drunken 42 **asinico** little ass (from Spanish *asnico*) 43 **scurvy-valiant** supremely worthless 44 **bought and sold** betrayed for a bribe 45 **barbarian** uncivilized or savage foreigner **use** continue, make it a habit

at thy heel, and tell what thou art by inches, thou thing of no
bowels, thou!

AJAX	You dog!	
THERSITES	You scurvy lord!	
50 AJAX	You cur!	*Beats him*
THERSITES	Mars his idiot! Do, rudeness, do, camel: do, do.	

Enter Achilles and Patroclus

ACHILLES   Why, how now, Ajax? Wherefore do you this?
How now, Thersites? What's the matter, man?

THERSITES   You see him there, do you?

55   ACHILLES   Ay, what's the matter?

THERSITES   Nay, look upon him.

ACHILLES   So I do: what's the matter?

THERSITES   Nay, but regard him well.

ACHILLES   Well, why, I do so.

60   THERSITES   But yet you look not well upon him, for whosomever
you take him to be, he is Ajax.

ACHILLES   I know that, fool.

THERSITES   Ay, but that fool knows not himself.

AJAX   Therefore I beat thee.

65   THERSITES   Lo, lo, lo, lo, what modicums of wit he utters! His
evasions have ears thus long. I have bobbed his brain more
than he has beat my bones: I will buy nine sparrows for a
penny, and his pia mater is not worth the ninth part of a
sparrow. This lord, Achilles — Ajax, who wears his wit in his
70   belly and his guts in his head — I'll tell you what I say of him.

ACHILLES   What?

THERSITES   I say, this Ajax—   *Ajax attempts to beat him*

---

46 tell reveal/count   **47 bowels** depths, sensitivity (given Ajax's size, plays ironically on the
sense of "substance, internal organs")   **49 scurvy** contemptible, worthless   **51 Mars his**
Mars' (Roman god of war)   **rudeness** rough, ill-mannered one   **camel** i.e. ungainly,
misshapen one   **52 Wherefore** why   **59 Well** all right, very well/closely, properly (Thersites'
sense in the previous line)   **60 well** approvingly   **61 Ajax** perhaps puns on "a jakes," i.e. a
toilet   **63 that fool** i.e. Ajax   **64 Therefore . . . thee** i.e. it is because I forgot myself that I beat
you (though Ajax unwittingly agrees that he is a fool)   **65 Lo** look   **modicums** tiny amounts
66 evasions verbal shuffling, dodges   **ears thus long** i.e. long ass's ears   **bobbed** cheated/
pummeled   **67 sparrows** i.e. creatures of little value   **68 pia mater** brain (literally the
membrane covering the brain)

ACHILLES	Nay, good Ajax.	*Intervenes*
THERSITES	Has not so much wit—	
75 | ACHILLES | Nay, I must hold you. | *To Ajax* |

THERSITES   As will stop the eye of Helen's needle, for whom he
comes to fight.

ACHILLES   Peace, fool!

THERSITES   I would have peace and quietness, but the fool will
80   not: he there, that he, look you there.

AJAX   O thou damned cur, I shall—

ACHILLES   Will you set your wit to a fool's?

THERSITES   No, I warrant you, for a fool's will shame it.

PATROCLUS   Good words, Thersites.

85   ACHILLES   What's the quarrel?

AJAX   I bade the vile owl go learn me the tenor of the
proclamation, and he rails upon me.

THERSITES   I serve thee not.

AJAX   Well, go to, go to.

90   THERSITES   I serve here voluntary.

ACHILLES   Your last service was sufferance, 'twas not voluntary:
no man is beaten voluntary. Ajax was here the voluntary,
and you as under an impress.

THERSITES   E'en so. A great deal of your wit, too, lies in your
95   sinews, or else there be liars. Hector shall have a great catch
if he knock out either of your brains: he were as good crack
a fusty nut with no kernel.

ACHILLES   What, with me too, Thersites?

THERSITES   There's Ulysses and old Nestor, whose wit was
100   mouldy ere your grandsires had nails on their toes, yoke you
like draught-oxen and make you plough up the war.

---

76 **stop** fill up   **eye** probably plays on the sense of "vagina"   80 **that he** him   82 **to** against;
wit may have genital connotations and **fools'** penises were proverbially supposed to be large
83 **warrant** assure   84 **Good words** i.e. speak more appropriately, be courteous   86 **owl** i.e.
dullard   **tenor** substance, nature   91 **service** performance of duty/military service/beating
sufferance compulsory/suffering   92 **the voluntary** voluntarily   93 **as . . . impress**
conscripted/marked with beatings   94 **E'en so** exactly   95 **there be liars** i.e. reports are
untrue   96 **were as good** might as well   97 **fusty** old, moldy   98 **with** i.e. will you argue
with   100 **ere** before   **grandsires** grandfathers   **yoke . . . war** i.e. they make you do the
work

ACHILLES	What? What?
THERSITES	Yes, good sooth. To, Achilles! To, Ajax! To—
AJAX	I shall cut out your tongue.
105 THERSITES	'Tis no matter, I shall speak as much as thou afterwards.
PATROCLUS	No more words, Thersites, peace!
THERSITES	I will hold my peace when Achilles' brach bids me, shall I?
110 ACHILLES	There's for you, Patroclus.
THERSITES	I will see you hanged like clodpolls ere I come any more to your tents: I will keep where there is wit stirring and leave the faction of fools. *Exit*
PATROCLUS	A good riddance.
115 ACHILLES	Marry, this, sir, is proclaimed through all our host: That Hector, by the fifth hour of the sun, Will with a trumpet 'twixt our tents and Troy Tomorrow morning call some knight to arms That hath a stomach, and such a one that dare
120	Maintain— I know not what: 'tis trash. Farewell.
AJAX	Farewell? Who shall answer him?
ACHILLES	I know not: 'tis put to lott'ry, otherwise He knew his man.
AJAX	O, meaning you? I will go learn more of it. *Exeunt*

[Act 2 Scene 2]   *running scene 4*

Enter Priam, Hector, Troilus, Paris and Helenus

PRIAM   After so many hours, lives, speeches spent,
Thus once again says Nestor from the Greeks:
'Deliver Helen, and all damage else —

---

103 good sooth in good truth   **To** the call of a plowman urging on his oxen   **108 peace** puns on "piece," i.e. genitals   **brach** bitch, i.e. (homosexual) whore   **110 There's** i.e. there's an insult   **111 clodpolls** idiots, blockheads   **112 keep** lodge, dwell   **115 host** army   **116 fifth . . . sun** i.e. eleven a.m.   **117 'twixt** between   **119 stomach** appetite for fighting, courage   **121 answer him** respond to the challenge/oppose him   **123 knew** would know   **2.2**   *Location: Troy*   **3 Deliver** release

As honour, loss of time, travail, expense,
5   Wounds, friends, and what else dear that is consumed
In hot digestion of this cormorant war —
Shall be struck off.' Hector, what say you to't?
HECTOR   Though no man lesser fears the Greeks than I,
As far as touches my particular,
10   Yet, dread Priam,
There is no lady of more softer bowels,
More spongy to suck in the sense of fear,
More ready to cry out 'Who knows what follows?'
Than Hector is. The wound of peace is surety,
15   Surety secure, but modest doubt is called
The beacon of the wise, the tent that searches
To th'bottom of the worst. Let Helen go:
Since the first sword was drawn about this question,
Every tithe soul 'mongst many thousand dimes,
20   Hath been as dear as Helen — I mean, of ours.
If we have lost so many tenths of ours
To guard a thing not ours nor worth to us,
Had it our name, the value of one ten,
What merit's in that reason which denies
25   The yielding of her up?
TROILUS   Fie, fie, my brother!
Weigh you the worth and honour of a king
So great as our dread father in a scale
Of common ounces? Will you with counters sum
30   The past proportion of his infinite,

---

4 As such as   **travail** labor, exertion   **5 dear** revered, valued   **6 cormorant** greedy,
voracious (from the large seabird of that name)   **7 struck off** canceled   **9 touches my**
particular I am concerned   **10 dread** deeply honored, revered   **11 bowels** sensitivity,
compassion   **14 surety** confidence, security   **15 secure** overconfident   **modest doubt**
reasonable caution   **16 tent** surgical probe   **17 worst** i.e. worst wound   **18 question** issue,
dispute   **19 tithe soul** tenth life/life taken as war's tithe   **tithe** the tenth of one's annual
income due to the Church   **dimes** tenths   **23 Had . . . name** even if it (Helen) were Trojan
one ten i.e. one Trojan life   **24 reason** argument, reasoning   **26 Fie** expression of disgust or
reproach   **28 scale . . . ounces** i.e. one designed to weigh light, inconsequential things
29 counters worthless tokens used to represent coins in calculation   **sum** add up, total
30 The . . . infinite the immeasurable value of his infinite worth

And buckle in a waist most fathomless
With spans and inches so diminutive
As fears and reasons? Fie, for godly shame!

HELENUS   No marvel, though you bite so sharp at reasons,
35   You are so empty of them. Should not our father
Bear the great sway of his affairs with reasons,
Because your speech hath none that tells him so?

TROILUS   You are for dreams and slumbers, brother priest.
You fur your gloves with reason. Here are your reasons:
40   You know an enemy intends you harm,
You know a sword employed is perilous,
And reason flies the object of all harm.
Who marvels then, when Helenus beholds
A Grecian and his sword, if he do set
45   The very wings of reason to his heels
And fly like chidden Mercury from Jove,
Or like a star disorbed? Nay, if we talk of reason,
Let's shut our gates and sleep: manhood and honour
Should have hard hearts, would they but fat their thoughts
50   With this crammed reason. Reason and respect
Makes livers pale and lustihood deject.

HECTOR   Brother, she is not worth what she doth cost
The holding.

TROILUS   What's aught but as 'tis valued?

55   HECTOR   But value dwells not in particular will:
It holds his estimate and dignity
As well wherein 'tis precious of itself
As in the prizer. 'Tis mad idolatry

---

31 **fathomless** too large to measure   32 **spans** measures of nine inches (roughly equivalent
to a handspan)   34 **reasons** may pun on "raisins"   36 **Bear . . . affairs** rule over matters of
state   37 **your . . . so** you urge him to act unreasonably   39 **fur . . . reason** i.e. live in
comfort, prefer appeasement for an easy life   42 **flies** flees   **object** sight   46 **chidden**
scolded   **Mercury** Jove's messenger, usually depicted with wings on his sandals   47 **disorbed**
out of its orbit   49 **hard** dishonorably callous, cruel/lean, deprived (many editors prefer
Quarto's "hare," i.e. timid)   **fat** fatten, feed up   50 **crammed** force-fed/overfed/fat   51 **livers**
considered the seat of the passions, including courage   **lustihood** vigor   53 **The holding** to
keep hold of   54 **aught** anything (worth)   **valued** i.e. by others, externally   55 **particular will**
individual preference   56 **his** its   **estimate and dignity** value and worth   57 **As well** both
of itself intrinsically   58 **As** and   **prizer** one who values it

To make the service greater than the god,
60   And the will dotes that is inclinable
To what infectiously itself affects,
Without some image of th'affected merit.
TROILUS   I take today a wife, and my election
Is led on in the conduct of my will;
65   My will enkindled by mine eyes and ears,
Two traded pilots 'twixt the dangerous shores
Of will and judgement. How may I avoid,
Although my will distaste what it elected,
The wife I chose? There can be no evasion
70   To blench from this and to stand firm by honour:
We turn not back the silks upon the merchant
When we have spoiled them; nor the remainder viands
We do not throw in unrespective sieve,
Because we now are full. It was thought meet
75   Paris should do some vengeance on the Greeks;
Your breath of full consent bellied his sails,
The seas and winds, old wranglers, took a truce
And did him service; he touched the ports desired,
And for an old aunt whom the Greeks held captive,
80   He brought a Grecian queen, whose youth and freshness
Wrinkles Apollo's and makes stale the morning.
Why keep we her? The Grecians keep our aunt:
Is she worth keeping? Why, she is a pearl

---

59 the service performance (of worship)   60 dotes is mad/is infatuated   is inclinable To
inclines toward   61 what . . . affects something it loves in a diseased manner/whatever
infectious object it loves   62 image . . . merit appearance of worth in that object   63 I if I
were to   election choice   64 in the conduct under the guidance   will wish, desire/
intention, determination/carnal appetite/genitals, usually "penis"   66 traded experienced
67 avoid reject, get rid of   68 distaste (now) dislikes   69 evasion evasive argument,
subterfuge   70 blench turn away, shrink   stand firm by i.e. retain, plays on "erection"
72 remainder viands leftover food   73 unrespective sieve undiscriminating basket (for
scraps)   74 meet fitting (puns on "meat," i.e. food)   76 bellied filled, swelled   77 wranglers
quarrelsome opponents   78 touched reached, landed at   79 for in retaliation for   aunt i.e.
Hesione, Ajax's mother and sister of Priam; she was rescued from a sea monster by Hercules
and given to the Greek Telamon; plays on slang sense of "prostitute," "bawd"   80 Grecian
queen i.e. Helen   81 Wrinkles Apollo's makes the sun god Apollo seem wrinkled

Whose price hath launched above a thousand ships,

85 And turned crowned kings to merchants.
If you'll avouch 'twas wisdom Paris went —
As you must needs, for you all cried 'Go, go' —
If you'll confess he brought home noble prize —
As you must needs, for you all clapped your hands

90 And cried 'Inestimable!' — why do you now
The issue of your proper wisdoms rate,
And do a deed that fortune never did,
Beggar the estimation which you prized
Richer than sea and land? O, theft most base,

95 That we have stol'n what we do fear to keep!
But thieves unworthy of a thing so stol'n,
That in their country did them that disgrace,
We fear to warrant in our native place!

Enter Cassandra [at a distance] with her hair about her ears

CASSANDRA   Cry, Trojans, cry!

100 PRIAM   What noise? What shriek is this?

TROILUS   'Tis our mad sister, I do know her voice.

CASSANDRA   Cry, Trojans!   *Coming forward*

HECTOR   It is Cassandra.

CASSANDRA   Cry, Trojans, cry! Lend me ten thousand eyes,

105 And I will fill them with prophetic tears.

HECTOR   Peace, sister, peace!

CASSANDRA   Virgins and boys, mid-age and wrinkled old,
Soft infancy, that nothing can but cry,
Add to my clamour! Let us pay betimes

110 A moiety of that mass of moan to come.
Cry, Trojans, cry! Practise your eyes with tears!

---

84 price . . . ships echoes Faustus' line to Helen in Marlowe's *Doctor Faustus* ("Was this the face that launched a thousand ships") **above** more than   **86 avouch** affirm   **87 must needs** must necessarily do   **91 issue** outcome   **proper** own   **rate** berate, condemn   **92 do . . . did** i.e. behave even more inconsistently than fortune   **93 Beggar the estimation** render worthless the valued object   **96 But** but we are/we are merely   **97 That . . . place** who insulted them in their own land and are afraid to justify the deed in ours   *hair . . . ears* a conventional sign of distress or madness   **107 mid-age** the middle-aged   **108 Soft** tender, vulnerable   **109 betimes** early, in advance   **110 moiety** part/half   **moan** grief, lamentation   **111 Practise** employ, make use of

Troy must not be, nor goodly Ilium stand:
Our firebrand brother, Paris, burns us all.
Cry, Trojans, cry! A Helen and a woe;
115   Cry, cry! Troy burns, or else let Helen go.   *Exit*

HECTOR   Now, youthful Troilus, do not these high strains
Of divination in our sister work
Some touches of remorse? Or is your blood
So madly hot that no discourse of reason,
120   Nor fear of bad success in a bad cause,
Can qualify the same?

TROILUS   Why, brother Hector,
We may not think the justness of each act
Such and no other than event doth form it,
125   Nor once deject the courage of our minds
Because Cassandra's mad: her brainsick raptures
Cannot distaste the goodness of a quarrel
Which hath our several honours all engaged
To make it gracious. For my private part,
130   I am no more touched than all Priam's sons:
And Jove forbid there should be done amongst us
Such things as might offend the weakest spleen
To fight for and maintain.

PARIS   Else might the world convince of levity
135   As well my undertakings as your counsels:
But I attest the gods, your full consent
Gave wings to my propension and cut off
All fears attending on so dire a project.

---

113 firebrand when pregnant, Paris' mother, Hecuba, dreamed that she would give birth to a firebrand that would burn down Troy   **116 high strains** exalted lyrical outpourings
117 work bring about, activate   **118 remorse** pity, regret   **blood** passion/temper (suggests sexual passion)   **120 success** outcome   **121 qualify the same** moderate, pacify it
123 think believe, deem   **124 Such . . . it** to be shaped solely by the way that things turn out
125 deject lessen   **126 raptures** fits   **127 distaste** make distasteful   **goodness** virtue, rightfulness   **128 several** various/individual   **129 gracious** righteous, honorable   **For . . .
part** in my personal case   **130 touched** affected   **132 Such . . . maintain** anything that might offend even the least courageous among us and make him unwilling to fight in its defense   **134 Else** otherwise   **convince** convict   **levity** wantonness, immorality   **135 As
well** both   **as** and   **counsels** advice, opinion   **136 attest** call to witness   **137 propension** inclination   **138 dire** dangerous

For what, alas, can these my single arms?
140 What propugnation is in one man's valour
To stand the push and enmity of those
This quarrel would excite? Yet, I protest,
Were I alone to pass the difficulties
And had as ample power as I have will,
145 Paris should ne'er retract what he hath done,
Nor faint in the pursuit.

PRIAM   Paris, you speak
Like one besotted on your sweet delights:
You have the honey still, but these the gall,
150 So to be valiant is no praise at all.

PARIS   Sir, I propose not merely to myself
The pleasures such a beauty brings with it,
But I would have the soil of her fair rape
Wiped off in honourable keeping her.
155 What treason were it to the ransacked queen,
Disgrace to your great worths and shame to me,
Now to deliver her possession up
On terms of base compulsion! Can it be
That so degenerate a strain as this
160 Should once set footing in your generous bosoms?
There's not the meanest spirit on our party
Without a heart to dare or sword to draw
When Helen is defended, nor none so noble
Whose life were ill bestowed or death unfamed

---

139 can . . . arms can my arms achieve alone   **arms** limbs/weapons   **140 propugnation**
defense, justification   **141 stand the push** withstand the attack   **143 pass** undergo
146 faint slacken   **148 besotted** intoxicated, drunk   **149 these** i.e. these other Trojans
gall bitterness (i.e. the hostilities resulting from Paris' abduction of Helen)   **150 So** therefore/
in this manner   **praise** virtue   **151 propose** bring up for consideration   **153 soil** stain,
dishonor   **her fair rape** the abduction of one so beautiful/the honorable abduction of her
(**rape**'s more sinister connotations are picked up in **ransacked**)   **154 honourable keeping her**
the honorable keeping of her   **155 were it** would it be   **ransacked** violated/carried off as
plunder   **157 her possession** our holding of her   **159 strain** trait, tendency   **160 generous**
noble   **161 meanest spirit** most low-born soul/most small-minded character   **party** side
162 Without who has not   **164 were ill bestowed** would be unworthily given   **death
unfamed** whose death would go uncelebrated

165   Where Helen is the subject. Then, I say,
Well may we fight for her whom, we know well,
The world's large spaces cannot parallel.

HECTOR   Paris and Troilus, you have both said well,
And on the cause and question now in hand

170   Have glozed, but superficially, not much
Unlike young men, whom Aristotle thought
Unfit to hear moral philosophy:
The reasons you allege do more conduce
To the hot passion of distempered blood

175   Than to make up a free determination
'Twixt right and wrong, for pleasure and revenge
Have ears more deaf than adders to the voice
Of any true decision. Nature craves
All dues be rendered to their owners: now,

180   What nearer debt in all humanity
Than wife is to the husband? If this law
Of nature be corrupted through affection,
And that great minds, of partial indulgence
To their benumbèd wills, resist the same,

185   There is a law in each well-ordered nation
To curb those raging appetites that are
Most disobedient and refractory.
If Helen then be wife to Sparta's king,
As it is known she is, these moral laws

190   Of nature and of nation speak aloud
To have her back returned: thus to persist
In doing wrong extenuates not wrong,

---

170 **glozed** expounded, explained   171 **Aristotle** famous Greek philosopher; in fact, he lived several centuries after the Trojan War   173 **allege** put forward   **conduce** lead, tend   174 **distempered** imbalanced (in which the four bodily fluids believed to govern individual temperament are disordered)   175 **free determination** unbiased judgment   177 **adders** in order to resist snake charmers, the adder supposedly blocked one ear with its tail and placed the other to the ground   179 **dues** debts   **rendered** given up, returned   180 **nearer** more pressing/more intimate   182 **affection** passion, desire   183 **that** if   **of partial** out of self-interested   184 **benumbèd** paralyzed, powerless   **the same** i.e. nature's law   187 **refractory** rebellious, stubborn   192 **extenuates not** does not lessen

But makes it much more heavy. Hector's opinion
Is this in way of truth, yet ne'ertheless,
195 My spritely brethren, I propend to you
In resolution to keep Helen still,
For 'tis a cause that hath no mean dependence
Upon our joint and several dignities.

TROILUS   Why, there you touched the life of our design:
200 Were it not glory that we more affected
Than the performance of our heaving spleens,
I would not wish a drop of Trojan blood
Spent more in her defence. But, worthy Hector,
She is a theme of honour and renown,
205 A spur to valiant and magnanimous deeds,
Whose present courage may beat down our foes,
And fame in time to come canonize us,
For I presume brave Hector would not lose
So rich advantage of a promised glory
210 As smiles upon the forehead of this action
For the wide world's revenue.

HECTOR   I am yours,
You valiant offspring of great Priamus.
I have a roisting challenge sent amongst
215 The dull and factious nobles of the Greeks
Will strike amazement to their drowsy spirits.
I was advertised their great general slept
Whilst emulation in the army crept:
This, I presume, will wake him.   *Exeunt*

---

193 heavy serious   **194 in way of** as a point of, in terms of   **195 spritely** animated, full of
spirit   **propend** incline, yield   **196 still** nevertheless/always   **197 hath . . . dependence** i.e.
depends in no small measure   **198 joint** collective   **several** individual   **dignities** honors
199 touched . . . design hit on the essence of our undertaking   **200 affected** were concerned
with, cultivated   **201 performance . . . spleens** working out of our impassioned anger
204 theme subject, cause (for action)   **205 magnanimous** heroic, courageous   **206 Whose
present courage** the ready courage of which   **207 canonize** memorialize, revere
210 smiles . . . forehead looks favorably in the face   **211 For** in exchange for   **revenue**
wealth   **214 roisting** rousing, swaggering   **216 Will** that will   **217 advertised** informed
general i.e. Agamemnon   **218 emulation** ignoble ambition, divisive rivalry

[Act 2 Scene 3]　　　　　　　　　　　*running scene 5*

Enter Thersites, solus

THERSITES　How now, Thersites? What, lost in the labyrinth of
thy fury? Shall the elephant Ajax carry it thus? He beats me,
and I rail at him. O, worthy satisfaction! Would it were
otherwise: that I could beat him, whilst he railed at me.
5　'Sfoot, I'll learn to conjure and raise devils, but I'll see some
issue of my spiteful execrations. Then there's Achilles, a rare
engineer. If Troy be not taken till these two undermine it, the
walls will stand till they fall of themselves. O thou great
thunder-darter of Olympus, forget that thou art Jove, the
10　king of gods and, Mercury, lose all the serpentine craft of thy
caduceus, if thou take not that little, little, less than little wit
from them that they have, which short-armed ignorance
itself knows is so abundant scarce, it will not in circumvention
deliver a fly from a spider without drawing the massy irons
15　and cutting the web. After this, the vengeance on the whole
camp! Or, rather, the bone-ache, for that, methinks, is the
curse dependent on those that war for a placket. I have said
my prayers and devil Envy say 'Amen'.— What ho? My lord
Achilles?

Enter Patroclus [from the tent]

20　PATROCLUS　Who's there? Thersites? Good Thersites, come in
and rail.　　　　　　　　　　　*Patroclus returns to the tent*

2.3 *Location: the Greek camp* **solus** "alone" (Latin)　**2 elephant** i.e. large, clumsy,
thick-skinned　**carry it** win the day　**3 rail** rant, verbally abuse　**satisfaction** recompense,
compensation (sarcastic)　**Would** I wish　**5 'Sfoot** by God's foot　**conjure** invoke　**but I'll
see** if it takes that to see　**6 issue** result　**execrations** curses　**rare** fine, splendid
7 engineer constructor of military works/contriver, plotter　**undermine** lay mines
underneath　**8 of themselves** by their own accord　**9 thunder-darter** thrower of
thunderbolts (Jove's personal weapon)　**10 craft** cunning/skill　**11 caduceus** Mercury's
wand, which featured two serpents entwined about it　**12 short-armed** inadequate, lacking in
reach　**13 circumvention** craft, power to outwit　**14 deliver** release　**massy** heavy, massive
irons swords　**15 After** following, as a result of　**16 bone-ache** i.e. syphilis, which weakens
the bones　**17 dependent on** hanging over/attendant upon　**placket** the slit at the front of a
skirt or petticoat, hence "woman/vagina"

THERSITES   If I could have remembered a gilt counterfeit, thou
wouldst not have slipped out of my contemplation. But it is
no matter: thyself upon thyself! The common curse of
25   mankind, folly and ignorance, be thine in great revenue!
Heaven bless thee from a tutor, and discipline come not near
thee! Let thy blood be thy direction till thy death! Then if she
that lays thee out says thou art a fair corpse, I'll be sworn
and sworn upon't she never shrouded any but lazars.
30   Amen.— Where's Achilles?   *Patroclus reemerges*

PATROCLUS   What, art thou devout? Wast thou in a   *from the tent*
prayer?

THERSITES   Ay, the heavens hear me!

Enter Achilles [from the tent]

ACHILLES   Who's there?

35   PATROCLUS   Thersites, my lord.

ACHILLES   Where, where? Art thou come? Why, my cheese, my
digestion, why hast thou not served thyself in to my table so
many meals? Come, what's Agamemnon?

THERSITES   Thy commander, Achilles. Then tell me, Patroclus,
40   what's Achilles?

PATROCLUS   Thy lord, Thersites: then tell me, I pray thee, what's
thyself?

THERSITES   Thy knower, Patroclus: then tell me, Patroclus,
what art thou?

45   PATROCLUS   Thou mayst tell that know'st.

ACHILLES   O, tell, tell.

THERSITES   I'll decline the whole question: Agamemnon
commands Achilles, Achilles is my lord, I am Patroclus'
knower, and Patroclus is a fool.

---

22 gilt counterfeit false coin   **23 slipped** plays on "slip," another term for a counterfeit coin
contemplation mind, thoughts (Thersites has forgotten to curse Patroclus along with Ajax and
Achilles)   **24 thyself upon thyself** i.e. may you be cursed by being yourself   **25 revenue**
abundance   **26 bless** save, protect   **discipline** learning, instruction   **27 blood** impulses,
passions (rather than reason)   **direction** guide   **28 lays thee out** prepares you for burial
fair virtuous/attractive/undiseased   **29 shrouded** wrapped in a shroud, prepared for burial
lazars lepers (sometimes confused with syphilitics)   **36 cheese** thought to aid digestion
37 served . . . meals i.e. come to see me for such a long time   **43 Thy knower** one who knows
you   **47 decline** go through in order (grammatical term)

50   PATROCLUS   You rascal!

      THERSITES   Peace, fool, I have not done.

      ACHILLES   He is a privileged man. Proceed, Thersites.

      THERSITES   Agamemnon is a fool, Achilles is a fool, Thersites is
      a fool, and, as aforesaid, Patroclus is a fool.

55   ACHILLES   Derive this: come.

      THERSITES   Agamemnon is a fool to offer to command Achilles,
      Achilles is a fool to be commanded of Agamemnon, Thersites
      is a fool to serve such a fool, and Patroclus is a fool positive.

      PATROCLUS   Why am I a fool?

      Enter Agamemnon, Ulysses, Nestor, Diomedes, Ajax and Calchas [at a distance]

60   THERSITES   Make that demand to the creator: it suffices me
      thou art. Look you, who comes here?

      ACHILLES   Patroclus, I'll speak with nobody. Come in with me,
      Thersites.   *Exit*

      THERSITES   Here is such patchery, such juggling and such
65   knavery! All the argument is a cuckold and a whore, a good
      quarrel to draw emulations, factions and bleed to death
      upon. Now, the dry serpigo on the subject, and war and
      lechery confound all!   [*Exit*]

      AGAMEMNON   Where is Achilles?   *Comes forward*

70   PATROCLUS   Within his tent, but ill disposed, my lord.

      AGAMEMNON   Let it be known to him that we are here.
      He shent our messengers, and we lay by
      Our appertainments, visiting of him:
      Let him be told of, so perchance he think

---

51 done finished   **52 privileged man** i.e. professional fool allowed to speak without restraint
55 Derive explain, trace the source of (grammatical term)   **56 offer** dare, presume/attempt
57 of by   **58 fool positive** absolute fool   **60 Make . . . to** ask that question of   **suffices** is
enough for   **64 patchery** trickery   **juggling** cheating, deceiving   **65 All the argument** the
entire subject (of the war)   **cuckold . . . whore** i.e. Menelaus and Helen   **cuckold** man with
an unfaithful wife   **66 draw** bring about, generate   **67 serpigo** skin disease/venereal
disease   **subject** whole business/the cause, Helen   **68 confound** destroy, overcome
70 ill disposed indisposed, unwell   **72 shent** abused, insulted   **lay by** put aside
73 appertainments prerogatives of rank   **visiting of** in visiting   **74 of** this   **so** i.e. in
case

75   We dare not move the question of our place,
           Or know not what we are.

PATROCLUS   I shall so say to him.   [*Exit*]

ULYSSES   We saw him at the opening of his tent:
           He is not sick.

80 **AJAX**   Yes, lion-sick, sick of proud heart: you may call it
           melancholy if you will favour the man, but, by my head, it is
           pride. But why, why? Let him show us the cause.— A word,
           my lord.   *Ajax and Agamemnon speak aside*

NESTOR   What moves Ajax thus to bay at him?

85 **ULYSSES**   Achilles hath inveigled his fool from him.

NESTOR   Who, Thersites?

ULYSSES   He.

NESTOR   Then will Ajax lack matter, if he have lost his
           argument.

90 **ULYSSES**   No, you see, he is his argument that has his
           argument — Achilles.

NESTOR   All the better: their fraction is more our wish than
           their faction, but it was a strong council that a fool could
           disunite.

95 **ULYSSES**   The amity that wisdom knits not, folly may easily
           untie.

Enter Patroclus

           Here comes Patroclus.

NESTOR   No Achilles with him?

ULYSSES   The elephant hath joints, but none for courtesy: his
100   legs are legs for necessity, not for flight.

PATROCLUS   Achilles bids me say, he is much sorry
           If anything more than your sport and pleasure

---

75 **move . . . place** insist on the issue of our authority   80 **lion-sick** i.e. sick with pride
84 **bay** bark, howl   85 **inveigled** lured away   88 **matter** subject matter/material for arguing
his argument subject matter/subject of his complaints, i.e. Thersites   90 **he . . . Achilles**
Achilles is his new cause for complaint as he has taken away his old one, Thersites
92 **fraction . . . faction** we prefer them quarreling to forming a faction against us   93 **it . . .
disunite** it must have been a strong faction if a fool could divide it (sarcastic)   95 **amity**
friendship, unity   99 **elephant . . . courtesy** elephants were thought to lack leg joints that
would enable them to kneel   102 **sport** recreation/exercise

Did move your greatness and this noble state
To call upon him; he hopes it is no other
105   But for your health and your digestion' sake,
An after-dinner's breath.

AGAMEMNON   Hear you, Patroclus:
We are too well acquainted with these answers,
But his evasion, winged thus swift with scorn,
110   Cannot outfly our apprehensions.
Much attribute he hath, and much the reason
Why we ascribe it to him, yet all his virtues,
Not virtuously of his own part beheld,
Do in our eyes begin to lose their gloss,
115   Yea, and like fair fruit in an unwholesome dish,
Are like to rot untasted. Go and tell him,
We came to speak with him; and you shall not sin
If you do say we think him over-proud
And under-honest, in self-assumption greater
120   Than in the note of judgement, and worthier than himself
Here tends the savage strangeness he puts on,
Disguise the holy strength of their command,
And underwrite in an observing kind
His humorous predominance. Yea, watch
125   His pettish lunes, his ebbs, his flows, as if
The passage and whole carriage of this action
Rode on his tide. Go tell him this, and add
That if he overhold his price so much,

---

103 noble state group of nobles   **104 it . . . other** i.e. it is for no other reason   **106 breath** i.e.
of fresh air   **110 apprehensions** understanding (plays on the sense "arrest")   **111 attribute**
reputation, honor   **113 of . . . beheld** upheld by him   **115 fair** fresh, attractive
unwholesome unsightly, contaminated   **116 like** likely   **117 sin** i.e. lie, do wrong
119 under-honest less than honorable   **self-assumption . . . judgement** more arrogant than
of good judgment/greater in his own estimation than those of good judgment know him to
be   **120 worthier . . . on** worthier men than he wait here on account of the uncivil aloofness
he affects   **122 command** authority   **123 underwrite . . . predominance** submit in a
deferential manner to his prevailing mood   **124 humorous** relating to the four bodily humors
thought to govern mood   **125 pettish lunes** petulant fits   **126 passage** progress   **carriage**
conduct   **action** enterprise, i.e. the war   **127 Rode . . . tide** i.e. relied on him   **128 overhold**
overestimate

We'll none of him; but let him, like an engine
130   Not portable, lie under this report:
'Bring action hither, this cannot go to war:
A stirring dwarf we do allowance give
Before a sleeping giant.' Tell him so.

PATROCLUS   I shall, and bring his answer presently.

135   **AGAMEMNON**   In second voice we'll not be satisfied:
We come to speak with him.— Ulysses, enter you.

Exit Ulysses [following Patroclus]

AJAX   What is he more than another?

AGAMEMNON   No more than what he thinks he is.

AJAX   Is he so much? Do you not think he thinks himself a
140   better man than I am?

AGAMEMNON   No question.

AJAX   Will you subscribe his thought, and say he is?

AGAMEMNON   No, noble Ajax: you are as strong, as valiant, as
wise, no less noble, much more gentle, and altogether more
145   tractable.

AJAX   Why should a man be proud? How doth pride grow?
I know not what it is.

AGAMEMNON   Your mind is the clearer, Ajax, and your virtues
the fairer. He that is proud eats up himself: pride is his own
150   glass, his own trumpet, his own chronicle, and whatever
praises itself but in the deed, devours the deed in the praise.

Enter Ulysses

AJAX   I do hate a proud man, as I hate the engendering of
toads.

NESTOR   Yet he loves himself: is't not strange?   *Aside*

155   **ULYSSES**   Achilles will not to the field tomorrow.

---

129 none of have nothing to do with   **engine** piece of military equipment   **130 lie under** be
subject to   **131 this** i.e. this **engine** (Achilles)   **132 stirring** active   **allowance** approval,
praise   **133 Before** over, rather than   **134 presently** immediately   **135 In second voice** i.e.
with a reply conveyed through a messenger   **142 subscribe** confirm, endorse   **144 gentle**
courteous, honorable   **148 the clearer** more innocent   **150 glass** mirror   **trumpet**
announcer   **chronicle** record   **151 but . . . deed** other than in performing worthy deeds
devours consumes the value of   **152 engendering** mating/offspring, spawn   **155 field**
battlefield

AGAMEMNON   What's his excuse?

ULYSSES   He doth rely on none,
But carries on the stream of his dispose
Without observance or respect of any,

160   In will peculiar and in self-admission.

AGAMEMNON   Why will he not upon our fair request
Untent his person and share the air with us?

ULYSSES   Things small as nothing, for request's sake only,
He makes important: possessed he is with greatness,

165   And speaks not to himself but with a pride
That quarrels at self-breath: imagined worth
Holds in his blood such swoll'n and hot discourse
That 'twixt his mental and his active parts
Kingdomed Achilles in commotion rages

170   And batters gainst itself. What should I say?
He is so plaguy proud that the death-tokens of it
Cry 'No recovery.'

AGAMEMNON   Let Ajax go to him.—
Dear lord, go you and greet him in his tent;

175   'Tis said he holds you well, and will be led
At your request a little from himself.

ULYSSES   O Agamemnon, let it not be so!
We'll consecrate the steps that Ajax makes
When they go from Achilles. Shall the proud lord

180   That bastes his arrogance with his own seam
And never suffers matter of the world
Enter his thoughts, save such as do revolve
And ruminate himself: shall he be worshipped

---

158 **stream . . . dispose** course of his inclination   159 **observance** notice/consideration/
respect   **respect** notice/regard for   160 **will peculiar** personal inclination, independent
will   **self-admission** self-approbation, self-centeredness   161 **fair** courteous/legitimate
162 **Untent his person** emerge from his tent   163 **for . . . only** simply because they are
requested   164 **greatness** self-worth   165 **speaks . . . self-breath** i.e. he is almost too proud
to speak   167 **hot** fired-up/passionate/angry   169 **Kingdomed Achilles** Achilles, as if he
were a kingdom   **commotion** rebellion/agitation   171 **plaguy** insufferably, damnably
death-tokens fatal symptoms   175 **holds** regards   176 **from himself** i.e. away from his
arrogant, self-absorbed behavior   178 **We'll consecrate** we would rather bless   179 **from**
away from   180 **seam** fat, grease   181 **suffers** allows   182 **revolve . . . himself** involve
contemplating and meditating on himself

Of that we hold an idol more than he?
185 No, this thrice-worthy and right valiant lord
Must not so stale his palm, nobly acquired,
Nor by my will assubjugate his merit,
As amply titled as Achilles is, by going to Achilles:
That were to enlard his fat-already pride
190 And add more coals to Cancer when he burns
With entertaining great Hyperion.
This lord go to him? Jupiter forbid,
And say in thunder 'Achilles go to him.'

NESTOR   O, this is well: he rubs the vein of him.   *Aside*
195 DIOMEDES   And how his silence drinks up this applause!   *Aside*
AJAX   If I go to him, with my armèd fist
I'll pash him o'er the face.
AGAMEMNON   O, no, you shall not go.
AJAX   An a be proud with me, I'll pheeze his pride.
200 Let me go to him.
ULYSSES   Not for the worth that hangs upon our quarrel.
AJAX   A paltry, insolent fellow!
NESTOR   How he describes himself!   *Aside*
AJAX   Can he not be sociable?
205 ULYSSES   The raven chides blackness.   *Aside*
AJAX   I'll let his humours blood.
AGAMEMNON   He will be the physician that should be   *Aside*
the patient.
AJAX   An all men were o'my mind—
ULYSSES   Wit would be out of fashion.   *Aside*

---

184 Of . . . he? by one whom we consider more worthy of worship (i.e. Ajax)   **186 stale** cheapen, lower the dignity of   **palm** honor (literally, palm leaf, a symbol of victory or prowess) **187 assubjugate** demean, debase   **188 As . . . is** granted that Achilles is well reputed **189 were** would be   **enlard** fatten, smear with grease   **fat-already** already bloated **190 add . . . Hyperion** increase summer's heat (the sun, Hyperion, enters the zodiacal sign of **Cancer** at the beginning of summer)   **194 rubs . . . him** stirs up his temperament, plays on his disposition   **196 armèd** armored/ready   **197 pash** smash, strike   **199 An a** if he   **proud** haughty   **pheeze** fix, do for   **201 worth . . . quarrel** all the cost attendant on our war with the Trojans   **205 The . . . blackness** i.e. Ajax condemns Achilles for faults he himself possesses (ravens are black)   **206 let . . . blood** draw his blood to balance his bodily humors (as doctors bled their patients)   **208 An** if

210 AJAX   A should not bear it so, a should eat swords first:
shall pride carry it?

NESTOR   An 'twould, you'd carry half.   *Aside*

ULYSSES   A would have ten shares.   *Aside*

AJAX   I will knead him: I'll make him supple.

215 NESTOR   He's not yet through warm. Force him with   *Aside*
praises: pour in, pour in, his ambition is dry.

ULYSSES   My lord, you feed too much on this
dislike.   *To Agamemnon*

NESTOR   Our noble general, do not do so.

DIOMEDES   You must prepare to fight without Achilles.

220 ULYSSES   Why, 'tis this naming of him doth him harm.
Here is a man — but 'tis before his face:
I will be silent.

NESTOR   Wherefore should you so?
He is not emulous, as Achilles is.

225 ULYSSES   Know the whole world, he is as valiant.

AJAX   A whoreson dog, that shall palter thus with us!
Would he were a Trojan!

NESTOR   What a vice were it in Ajax now—

ULYSSES   If he were proud—

230 DIOMEDES   Or covetous of praise—

ULYSSES   Ay, or surly borne—

DIOMEDES   Or strange, or self-affected!

ULYSSES   Thank the heavens, lord, thou art of sweet
composure:
Praise him that got thee, she that gave thee suck:

---

210 A he   **bear it** behave   **eat swords** i.e. be stabbed (possibly puns on "eat his words")
211 carry it prevail   **212 An 'twould** if it did   **carry half** i.e. bear half the load of pride
213 ten shares ten tenths, all of it   **214 knead** mold (like dough), i.e. strike   **215 through**
thoroughly   **Force** stuff, cram   **216 dry** shriveled/thirsty   **217 feed . . . dislike** brood too
much on Achilles' dissension   **220 naming of him** repeated reference to Achilles, constant
citing of his heroism   **221 a man** i.e. Ajax   **224 emulous** greedy for praise, filled with
ambitious rivalry   **225 Know . . . world** let the whole world know   **226 palter** equivocate, be
evasive   **231 surly borne** bore himself in an arrogant manner   **232 strange** aloof, distant
self-affected egotistical, self-loving   **233 lord** i.e. Ajax   **composure** temperament   **234 got**
begot, conceived   **gave thee suck** suckled you

235   Fame be thy tutor, and thy parts of nature
    Thrice famed beyond, beyond all erudition:
    But he that disciplined thy arms to fight,
    Let Mars divide eternity in twain,
    And give him half, and for thy vigour,
240   Bull-bearing Milo his addition yield
    To sinewy Ajax. I will not praise thy wisdom,
    Which, like a bourn, a pale, a shore, confines
    Thy spacious and dilated parts. Here's Nestor —
    Instructed by the antiquary times —
245   He must, he is, he cannot but be wise:
    Put pardon, father Nestor, were your days
    As green as Ajax' and your brain so tempered,
    You should not have the eminence of him,
    But be as Ajax.

250   AJAX   Shall I call you father?

      ULYSSES   Ay, my good son.

      DIOMEDES   Be ruled by him, Lord Ajax.

      ULYSSES   There is no tarrying here: the hart Achilles
    Keeps thicket. Please it our general
255   To call together all his state of war.
    Fresh kings are come to Troy; tomorrow
    We must with all our main of power stand fast.
    And here's a lord— come knights from east to west,
    And cull their flower, Ajax shall cope the best.

260   AGAMEMNON   Go we to council. Let Achilles sleep:
    Light boats may sail swift, though greater bulks draw deep.

                            Exeunt

---

235 Fame renown, honor   **thy . . . erudition** may your natural qualities exceed three-fold anything learned   **237 disciplined** trained   **238 eternity** i.e. eternal fame   **twain** two **240 Milo** Greek athlete of the sixth century BC, famed for carrying a bull on his shoulders **addition** title, claim to fame   **242 bourn** boundary   **pale** fenced area, enclosure   **shore** border, shoreline   **confines** encloses, contains   **243 dilated parts** extensive qualities (sarcastically plays on Ajax's large physical size)   **244 antiquary** ancient   **247 green** youthful   **tempered** molded, composed   **248 have . . . of** be superior to   **252 ruled** guided, directed   **253 tarrying** (point in) delaying   **hart** male deer   **254 Keeps** stays hidden in the **255 state** council   **257 main of power** full force   **259 cull their flower** select their very best **cope** match/encounter (in combat)   **261 draw deep** require deeper water (due to their weight)

[Act 3 Scene 1]

Music sounds within. Enter Pandarus and a Servant

PANDARUS   Friend, you! Pray you, a word: do not you follow the
young lord Paris?

SERVANT   Ay, sir, when he goes before me.

PANDARUS   You depend upon him, I mean?

5   SERVANT   Sir, I do depend upon the lord.

PANDARUS   You depend upon a noble gentleman: I must needs
praise him.

SERVANT   The lord be praised!

PANDARUS   You know me, do you not?

10   SERVANT   Faith, sir, superficially.

PANDARUS   Friend, know me better: I am the Lord Pandarus.

SERVANT   I hope I shall know your honour better.

PANDARUS   I do desire it.

SERVANT   You are in the state of grace?

15   PANDARUS   Grace? Not so, friend: honour and lordship are my
title. What music is this?

SERVANT   I do but partly know, sir: it is music in parts.

PANDARUS   Know you the musicians?

SERVANT   Wholly, sir.

20   PANDARUS   Who play they to?

SERVANT   To the hearers, sir.

PANDARUS   At whose pleasure, friend?

SERVANT   At mine, sir, and theirs that love music.

PANDARUS   Command, I mean, friend.

25   SERVANT   Who shall I command, sir?

3.1   *Location: Troy*   1 follow serve, attend (the servant plays on the literal sense)
4 depend upon serve, wait on   **5 the lord** i.e. Paris, but plays on the sense of "God"   **6 must
needs** must   **10 superficially** slightly/by sight   **12 know . . . better** get to know your
lordship better/see you become a better man   **14 You . . . grace?** Are you in receipt of the
divine favor necessary for salvation? (but Pandarus understands "Are you a duke eligible to be
addressed as 'your grace'?")   **15 Grace? Not so** here Pandarus declares such a title
inappropriate for his rank   **22 pleasure** command (the servant deliberately understands
"enjoyment")   **25 Who . . . sir?** the servant willfully misunderstands Pandarus to be giving
him an instruction

PANDARUS   Friend, we understand not one another: I am too courtly and thou art too cunning. At whose request do these men play?

SERVANT   That's to't indeed, sir. Marry, sir, at the request of
30   Paris, my lord, who's there in person; with him, the mortal Venus, the heart-blood of beauty, love's invisible soul—

PANDARUS   Who? My cousin Cressida?

SERVANT   No, sir, Helen: could you not find out that by her attributes?

35   PANDARUS   It should seem, fellow, that thou hast not seen the lady Cressida. I come to speak with Paris from the Prince Troilus: I will make a complimental assault upon him, for my business seethes.

SERVANT   Sodden business. There's a stewed phrase indeed!

Enter Paris and Helen [with Attendants]

40   PANDARUS   Fair be to you, my lord, and to all this fair company. Fair desires in all fair measure fairly guide them, especially to you, fair queen. Fair thoughts be your fair pillow.

HELEN   Dear lord, you are full of fair words.

PANDARUS   You speak your fair pleasure, sweet queen. Fair
45   prince, here is good broken music.

PARIS   You have broke it, cousin, and, by my life, you shall make it whole again: you shall piece it out with a piece of your performance. Nell, he is full of harmony.

PANDARUS   Truly, lady, no.

50   HELEN   O, sir—

---

27 courtly refined, possessed of the manners and language of the court   **too cunning** clever, skillful/devious   **29 to't** to the point   **31 Venus** Roman goddess of love   **heart-blood** i.e. life blood, essence   **33 find out that** work that out   **37 complimental** courteous   **38 seethes** boils with urgency (with **sodden** and **stewed** the servant picks up on connotations of the "boiling" effects of syphilis and of the sweating treatments used to try and cure it)   **39 Sodden** boiled/limp, flaccid (phallic connotations)   **business** may play on the sense of "sexual activity"; conceivably plays on a sense of "penis"   **stewed** saturated (puns on a "stew" or brothel)   **40 Fair** i.e. fair wishes (sense shifts to "elegant" and then "pleasing")   **41 fair measure** just proportion   **fairly** favorably   **43 fair** charming, flattering   **44 pleasure** thoughts, wishes   **45 broken** arranged in parts, for different instruments or voices   **46 broke** interrupted   **cousin** friendly form of address among social equals   **47 piece it out** put it back together   **piece** part of a song   **48 Nell** nickname for Helen   **harmony** tuneful singing/agreeable sentiments

PANDARUS	Rude, in sooth, in good sooth, very rude.
PARIS	Well said, my lord. Well, you say so in fits.
PANDARUS	I have business to my lord, dear queen. My lord, will you vouchsafe me a word?
55 HELEN	Nay, this shall not hedge us out: we'll hear you sing, certainly.
PANDARUS	Well, sweet queen, you are pleasant with me. But, marry, thus, my lord: my dear lord and most esteemed friend, your brother Troilus—
60 HELEN	My lord Pandarus, honey-sweet lord—
PANDARUS	Go to, sweet queen, go to.— Commends himself most affectionately to you— *To Paris*
HELEN	You shall not bob us out of our melody: if you do, our melancholy upon your head!
65 PANDARUS	Sweet queen, sweet queen: that's a sweet queen, i'faith.
HELEN	And to make a sweet lady sad is a sour offence.
PANDARUS	Nay, that shall not serve your turn, that shall it not, in truth, la. Nay, I care not for such words, no, no. And, my lord, he desires you, that if the king call for him at supper, you will make his excuse.
HELEN	My lord Pandarus—
PANDARUS	What says my sweet queen, my very very sweet queen?
75 PARIS	What exploit's in hand? Where sups he tonight?
HELEN	Nay, but, my lord—
PANDARUS	What says my sweet queen? My cousin will fall out with you.
HELEN	You must not know where he sups. *To Paris*

---

51 **Rude** (I am) unaccomplished, unpolished   52 **fits** spurts, fits and starts (plays on the sense of "section of a poem or song")   53 **to** with   54 **vouchsafe** permit, grant   55 **hedge us out** exclude, get rid of me   57 **pleasant** merry, jocular   61 **queen** plays on "quean" meaning "prostitute"   63 **bob** cheat, swindle   64 **melancholy** ill temper, sullenness   67 **sour** i.e. the antithesis of **sweet**   68 **serve your turn** meet your purpose, i.e. win the argument   69 **la** exclamation used for emphasis   70 **desires** requests   75 **in hand** under way   **sups** dines
77 **My . . . you** my friend Paris will get cross with you (for your repeated interruptions)

80	PARIS	With my disposer Cressida?
	PANDARUS	No, no; no such matter, you are wide. Come, your disposer is sick.
	PARIS	Well, I'll make excuse.
	PANDARUS	Ay, good my lord. Why should you say Cressida? No,
85		your poor disposer's sick.
	PARIS	I spy.
	PANDARUS	You spy? What do you spy?— Come, give me an instrument.— Now, sweet queen. *He is handed*
	HELEN	Why, this is kindly done. *a musical*
90	PANDARUS	My niece is horrible in love with a thing *instrument* you have, sweet queen.
	HELEN	She shall have it, my lord, if it be not my lord Paris.
	PANDARUS	He? No, she'll none of him: they two are twain.
	HELEN	Falling in after falling out may make them three.
95	PANDARUS	Come, come, I'll hear no more of this. I'll sing you a song now.
	HELEN	Ay, ay, prithee now. By my troth, sweet lord, thou hast a fine forehead.
	PANDARUS	Ay, you may, you may.
100	HELEN	Let thy song be love: this love will undo us all. O Cupid, Cupid, Cupid!
	PANDARUS	Love? Ay, that it shall, i'faith.
	PARIS	Ay, good now, 'Love, love, nothing but love'.
	PANDARUS	In good troth, it begins so.
105		Love, love, nothing but love, still more! *Sings*
		For, O, love's bow

---

80 disposer unclear meaning; perhaps "one who controls arrangements" hence possibly "courtly mistress" or, similarly, "one who may dispose of me as she wishes" (said playfully) **81 wide** i.e. of the mark   **83 make excuse** i.e. on behalf of Troilus   **86 I spy** i.e. I see what's going on here   **90 horrible** horribly, extremely   **thing** plays on the sense of "penis" **93 twain** at odds, have nothing in common (Helen plays on the literal sense of "two") **94 Falling . . . out** making up after arguing (**falling in** plays on the notion of sexual penetration)   **make them three** i.e. result in childbirth   **98 fine forehead** commanding countenance   **99 you may** i.e. you may have your joke, so you say   **100 be** be about   **undo** ruin   **103 good now** please, be so good   **106 love's** i.e. Cupid's   **bow** plays on the sense of "penis"

Shoots buck and doe:
The shaft confounds,
Not that it wounds,
110   But tickles still the sore.
These lovers cry, O ho, they die!
Yet that which seems the wound to kill,
Doth turn O ho, to ha, ha, he!
So dying love lives still:
115   O ho, awhile, but ha, ha, ha!
O ho, groans out for ha, ha, ha!—
Hey-ho!

HELEN   In love, i'faith, to the very tip of the nose.

PARIS   He eats nothing but doves, love, and that breeds hot
120   blood, and hot blood begets hot thoughts, and hot thoughts
beget hot deeds, and hot deeds is love.

PANDARUS   Is this the generation of love? Hot blood, hot
thoughts, and hot deeds? Why, they are vipers: is love a
generation of vipers?— Sweet lord, who's afield today?

125   PARIS   Hector, Deiphobus, Helenus, Antenor, and all the
gallantry of Troy: I would fain have armed today, but my Nell
would not have it so. How chance my brother Troilus went
not?

HELEN   He hangs the lip at something; you know all, Lord
130   Pandarus.

PANDARUS   Not I, honey-sweet queen. I long to hear how they
sped today.— You'll remember your brother's excuse?

PARIS   To a hair.

---

107 Shoots plays on the sense of "ejaculates (in)"   **buck and doe** male and female (deer)
108 shaft arrow of love/penis   **confounds, Not that** does not damage what   **110 tickles**
sexually excites   **still** continually   **the sore** wound/vagina (**sore** plays on the sense of "four-
year-old male deer")   **111 O, ho** i.e. groans of pain/cries of sexual pleasure   **die** plays on the
sense of "orgasm"   **112 to kill** that will prove fatal   **113 ha, ha, he** i.e. laughter/increasingly
excited sexual cries   **116 O . . . out** possibly also suggestive of the subsequent pains of
childbirth   **118 In love** you're in love   **tip . . . nose** i.e. completely (**nose** plays on the sense of
"penis")   **119 doves** birds associated with love; they pulled Venus' chariot   **hot blood** sexual
desire   **120 begets** conceives   **122 generation of love** how love is created   **124 vipers**
proverbially vicious offspring   **afield** on the battlefield   **126 gallantry** gallant warriors   **fain**
gladly   **127 chance** comes it   **129 He . . . lip** Pandarus pouts, looks vexed/Troilus is sulking
132 sped fared/succeeded   **133 To a hair** i.e. down to the last detail

PANDARUS	Farewell, sweet queen.
135 HELEN	Commend me to your niece.
PANDARUS	I will, sweet queen. [*Exit*]

Sound a retreat

PARIS   They're come from field: let us to Priam's hall
To greet the warriors. Sweet Helen, I must woo you
To help unarm our Hector: his stubborn buckles,
140   With these your white enchanting fingers touched,
Shall more obey than to the edge of steel
Or force of Greekish sinews. You shall do more
Than all the island kings: disarm great Hector.

HELEN   'Twill make us proud to be his servant, Paris.
145   Yea, what he shall receive of us in duty
Gives us more palm in beauty than we have,
Yea, overshines ourself.

PARIS   Sweet, above thought I love thee.   *Exeunt*

[Act 3 Scene 2]   *running scene 7*

Enter Pandarus and Troilus' Man

PANDARUS   How now? Where's thy master? At my cousin
Cressida's?

MAN   No, sir, he stays for you to conduct him thither.

Enter Troilus

PANDARUS   O, here he comes.—How now, how now?

5   TROILUS   Sirrah, walk off.   [*Exit Troilus' Man*]

PANDARUS   Have you seen my cousin?

TROILUS   No, Pandarus: I stalk about her door,
Like a strange soul upon the Stygian banks

---

138 woo entreat   **139 unarm** remove armor from   **141 more obey** be more obedient   **edge**
sword edge   **143 island kings** kings from the Greek islands   **145 of us** from me   **146 palm**
honor   **in . . . have** than I have from my beauty   **148 above thought** beyond thought itself
(perhaps suggests the rashness of Paris' actions in obtaining Helen)   **3.2   *Man*** manservant
3 stays waits   **conduct** escort   **5 Sirrah** sir (used to a social inferior)   **6 cousin** i.e. niece
(the term could designate any close relative)   **7 stalk** move stealthily (hunting term, used of
an approach to the prey)   **8 strange** foreign, newly arrived   **Stygian banks** banks of the
Styx, the river that the souls of the dead had to cross to reach the underworld

Staying for waftage. O, be thou my Charon,
10   And give me swift transportance to those fields
Where I may wallow in the lily-beds
Proposed for the deserver. O gentle Pandarus,
From Cupid's shoulder pluck his painted wings
And fly with me to Cressid!

15 PANDARUS   Walk here i'th'orchard, I'll bring her straight.

Exit Pandarus

TROILUS   I am giddy; expectation whirls me round.
Th'imaginary relish is so sweet
That it enchants my sense: what will it be,
When that the wat'ry palates taste indeed
20   Love's thrice-repurèd nectar? Death, I fear me,
Swooning destruction, or some joy too fine,
Too subtle-potent, tuned too sharp in sweetness,
For the capacity of my ruder powers;
I fear it much, and I do fear besides,
25   That I shall lose distinction in my joys,
As doth a battle, when they charge on heaps
The enemy flying.

Enter Pandarus

PANDARUS   She's making her ready, she'll come straight. You
must be witty now: she does so blush, and fetches her wind
30   so short, as if she were fraid with a sprite. I'll fetch her. It is

---

9 **waftage** conveyance by water   **Charon** the ferryman who transported departed souls to the underworld   10 **fields** the Elysian fields, the dwelling place of blessed souls in the underworld
11 **lily-beds** with connotations of the sexual bed/vagina   12 **Proposed** promised
13 **painted** brightly colored/artificial/as depicted in paintings   15 **i'th'orchard** in the garden
straight straightaway   17 **imaginary relish** imagined taste   18 **sense** senses/power of
reason   **be** be like   19 **wat'ry** tasteless/watering in anticipation   **indeed** in reality
20 **thrice-repurèd** thrice-refined, purified   **nectar** with connotations of sexual juices   **Death**
with connotations of orgasm   21 **fine** refined, pure   22 **subtle-potent** powerfully refined
sharp high-pitched (plays on the sense of "pungent-tasting, acidic" to provide antithesis with
sweetness)   23 **capacity** capability, understanding   **ruder** coarser, more uncultivated
powers faculties   25 **lose . . . joys** be unable to distinguish one pleasure from another
26 **battle** battalion   **on heaps** in a mass, all together   27 **flying** retreating   28 **her** herself
29 **witty** sharp, clever, amusing   **fetches . . . short** is so breathless   30 **fraid with** frightened
by   **sprite** ghost

the prettiest villain: she fetches her breath so short as a new-
ta'en sparrow.   *Exit Pandarus*

TROILUS   Even such a passion doth embrace my bosom:
My heart beats thicker than a feverous pulse,
35 And all my powers do their bestowing lose,
Like vassalage at unawares encount'ring
The eye of majesty.

Enter Pandarus and Cressida [veiled]

PANDARUS   Come, come, what need you blush? Shame's a baby.
Here she is now: swear the oaths now to her that you have
40 sworn to me.— What, are you gone again? You must be
watched ere you be made tame, must you? Come your ways,
come your ways, an you draw backward, we'll put you
i'th'fills.— Why do you not speak to her? Come, draw this
curtain, and let's see your picture. Alas the day, how loath
45 you are to offend daylight! An 'twere dark, you'd close
sooner. So, so, rub on, and kiss the mistress. How now, a kiss
in fee-farm? Build there, carpenter, the air is sweet. Nay, you
shall fight your hearts out ere I part you. The falcon as the
tercel, for all the ducks i'th'river. Go to, go to.
50 TROILUS   You have bereft me of all words, lady.

PANDARUS   Words pay no debts, give her deeds. But she'll bereave
you o'th'deeds too, if she call your activity in question.

---

31 prettiest most delightful, charming   **villain** here a playful term   **new-ta'en** newly
captured   **32 sparrow** proverbially lecherous birds, sacred to Venus   **33 Even** exactly
34 thicker faster   **35 bestowing** use, function   **36 vassalage** subordination, a servant
at unawares unexpectedly   **41 watched** kept awake (a method used to **tame** and train hawks)
Come your ways come along   **42 draw backward** retreat, shy away   **43 i'th'fills** in the shafts
of a cart (like a horse)   **draw this curtain** i.e. draw back your veil (paintings are sometimes
kept behind curtains to protect them from the light)   **44 picture** i.e. face   **45 close** come
close/embrace intimately/bring matters to a close   **46 rub . . . mistress** a bowling metaphor:
to **rub** is to negotiate obstacles in the way of the ball (playing on the idea of sexual friction),
and to **kiss the mistress** to touch the target ball (with obvious sexual suggestion)   **kiss in
fee-farm** i.e. a prolonged kiss   **47 fee-farm** the absolute possession of land subject to a fixed
rent   **air** i.e. Cressida's breath   **48 fight . . . out** compete to outdo one another in love
(fighting plays on the notion of sexual grappling)   **falcon . . . tercel** i.e. female is as vigorous
as the male   **49 tercel** a male hawk   **for . . . river** I'll bet you all the ducks on the river
50 bereft deprived   **51 pay no debts** i.e. count for little (to **pay** one's **debt** also means to have
sex)   **deeds** actions/sexual acts/legal documents   **52 activity** sexual performance

What, billing again? Here's 'In witness whereof the parties
interchangeably.' Come in, come in: I'll go get a fire.   [*Exit*]

55   CRESSIDA   Will you walk in, my lord?

TROILUS   O Cressida, how often have I wished me thus!

CRESSIDA   Wished, my lord? The gods grant— O my lord!

TROILUS   What should they grant? What makes this pretty
abruption? What too curious dreg espies my sweet lady in
60   the fountain of our love?

CRESSIDA   More dregs than water, if my fears have eyes.

TROILUS   Fears make devils of cherubims: they never see truly.

CRESSIDA   Blind fear, that seeing reason leads, finds safer
footing than blind reason stumbling without fear: to fear the
65   worst oft cures the worse.

TROILUS   O, let my lady apprehend no fear: in all Cupid's
pageant there is presented no monster.

CRESSIDA   Nor nothing monstrous neither?

TROILUS   Nothing, but our undertakings, when we vow to
70   weep seas, live in fire, eat rocks, tame tigers; thinking it harder
for our mistress to devise imposition enough than for us to
undergo any difficulty imposed. This is the monstruosity in
love, lady, that the will is infinite and the execution confined,
that the desire is boundless and the act a slave to limit.

75   CRESSIDA   They say all lovers swear more performance than
they are able, and yet reserve an ability that they never
perform, vowing more than the perfection of ten and

---

53 billing kissing, caressing (like doves)/drawing up a legal document/entering items in a
financial account   **'In . . . interchangeably'** phrase used in indentures (legal contract that
was halved along a zigzag line to form two documents that, when placed together, were a
unique match—in this context, may suggest sexual coupling)   **54 fire** suggestive of sexual
passion   **58 pretty** artful/charming   **59 abruption** breaking off   **curious** subtle, well-hidden
dreg impurity, sediment   **63 seeing reason leads** is guided by clear-sighted reason
66 apprehend conceive of, perceive/fear   **in . . . pageant** spectacle, show, entertainment
68 nothing monstrous nothing unnatural (possibly plays on phallic connotations of
monstrous and "thing" to suggest "no huge penis")   **69 undertakings** (lover's)
responsibilities, vows (plays on the sense of "copulations")   **71 imposition enough** sufficiently
difficult tasks   **72 monstruosity in** extraordinary nature of (variant form of "monstrosity")
73 will desire/sexual appetite/penis   **execution confined** acting on it limited   **74 the act**
human endeavor/the sexual act   **76 reserve** keep back   **77 the . . . ten** the ability of ten
other lovers/the maximum, 100 percent

discharging less than the tenth part of one. They that have
the voice of lions and the act of hares, are they not monsters?

80   TROILUS   Are there such? Such are not we: praise us as we are
tasted, allow us as we prove, our head shall go bare till merit
crown it. No perfection in reversion shall have a praise in
present: we will not name desert before his birth, and, being
born, his addition shall be humble. Few words to fair faith.

85   Troilus shall be such to Cressid as what envy can say worst
shall be a mock for his truth, and what truth can speak
truest not truer than Troilus.

CRESSIDA   Will you walk in, my lord?

Enter Pandarus

PANDARUS   What, blushing still? Have you not done talking yet?

90   CRESSIDA   Well, uncle, what folly I commit, I dedicate to you.

PANDARUS   I thank you for that: if my lord get a boy of you,
you'll give him me. Be true to my lord: if he flinch, chide me
for it.

TROILUS   You know now your hostages: your uncle's word

95   and my firm faith.

PANDARUS   Nay, I'll give my word for her too: our kindred,
though they be long ere they are wooed, they are constant
being won. They are burrs, I can tell you: they'll stick where
they are thrown.

100   CRESSIDA   Boldness comes to me now, and brings me heart.
Prince Troilus, I have loved you night and day
For many weary months.

TROILUS   Why was my Cressid then so hard to win?

---

80 such such men   **Such . . . we** I am not one   **81 tasted** tested/sampled sexually   **allow**
praise/accept, approve   **prove** plays on the sense of "perform sexually"   **head** may play on
the sense of "head of the penis" (which will be "crowned" vaginally)   **82 crown it** i.e. with a
victor's wreaths   **perfection in reversion** promise of future achievement   **83 desert**
deserving, merit   **84 addition** title, name   **Few . . . faith** truth needs few words (proverbial)
85 as . . . truth that the worst malice can do is mock Troilus' faith and constancy   **90 folly**
foolishness/lechery   **I . . . you** bestow as a gift to you/hold you responsible for   **91 get** begets,
conceives   **92 give him me** i.e. name him after me   **flinch** fall short, recoil (also suggests
detumescence or sexual reluctance)   **98 burrs** prickly seed-heads that stick easily to clothing
99 thrown plays on the sense of "thrown down sexually, seduced"   **100 Boldness** courage/
sexual immodesty

CRESSIDA   Hard to seem won: but I was won, my lord,
105   With the first glance that ever — pardon me —
    If I confess much, you will play the tyrant.
    I love you now, but not, till now, so much
    But I might master it; in faith, I lie:
    My thoughts were like unbridled children grown
110   Too headstrong for their mother. See, we fools!
    Why have I blabbed? Who shall be true to us,
    When we are so unsecret to ourselves?
    But, though I loved you well, I wooed you not,
    And yet, good faith, I wished myself a man,
115   Or that we women had men's privilege
    Of speaking first. Sweet, bid me hold my tongue,
    For in this rapture I shall surely speak
    The thing I shall repent. See, see, your silence,
    Cunning in dumbness, from my weakness draws
120   My soul of counsel from me. Stop my mouth.
TROILUS   And shall, albeit sweet music issues thence.   *Kisses her*
PANDARUS   Pretty, i'faith.
CRESSIDA   My lord, I do beseech you pardon me:
    'Twas not my purpose, thus to beg a kiss.
125   I am ashamed. O heavens, what have I done?
    For this time will I take my leave, my lord.
TROILUS   Your leave, sweet Cressid?
PANDARUS   Leave? An you take leave till tomorrow morning—
CRESSIDA   Pray you content you.
130   TROILUS   What offends you, lady?
CRESSIDA   Sir, mine own company.
TROILUS   You cannot shun yourself.
CRESSIDA   Let me go and try:
    I have a kind of self resides with you,
135   But an unkind self, that itself will leave

---

106 play the tyrant i.e. have mastery over me/behave in a cruel manner   **108 But . . . it** that I
could not control it   **109 unbridled** uncontrolled, not reined in   **115 privilege** advantage/
license   **119 Cunning** skilled, clever   **120 soul of counsel** innermost secret thoughts
121 shall I shall   **126 this time** the time being   **129 content you** be contented, be quiet
135 unkind unnatural

To be another's fool. Where is my wit?
I would be gone: I speak I know not what.

TROILUS   Well know they what they speak that speaks so
    wisely.

CRESSIDA   Perchance, my lord, I show more craft than love,
140   And fell so roundly to a large confession
    To angle for your thoughts: but you are wise,
    Or else you love not, for to be wise and love
    Exceeds man's might: that dwells with gods above.

TROILUS   O, that I thought it could be in a woman —
145   As, if it can, I will presume in you —
    To feed for aye her lamp and flames of love,
    To keep her constancy in plight and youth,
    Outliving beauty's outward, with a mind
    That doth renew swifter than blood decays!
150   Or that persuasion could but thus convince me
    That my integrity and truth to you
    Might be affronted with the match and weight
    Of such a winnowed purity in love,
    How were I then uplifted! But, alas,
155   I am as true as truth's simplicity
    And simpler than the infancy of truth.

CRESSIDA   In that I'll war with you.

TROILUS   O virtuous fight,
    When right with right wars who shall be most right!
160   True swains in love shall in the world to come
    Approve their truths by Troilus: when their rhymes,
    Full of protest, of oath and big compare,

---

136 fool plaything   **138 Well . . . wisely** those who speak so wisely must know what they are
saying   **139 Perchance** perhaps (you think)   **craft** skill/cunning   **140 roundly** openly,
frankly   **large** unrestrained, outspoken/full   **141 wise** i.e. as you didn't take the bait
143 that that ability (to be wise and in love)   **145 presume** presume that it is   **146 aye** ever
147 plight youthful good health   **148 outward** outward appearance   **149 renew swifter**
renew itself more quickly   **blood decays** passion wanes/aging occurs   **152 affronted**
matched, set face to face   **153 winnowed** refined (like wheat separated from chaff)
154 were I would I be   **155 truth's simplicity** simple truth   **156 simpler . . . truth** more
sincere than truth at its purest   **160 swains** lovers   **161 Approve** attest, confirm   **their . . .
Troilus** with reference to Troilus   **162 protest** declarations of love   **big compare** extravagant
comparisons

Wants similes, truth tired with iteration,
As true as steel, as plantage to the moon,
165   As sun to day, as turtle to her mate,
As iron to adamant, as earth to th'centre,
Yet, after all comparisons of truth,
As truth's authentic author to be cited,
'As true as Troilus' shall crown up the verse,
170   And sanctify the numbers.
CRESSIDA   Prophet may you be!
If I be false, or swerve a hair from truth,
When time is old and hath forgot itself,
When waterdrops have worn the stones of Troy,
175   And blind oblivion swallowed cities up,
And mighty states characterless are grated
To dusty nothing, yet let memory,
From false to false, among false maids in love,
Upbraid my falsehood! When they've said 'As false
180   As air, as water, as wind, as sandy earth,
As fox to lamb, as wolf to heifer's calf,
Pard to the hind, or stepdame to her son',
'Yea', let them say, to stick the heart of falsehood,
'As false as Cressid.'
185   PANDARUS   Go to, a bargain made: seal it, seal it, I'll be the
witness. Here I hold your hand, here my cousin's. If ever you
prove false one to another, since I have taken such pains to
bring you together, let all pitiful goers-between be called to
the world's end after my name: call them all panders; let all
190   constant men be Troiluses, all false women Cressids, and all
brokers-between panders! Say, 'Amen.'

---

163 **Wants** lack   **tired** having been exhausted, rendered clichéd   **iteration** repetition
164 **plantage** plant life, vegetation (which supposedly grew more effectively under moonlight)
165 **turtle** turtledove (a proverbially faithful bird)   166 **adamant** legendary magnetic
rock   **th'centre** its center (thought to be the point to which everything was drawn)
167 **comparisons** i.e. similes   168 **authentic** most authoritative, legitimate   169 **crown up**
add the final touches to/dignify   170 **numbers** poetic meter   172 **false** untrue, unfaithful
a hair i.e. even a very tiny amount   176 **characterless** featureless/leaving no trace, no written
records   **grated** eroded   182 **Pard** leopard   **hind** female deer   **stepdame** stepmother
183 **stick the heart** pierce the center   185 **seal it** plays on the sense of "have sex"

TROILUS   Amen.

CRESSIDA   Amen.

PANDARUS   Amen. Whereupon I will show you a chamber with
195   a bed, which bed, because it shall not speak of your pretty
encounters, press it to death. Away! And Cupid grant all
tongue-tied maidens here Bed, chamber and pander to
provide this gear!   *Exeunt*

[Act 3 Scene 3]   *running scene 8*

*Enter Ulysses, Diomedes, Nestor, Agamemnon, Menelaus and Calchas.
Flourish*

CALCHAS   Now, princes, for the service I have done you,
Th'advantage of the time prompts me aloud
To call for recompense. Appear it to your mind
That through the sight I bear in things to come,
5   I have abandoned Troy, left my possession,
Incurred a traitor's name, exposed myself,
From certain and possessed conveniences,
To doubtful fortunes, sequest'ring from me all
That time, acquaintance, custom and condition
10   Made tame and most familiar to my nature,
And here, to do you service, am become
As new into the world, strange, unacquainted.
I do beseech you, as in way of taste,
To give me now a little benefit
15   Out of those many registered in promise,
Which, you say, live to come in my behalf.

195 because so that   **196 encounters** sexual activities   **press . . . death** punish it severely
(alludes to a punishment that involved pressing a suspect with heavy weights until he pleaded
innocent or guilty, or died; plays on the sense of "have sex until you orgasm")   **197 maidens**
virgins/young women   **here** generally/in the audience   **198 gear** necessary equipment/
genitals   **3.3   *Location: the Greek camp*   2 advantage** opportunity, right moment
3 Appear it let it appear   **4 sight** foresight, visionary power   **5 possession** property,
belongings   **7 From** by turning from   **conveniences** advantages   **8 sequest'ring**
separating, removing   **9 condition** social position and circumstances   **10 tame** familiar,
customary   **12 As** as though   **strange** foreign, unfamiliar   **unacquainted** unfamiliar/
without acquaintances   **13 taste** foretaste, i.e. advance payment   **15 registered in promise**
recorded as pledges   **16 live to come** await fulfillment

AGAMEMNON   What wouldst thou of us, Trojan? Make demand.

CALCHAS   You have a Trojan prisoner, called Antenor,
Yesterday took: Troy holds him very dear.
20   Oft have you — often have you thanks therefore —
Desired my Cressid in right great exchange,
Whom Troy hath still denied. But this Antenor,
I know is such a wrest in their affairs
That their negotiations all must slack,
25   Wanting his manage, and they will almost
Give us a prince of blood, a son of Priam,
In change of him: let him be sent, great princes,
And he shall buy my daughter, and her presence
Shall quite strike off all service I have done,
30   In most accepted pain.

AGAMEMNON   Let Diomedes bear him,
And bring us Cressid hither: Calchas shall have
What he requests of us. Good Diomed,
Furnish you fairly for this interchange.
35   Withal bring word if Hector will tomorrow
Be answered in his challenge: Ajax is ready.

DIOMEDES   This shall I undertake, and 'tis a burden
Which I am proud to bear.   *Exit [Diomedes with Calchas]*

Enter Achilles and Patroclus in their tent

ULYSSES   Achilles stands i'th'entrance of his tent;
40   Please it our general to pass strangely by him,
As if he were forgot, and, princes all,
Lay negligent and loose regard upon him;
I will come last. 'Tis like he'll question me

---

19 took captured   **20 often . . . therefore** you have often been thanked for doing so
21 in . . . exchange in exchange for a Trojan of rank   **23 wrest** tuning implement (i.e.
Antenor is essential to the harmonious operation of Trojan affairs)   **24 slack** slow down,
become less effective (like slack strings on an untuned instrument)   **25 Wanting his manage**
lacking his guidance   **26 blood** royal lineage   **27 change of** exchange for   **29 strike off**
cancel out, pay for   **30 In . . . pain** with most willing effort   **31 bear him** i.e. take Antenor
back   **34 Furnish you fairly** equip yourself fully   **interchange** exchange   **35 Withal** in
addition   **36 Be answered in** meet the man who will answer   **40 Please it** if it please
strangely distantly, as if he were a stranger   **42 loose** casual, careless   **regard** looks
43 like likely

Why such unplausive eyes are bent, why turned on him.
45   If so, I have derision medicinable
To use between your strangeness and his pride,
Which his own will shall have desire to drink;
It may do good: pride hath no other glass
To show itself but pride, for supple knees
50   Feed arrogance and are the proud man's fees.

AGAMEMNON   We'll execute your purpose, and put on
A form of strangeness as we pass along:
So do each lord, and either greet him not
Or else disdainfully, which shall shake him more
55   Than if not looked on. I will lead the way.

ACHILLES   What, comes the general to speak with me?
You know my mind: I'll fight no more gainst Troy.

AGAMEMNON   What says Achilles? Would he aught with us?

NESTOR   Would you, my lord, aught with the general?

60   ACHILLES   No.

NESTOR   Nothing, my lord.

AGAMEMNON   The better.   [*Exeunt Agamemnon and Nestor*]

ACHILLES   Good day, good day.   *To Menelaus*

MENELAUS   How do you? How do you?   [*Exit*]

65   ACHILLES   What, does the cuckold scorn me?

AJAX   How now, Patroclus?

ACHILLES   Good morrow, Ajax.

AJAX   Ha?

ACHILLES   Good morrow.

70   AJAX   Ay, and good next day too.   *Exit*

ACHILLES   What mean these fellows? Know they not Achilles?

PATROCLUS   They pass by strangely: they were used to bend
To send their smiles before them to Achilles,
To come as humbly as they used to creep
75   To holy altars.

---

44 unplausive disapproving, disdainful   **45 derision medicinable** i.e. a way to use scorn to
cure him   **48 glass** mirror   **49 supple . . . fees** i.e. submissive behavior such as kneeling
only encourages arrogance and is the reward the proud man expects   **51 purpose** plan
52 form appearance   **54 shake** affect, unsettle   **58 aught** have anything to do   **62 The
better** so much the better   **71 Know** recognize   **72 used** accustomed

ACHILLES   What, am I poor of late?
    'Tis certain, greatness, once fall'n out with fortune,
    Must fall out with men too: what the declined is
    He shall as soon read in the eyes of others
80   As feel in his own fall, for men, like butterflies,
    Show not their mealy wings but to the summer,
    And not a man, for being simply man,
    Hath any honour, but honoured for those honours
    That are without him, as place, riches and favour,
85   Prizes of accident as oft as merit,
    Which when they fall, as being slippery standers,
    The love that leaned on them as slippery too,
    Doth one pluck down another and together
    Die in the fall. But 'tis not so with me;
90   Fortune and I are friends: I do enjoy
    At ample point all that I did possess,
    Save these men's looks, who do, methinks, find out
    Something not worth in me such rich beholding
    As they have often given. Here is Ulysses:
95   I'll interrupt his reading.— How now Ulysses?

ULYSSES   Now, great Thetis' son!

ACHILLES   What are you reading?

ULYSSES   A strange fellow here
    Writes me that man, how dearly ever parted,
100   How much in having, or without or in,
    Cannot make boast to have that which he hath,
    Nor feels not what he owes, but by reflection,

---

76 poor devalued, insignificant   **78 the declined** man whose fortune has declined, one brought low   **81 mealy** powdery (as if covered with meal or flour)   **but** except   **83 but . . . him** except the honor bestowed by external recognition   **84 as** such as   **place** position, rank   **85 of accident** gained by chance, fate   **86 they** i.e. such men   **as . . . standers** like those standing on slippery ground (may play on the sense of "lecherous erections," in which case **Die . . . fall** plays on the sense of "orgasm and lose the erection," **enjoy** and **possess** resonate sexually and **ample point** plays on the sense of "fully erect penis")   **87 love** i.e. adulation of others   **slippery** sense now also includes "fickle"   **91 At ample point** to the full (possibly puns on sexual sense of **point** as penis)   **92 Save** except   **93 such rich beholding** of such high regard   **99 Writes me** writes (**me** is emphatic)   **how . . . parted** however richly endowed with personal qualities   **100 or . . . in** either externally or internally   **102 owes** owns, possesses   **but by reflection** except in how his qualities are reflected in others' responses to him

As when his virtues shining upon others
Heat them and they retort that heat again
105 To the first giver.

ACHILLES   This is not strange, Ulysses.
The beauty that is borne here in the face
The bearer knows not, but commends itself
Not going from itself, but eye to eye opposed
110 Salutes each other with each other's form.
For speculation turns not to itself
Till it hath travelled and is mirrored there
Where it may see itself. This is not strange at all.

ULYSSES   I do not strain it at the position —
115 It is familiar — but at the author's drift,
Who in his circumstance expressly proves
That no man is the lord of anything —
Though in and of him there is much consisting —
Till he communicate his parts to others,
120 Nor doth he of himself know them for aught
Till he behold them formed in th'applause
Where they are extended, who, like an arch, reverb'rate
The voice again, or, like a gate of steel
Fronting the sun, receives and renders back
125 His figure and his heat. I was much wrapt in this,
And apprehended here immediately
The unknown Ajax.

---

104 retort reflect, cast back   **108 but** unless it/but instead it   **109 Not . . . form** not in leaving and looking back at itself, but through facing another person, which enables the gazers to see themselves mirrored in each other's eyes   **111 speculation** the power of sight/contemplation, thought   **112 travelled** plays on the sense of "travailed," i.e. labored/become learned through study   **113 strange** odd/unfamiliar   **114 strain . . . position** have difficulty accepting the hypothesis   **115 drift** application (of the argument)   **116 his circumstance** the surrounding details of his argument   **118 in . . . consisting** he is composed of many fine qualities   **119 parts** personal qualities   **120 know . . . aught** recognize them as anything significant   **121 th'applause . . . extended** the praise of those who have seen them displayed   **122 who** refers to those applauding or to the applause itself **an arch** i.e. of a city gate or bridge   **123 voice** praise/vote of approval   **gate** door **124 Fronting** facing   **renders** returns   **125 His figure** the sun's shape   **wrapt in** involved in, engaged by   **126 apprehended** thought of, recognized   **127 unknown** little known, unacknowledged

Heavens, what a man is there! A very horse,
That has he knows not what. Nature, what things there are
130   Most abject in regard and dear in use!
What things again most dear in the esteem
And poor in worth! Now shall we see tomorrow —
An act that very chance doth throw upon him —
Ajax renowned! O heavens, what some men do,
135   While some men leave to do!
How some men creep in skittish fortune's hall,
Whiles others play the idiots in her eyes!
How one man eats into another's pride,
While pride is fasting in his wantonness!
140   To see these Grecian lords! Why, even already
They clap the lubber Ajax on the shoulder,
As if his foot were on brave Hector's breast
And great Troy shrinking.

ACHILLES   I do believe it, for they passed by me
145   As misers do by beggars, neither gave to me
Good word nor look. What, are my deeds forgot?

ULYSSES   Time hath, my lord, a wallet at his back,
Wherein he puts alms for oblivion,
A great-sized monster of ingratitudes:
150   Those scraps are good deeds past, which are devoured
As fast as they are made, forgot as soon
As done: perseverance, dear my lord,
Keeps honour bright: to have done is to hang
Quite out of fashion, like a rusty mail
155   In monumental mock'ry. Take the instant way,

128 **horse** i.e. strong (perhaps slyly alludes to Ajax being large and stupid)   129 **That . . . what** i.e. who knows not what strength he possesses (perhaps also a dig at Ajax's ignorance)
130 **Most . . . use** that are considered contemptible but are of immense practical value
131 **again** also/conversely   135 **leave to do** give up/neglect (a reference to Achilles)
136 **creep . . . hall** creep furtively into fickle fortune's domain   137 **idiots** jesters, clowns, fools
138 **pride** glory   139 **is . . . wantonness** starves on account of his willful behavior
141 **lubber** clumsy lout   143 **shrinking** recoiling in fear   147 **wallet** bag, knapsack
148 **alms for oblivion** i.e. admirable deeds destined to be forgotten   **alms** charitable offerings
153 **to have done** i.e. to have done a good deed in the past   154 **mail** piece of armor made of chain-mail links   155 **in monumental mock'ry** as a mocking trophy to forgotten glory
instant immediate, direct

For honour travels in a strait so narrow
Where one but goes abreast. Keep then the path,
For emulation hath a thousand sons
That one by one pursue: if you give way,
160   Or hedge aside from the direct forthright,
Like to an entered tide they all rush by
And leave you hindmost,
Or like a gallant horse fall'n in first rank,
Lie there for pavement to the abject rear,
165   O'er-run and trampled on: then what they do in present,
Though less than yours in past, must o'ertop yours,
For time is like a fashionable host
That slightly shakes his parting guest by th'hand,
And with his arms outstretched as he would fly,
170   Grasps in the comer. The welcome ever smiles,
And farewell goes out sighing. O, let not virtue seek
Remuneration for the thing it was.
For beauty, wit,
High birth, vigour of bone, desert in service,
175   Love, friendship, charity, are subjects all
To envious and calumniating time.
One touch of nature makes the whole world kin,
That all with one consent praise new-born gawds,
Though they are made and moulded of things past,
180   And give to dust that is a little gilt
More laud than gilt o'er-dusted.

---

156 strait narrow passage, confined path   157 one . . . abreast i.e. one must go in single file
Keep . . . path i.e. stick to the path/keep moving along the path   158 emulation ambitious
rivalry   160 hedge aside deviate, shift   forthright straight path   161 entered inrushing,
broken through   162 hindmost last   163 rank line of attacking troops   164 for . . . rear as
a paved thoroughfare for the contemptible troops in the back ranks   168 slightly casually,
inattentively   169 as . . . fly as if he was about to fly   170 Grasps in embraces   ever always
172 Remuneration payment, reward   174 vigour of bone bodily strength   desert in service
worthy deeds in war   176 calumniating slandering, defaming   177 touch of nature natural
trait/human weakness   makes . . . kin unites all people   178 with one consent in mutual
agreement, with one voice   new-born gawds trifling novelties, fashionable trinkets (gawds
puns on "gods")   180 dust . . . gilt i.e. worthless objects that are covered with a thin veneer of
gold   181 laud praise, honor   gilt o'er-dusted true gold covered with dust   (here gilt as
gold)

The present eye praises the present object.
Then marvel not, thou great and complete man,
That all the Greeks begin to worship Ajax;
185   Since things in motion begin to catch the eye
Than what not stirs. The cry went out on thee,
And still it might, and yet it may again,
If thou wouldst not entomb thyself alive
And case thy reputation in thy tent;
190   Whose glorious deeds, but in these fields of late,
Made emulous missions 'mongst the gods themselves
And drave great Mars to faction.

ACHILLES   Of this my privacy
I have strong reasons.

195   ULYSSES   But gainst your privacy
The reasons are more potent and heroical:
'Tis known, Achilles, that you are in love
With one of Priam's daughters.

ACHILLES   Ha? Known?

200   ULYSSES   Is that a wonder?
The providence that's in a watchful state
Knows almost every grain of Pluto's gold,
Finds bottom in th'uncomprehensive deeps,
Keeps place with thought, and almost, like the gods,
205   Do thoughts unveil in their dumb cradles.
There is a mystery — with whom relation
Durst never meddle — in the soul of state;
Which hath an operation more divine
Than breath or pen can give expressure to:

---

182 **present object** item immediately within its view   183 **complete** accomplished
186 **cry . . . thee** you were once acclaimed   189 **case** enclose, conceal   190 **but . . . late** even
lately on the battlefield   191 **Made emulous missions** caused forays into the battle provoked
by envy/rivalry   192 **drave** drove   **to faction** to take sides   198 **one . . . daughters** i.e.
Polyxena   201 **providence** foresight, forethought   202 **Pluto** the wealthy Greek god of the
underworld   203 **th'uncomprehensive deeps** the fathomless seas   204 **Keeps place** keeps
up   205 **thoughts . . . cradles** i.e. discerns thoughts even before they can be fully formulated
or uttered   206 **mystery** inexplicable essence/art, skill/trade secret   **with . . . meddle** that is
never discussed   **relation** report, narration   207 **state** affairs of state, government, statecraft
208 **operation** effect, function, power   209 **expressure** expression

210 All the commerce that you have had with Troy
As perfectly is ours as yours, my lord,
And better would it fit Achilles much
To throw down Hector than Polyxena.
But it must grieve young Pyrrhus now at home,
215 When fame shall in our island sound her trump,
And all the Greekish girls shall tripping sing,
'Great Hector's sister did Achilles win,
But our great Ajax bravely beat down him.'
Farewell, my lord: I as your lover speak;
220 The fool slides o'er the ice that you should break.   [*Exit*]

PATROCLUS   To this effect, Achilles, have I moved you:
A woman impudent and mannish grown
Is not more loathed than an effeminate man
In time of action. I stand condemned for this;
225 They think my little stomach to the war
And your great love to me restrains you thus:
Sweet, rouse yourself; and the weak wanton Cupid
Shall from your neck unloose his amorous fold,
And, like a dew-drop from the lion's mane,
230 Be shook to airy air.

ACHILLES   Shall Ajax fight with Hector?

PATROCLUS   Ay, and perhaps receive much honour by him.

ACHILLES   I see my reputation is at stake,
My fame is shrewdly gored.

235 PATROCLUS   O, then, beware:
Those wounds heal ill that men do give themselves.
Omission to do what is necessary

---

210 **commerce** dealings, transactions   211 **perfectly . . . yours** is as well known to us as to
you   212 **fit** befit, suit   213 **throw . . . Polyxena** defeat Hector in battle than to seduce
Polyxena   214 **Pyrrhus** Achilles' son   215 **trump** trumpet   216 **Greekish girls** women of
Greece (suggests also wanton women)   **tripping** skipping, with dancing steps   218 **him** i.e.
Hector (also suggestive of Ajax bettering Achilles; while Ajax defeats Hector, Achilles will
beat—i.e. have sex with—Polyxena)   219 **lover** friend, supporter   220 **The . . . break** i.e.
Ajax deals incompetently with matters you would deal with properly/Ajax is such an idiot that
he escapes dangers that would prove fatal to a man of your stature   221 **moved** encouraged,
urged   222 **impudent** shameless   225 **stomach to** appetite for   227 **wanton** willful/lustful
(may act as noun or verb)   228 **fold** embrace   232 **by him** i.e. by defeating him   234 **fame**
reputation, renown   **shrewdly gored** severely wounded   236 **ill** badly

Seals a commission to a blank of danger,
And danger, like an ague, subtly taints
240   Even then when we sit idly in the sun.

ACHILLES   Go call Thersites hither, sweet Patroclus:
I'll send the fool to Ajax and desire him
T'invite the Trojan lords after the combat
To see us here unarmed. I have a woman's longing,
245   An appetite that I am sick withal,
To see great Hector in his weeds of peace,

Enter Thersites

To talk with him and to behold his visage,
Even to my full of view.— A labour saved!   *Sees Thersites*

THERSITES   A wonder!
250   ACHILLES   What?

THERSITES   Ajax goes up and down the field, asking for himself.

ACHILLES   How so?

THERSITES   He must fight singly tomorrow with Hector, and is
so prophetically proud of an heroical cudgelling that he
255   raves in saying nothing.

ACHILLES   How can that be?

THERSITES   Why, he stalks up and down like a peacock, a stride
and a stand: ruminates like an hostess that hath no arithmetic
but her brain to set down her reckoning: bites his lip with a
260   politic regard, as who should say 'There were wit in this head,
an 'twould out'; and so there is, but it lies as coldly in him as
fire in a flint, which will not show without knocking. The
man's undone for ever; for if Hector break not his neck
i'th'combat, he'll break't himself in vainglory. He knows not

---

238 **Seals . . . danger** gives danger full license, gives it a blank warrant which it may fill in as it
wishes   239 **ague** fever characterized by shaking   **taints** infects   244 **woman's longing** i.e.
cravings like those experienced in pregnancy   245 **withal** with   246 **weeds** clothes
248 **Even . . . view** until my gaze is entirely satisfied   251 **himself** i.e. Ajax, perhaps punning
on "a jakes"   254 **prophetically proud** proud in anticipation   255 **raves . . . nothing** rants
incoherently   257 **peacock** proverbially proud bird   **a . . . stand** stopping and starting
258 **hostess** tavern landlady   **arithmetic** ability to calculate   259 **her reckoning** the bill
260 **politic regard** calculated expression, wise look   **as** as one   261 **an 'twould out** if only it
would emerge   262 **knocking** being struck (refers to the flint and to beating Ajax)
263 **undone** ruined, destroyed, brought down   264 **knows** recognizes

265 me: I said, 'Good morrow, Ajax'; and he replies, 'Thanks,
     Agamemnon.' What think you of this man that takes me for
     the general? He's grown a very land-fish, language-less, a
     monster. A plague of opinion! A man may wear it on both
     sides, like a leather jerkin.

270 ACHILLES Thou must be my ambassador to him, Thersites.

     THERSITES Who, I? Why, he'll answer nobody. He professes not
     answering: speaking is for beggars, he wears his tongue in's
     arms. I will put on his presence; let Patroclus make his
     demands to me, you shall see the pageant of Ajax.

275 ACHILLES To him, Patroclus; tell him I humbly desire the
     valiant Ajax to invite the most valorous Hector to come
     unarmed to my tent, and to procure safe conduct for his
     person of the magnanimous and most illustrious six-or-
     seven-times-honoured captain-general of the Grecian army,

280 Agamemnon, et cetera. Do this.

     PATROCLUS Jove bless great Ajax!

     THERSITES Hum!

     PATROCLUS I come from the worthy Achilles—

     THERSITES Ha!

285 PATROCLUS Who most humbly desires you to invite Hector to
     his tent—

     THERSITES Hum!

     PATROCLUS And to procure safe conduct from Agamemnon.

     THERSITES Agamemnon?

290 PATROCLUS Ay, my lord.

     THERSITES Ha?

     PATROCLUS What say you to't?

     THERSITES God buy you, with all my heart.

     PATROCLUS Your answer, sir.

---

267 land-fish fish living on land, i.e. an unnatural creature   **268 of opinion** on reputation/
self-regard   **269 leather jerkin** close-fitting leather jacket (here presumably reversible)
271 professes not does not engage in   **272 wears . . . arms** gives his answer with his
weapons   **273 put on** imitate   **presence** bearing, demeanor, appearance   **274 demands**
requests, questions   **275 To him** set to it, tackle him   **282 Hum!** i.e. hmm   **293 God buy
you** God be with you, i.e. goodbye

295 THERSITES   If tomorrow be a fair day, by eleven o'clock it will
go one way or other: howsoever, he shall pay for me ere he
has me.

PATROCLUS   Your answer, sir.

THERSITES   Fare you well, with all my heart.

300 ACHILLES   Why, but he is not in this tune, is he?

THERSITES   No, but he's out o'tune thus. What music will be in
him when Hector has knocked out his brains, I know not,
but I am sure none, unless the fiddler Apollo get his sinews to
make catlings on.

305 ACHILLES   Come, thou shalt bear a letter to him straight.

THERSITES   Let me carry another to his horse; for that's the
more capable creature.

ACHILLES   My mind is troubled, like a fountain stirred,
And I myself see not the bottom of it.

[Exeunt Achilles and Patroclus]

310 THERSITES   Would the fountain of your mind were clear again,
that I might water an ass at it! I had rather be a tick in a
sheep than such a valiant ignorance.   *[Exit]*

[Act 4 Scene 1]

Enter at one door Aeneas with a torch, at another Paris, Deiphobus,
Antenor, Diomedes the Grecian, with torches

PARIS   See, ho! Who is that there?

DEIPHOBUS   It is the lord Aeneas.

AENEAS   Is the prince there in person?
Had I so good occasion to lie long

5   As you, Prince Paris, nothing but heavenly business
Should rob my bed-mate of my company.

---

296 **howsoever** in either case   **pay for me** i.e. receive a beating   297 **has** defeats   300 **tune**
i.e. mood   303 **fiddler** fiddle player   **Apollo** Greek god of music   304 **catlings** catgut, used
to make strings for musical instruments   **on** out of   307 **capable** receptive, intelligent
308 **stirred** i.e. disturbed with sediment   312 **valiant** hearty, utter   **ignorance** ignorant fool
4.1   *Location: Troy*   **torch** torch (held by Aeneas)/torchbearer   4 **occasion** opportunity/
reason   **lie** i.e. in bed   5 **heavenly business** i.e. worship or deeds for the gods

DIOMEDES	That's my mind too. Good morrow, Lord Aeneas.
PARIS	A valiant Greek, Aeneas: take his hand.
	Witness the process of your speech, within

10 You told how Diomed, in a whole week by days,
Did haunt you in the field.

AENEAS Health to you, valiant sir,
During all question of the gentle truce,
But when I meet you armed, as black defiance

15 As heart can think or courage execute.

DIOMEDES The one and other Diomed embraces.
Our bloods are now in calm, and, so long, health!
But when contention and occasion meets,
By Jove, I'll play the hunter for thy life

20 With all my force, pursuit and policy.

AENEAS And thou shalt hunt a lion that will fly
With his face backward. In humane gentleness,
Welcome to Troy. Now, by Anchises' life,
Welcome indeed! By Venus' hand I swear,

25 No man alive can love in such a sort
The thing he means to kill more excellently.

DIOMEDES We sympathize. Jove, let Aeneas live —
If to my sword his fate be not the glory —
A thousand complete courses of the sun!

30 But, in mine emulous honour, let him die
With every joint a wound, and that tomorrow!

AENEAS We know each other well.

DIOMEDES We do, and long to know each other worse.

---

7 mind opinion   **9 Witness . . . speech** bear witness to the drift of your own remarks (regarding Diomedes' worth)   **10 by days** daily   **11 haunt** pursue   **13 question of** discussions permitted during   **gentle** noble/peaceful   **15 think** conceive of/intend   **execute** carry out (plays on the sense of "kill")   **16 The . . . other** i.e. both sentiments (health and defiance)   **17 bloods** tempers   **so long** i.e. while the truce lasts   **18 contention** dispute, conflict   **occasion** opportunity   **20 policy** cunning/strategy   **22 backward** i.e. courageously facing the pursuer   **23 Anchises** Aeneas' father   **24 Venus** the goddess was Aeneas' mother   **25 No . . . excellently** no man alive can love in such a manner, so excellently the thing he means to kill   **27 sympathize** agree, are in accord   **28 If . . . glory** if I am not to have the glory of killing him   **29 complete . . . sun** i.e. years   **30 in mine** for, in the cause of **emulous** ambitious, rivalrous   **32 know** understand   **33 know . . . worse** see the other one in a worse state/meet as enemies

PARIS   This is the most despiteful'st gentle greeting,
35   The noblest hateful love, that e'er I heard of.
        What business, lord, so early?
AENEAS   I was sent for to the king; but why, I know not.
PARIS   His purpose meets you: it was to bring this Greek
        To Calchas' house, and there to render him,
40   For the enfreed Antenor, the fair Cressid.
        Let's have your company, or, if you please,
        Haste there before us.—
                                    I constantly do think —   *Aside to*
        Or rather, call my thought a certain knowledge —   *Aeneas*
        My brother Troilus lodges there tonight:
45   Rouse him and give him note of our approach,
        With the whole quality whereof. I fear
        We shall be much unwelcome.
AENEAS   That I assure you:
        Troilus had rather Troy were borne to Greece
50   Than Cressid borne from Troy.
PARIS   There is no help:
        The bitter disposition of the time
        Will have it so. On, lord, we'll follow you.
AENEAS   Good morrow, all.   *Exit Aeneas*
55 PARIS   And tell me, noble Diomed, faith, tell me true,
        Even in the soul of sound good-fellowship,
        Who, in your thoughts, merits fair Helen most,
        Myself or Menelaus?
DIOMEDES   Both alike:
60   He merits well to have her that doth seek her,
        Not making any scruple of her soilure,
        With such a hell of pain and world of charge.
        And you as well to keep her that defend her,

---

34 despiteful'st gentle malicious courteous   **39 render** give   **42 constantly** assuredly, firmly
43 call my thought let my thought be called   **45 note** notice, news   **46 quality whereof**
reason for it   **52 disposition** nature/arrangements   **54 morrow** morning   **60 He** i.e.
Menelaus   **61 making . . . of** worrying about, entertaining moral doubts about   **soilure**
defilement, sexual dishonoring   **62 With . . . charge** and the pain and cost of war

Not palating the taste of her dishonour,

65   With such a costly loss of wealth and friends.
He, like a puling cuckold, would drink up
The lees and dregs of a flat tamèd piece:
You, like a lecher, out of whorish loins
Are pleased to breed out your inheritors.

70   Both merits poised, each weighs no less nor more,
But he as he, the heavier for a whore.

PARIS   You are too bitter to your countrywoman.

DIOMEDES   She's bitter to her country. Hear me, Paris:
For every false drop in her bawdy veins

75   A Grecian's life hath sunk, for every scruple
Of her contaminated carrion weight,
A Trojan hath been slain. Since she could speak,
She hath not given so many good words breath
As for her Greeks and Trojans suffered death.

80   **PARIS**   Fair Diomed, you do as chapmen do,
Dispraise the thing that you desire to buy:
But we in silence hold this virtue well:
We'll not commend what we intend to sell.
Here lies our way.   *Exeunt*

[Act 4 Scene 2]   *running scene 10*

Enter Troilus and Cressida

TROILUS   Dear, trouble not yourself: the morn is cold.

CRESSIDA   Then, sweet my lord, I'll call mine uncle down;
He shall unbolt the gates.

---

64 palating tasting, affected by   **66 puling** whimpering, whining   **67 lees and dregs**
remains, sediment   **flat tamèd piece** wine cask that has been left open (**tamèd**) and the
contents of which have become stale; plays on the sense of "sexually conquered woman"
(**piece**), with **flat** suggesting unresponsive submission   **68 whorish loins** i.e. Helen's
69 breed out conceive, create/taint and dilute the lineage of   **70 poised** balanced   **71 he as**
he i.e. both men are equal   **the heavier** both are more sorrowful   **whore** plays on the
antithesis of "light" (i.e. sexually immoral), a common descriptor for whores   **75 sunk** i.e.
been lost   **scruple** tiny amount   **76 carrion** putrefied, rotten (also a term for a whore)
78 breath utterance   **80 chapmen** traders, merchants   **81 Dispraise** disparage, belittle
82 But . . . sell i.e. we won't play the tradesman   **hold** uphold   **83 commend** praise/hand
over   **84 way** path, route

TROILUS   Trouble him not.

5   To bed, to bed: sleep kill those pretty eyes,
               And give as soft attachment to thy senses
               As infants empty of all thought!

CRESSIDA   Good morrow, then.

TROILUS   I prithee now, to bed.

10   CRESSIDA Are you aweary of me?

TROILUS   O Cressida! But that the busy day,
               Waked by the lark, hath roused the ribald crows,
               And dreaming night will hide our joys no longer,
               I would not from thee.

15   CRESSIDA Night hath been too brief.

TROILUS   Beshrew the witch! With venomous wights she stays
               As hideously as hell, but flies the grasps of love
               With wings more momentary-swift than thought.
               You will catch cold and curse me.

20   CRESSIDA Prithee, tarry: you men will never tarry.
               O foolish Cressid! I might have still held off,
               And then you would have tarried. Hark, there's one up.

PANDARUS   What's all the doors open here?   *Within*

TROILUS   It is your uncle.

Enter Pandarus

25   CRESSIDA A pestilence on him! Now will he be mocking:
               I shall have such a life!

PANDARUS   How now, how now? How go maidenheads?
               Hear, you maid! Where's my cousin Cressid?

CRESSIDA   Go hang yourself, you naughty mocking uncle!

30   You bring me to do – – – – and then you flout me too.

4.2   5 kill subdue, overpower   **6 soft attachment** gentle confinement   **7 As** as have/as to
those of   **11 But** were it not   **busy** active/interfering   **12 ribald** raucously abusive,
irreverent   **14 from** go from   **16 Beshrew** curse   **venomous wights** malignant people
stays lingers   **17 grasps** clutches/embraces   **18 momentary-swift** fleeting   **20 tarry** linger,
delay   **21 held off** i.e. from intercourse   **23 What's** i.e. why are   **25 pestilence** plague
26 life i.e. hard time of it   **27 how go** how is it with/what is the current price for
maidenheads virginities   **28 Hear . . . Cressid?** Pandarus pretends not to recognize
Cressida now that she is no longer a virgin   **29 naughty** wicked (perhaps also "licentious")
30 – – – – the original text has this sequence of dashes to suggest an obscenity   **flout** insult,
mock, taunt

PANDARUS   To do what? To do what? Let her say what: what
have I brought you to do?

CRESSIDA   Come, come, beshrew your heart! You'll ne'er be
good,
Nor suffer others.

35   PANDARUS   Ha, ha! Alas, poor wretch! Ah, poor *chipochia*! Hast
not slept tonight? Would he not — a naughty man — let it
sleep? A bugbear take him!   *One knocks*

CRESSIDA   Did not I tell you? Would he were knocked i'th'head!
Who's that at door? Good uncle, go and see.—

40   My lord, come you again into my chamber.
You smile and mock me, as if I meant naughtily.

TROILUS   Ha, ha!

CRESSIDA   Come, you are deceived, I think of no such thing.
How earnestly they knock! Pray you, come in: *Knock*

45   I would not for half Troy have you seen here.
                                     Exeunt [*Troilus and Cressida*]

PANDARUS   Who's there? What's the matter? Will you beat
down the door? How now, what's the matter?

[*Enter Aeneas*]

AENEAS   Good morrow, lord, good morrow.

PANDARUS   Who's there? My lord Aeneas? By my troth,
50   I knew you not: what news with you so early?

AENEAS   Is not Prince Troilus here?

PANDARUS   Here? What should he do here?

AENEAS   Come, he is here, my lord, do not deny him:
It doth import him much to speak with me.

---

31 **do** plays on the sense of "have sex with"   34 **suffer others** allow others to be
35 *chipochia* vulva, vagina (from Italian *poccia dell'amore*, woman's genitalia); most editors
incorrectly emend to *capocchia*, "foreskin," which would require the line to be addressed to
Troilus   37 **bugbear** hobgoblin, bogeyman (used to frighten children; Pandarus continues
teasingly speaking in a manner appropriate to small children)   38 **knocked i'th'head** bashed
over the head (perhaps Cressida unconsciously employs sexual language: "to knock" could
mean to have sex and **head** could refer to the head of a penis)   41 **meant naughtily** had
wicked intentions, i.e. was inviting you in for sex (in addition, to **come** could mean "to orgasm"
and **chamber** could mean "vagina")   43 **thing** perhaps plays on the sense of "penis"
50 **knew** recognized   54 **import** concern

55   PANDARUS   Is he here, say you? 'Tis more than I know, I'll be
sworn. For my own part, I came in late. What should he do
here?

AENEAS   Who, nay then! Come, come, you'll do him wrong
ere you're ware: you'll be so true to him, to be false to him.

60   Do not you know of him, but yet go fetch him hither. Go.

Enter Troilus

TROILUS   How now? What's the matter?

AENEAS   My lord, I scarce have leisure to salute you,
My matter is so rash: there is at hand
Paris your brother, and Deiphobus,

65   The Grecian Diomed, and our Antenor
Delivered to us, and for him forthwith,
Ere the first sacrifice, within this hour,
We must give up to Diomedes' hand
The lady Cressida.

70   TROILUS   Is it concluded so?

AENEAS   By Priam and the general state of Troy:
They are at hand and ready to effect it.

TROILUS   How my achievements mock me!
I will go meet them. And, my lord Aeneas,

75   We met by chance; you did not find me here.

AENEAS   Good, good, my lord, the secrets of nature
Have not more gift in taciturnity.   *Exeunt [Troilus and Aeneas]*

Enter Cressida

PANDARUS   Is't possible? No sooner got but lost? The devil take
Antenor! The young prince will go mad. A plague upon

80   Antenor! I would they had broke's neck!

CRESSIDA   How now? What's the matter? Who was here?

---

58 Who a form of "ho" or "whoa" (expressions of impatience)   **59 ere you're ware**
unintentionally, before you know it   **you'll . . . him** i.e. in trying to be loyal you will end up
doing him a disservice   **60 Do . . . him** i.e. very well, so you don't know where he is (Aeneas
will play along with Pandarus' lie)   **yet** nevertheless   **63 rash** urgent   **67 sacrifice** religious
observance, offering to the gods (made at regular intervals throughout the day)
70 concluded decided, settled   **71 state** council   **73 achievements** accomplishments,
success/sexual conquest   **77 Have . . . taciturnity** are not more gifted than in keeping silent
80 broke's broken his

| | PANDARUS | Ah, ha! |

PANDARUS   Ah, ha!

CRESSIDA   Why sigh you so profoundly? Where's my lord?
Gone! Tell me, sweet uncle, what's the matter?

85   PANDARUS   Would I were as deep under the earth as I am above!

CRESSIDA   O the gods! What's the matter?

PANDARUS   Prithee, get thee in: would thou hadst ne'er been
born! I knew thou wouldst be his death. O, poor gentleman!
A plague upon Antenor!

90   CRESSIDA   Good uncle, I beseech you, on my knees I beseech
you, what's the matter?

PANDARUS   Thou must be gone, wench, thou must be gone;
thou art changed for Antenor. Thou must to thy father, and
be gone from Troilus: 'twill be his death, 'twill be his bane: he
95   cannot bear it.

CRESSIDA   O you immortal gods! I will not go.

PANDARUS   Thou must.

CRESSIDA   I will not, uncle. I have forgot my father:
I know no touch of consanguinity:
100   No kin, no love, no blood, no soul so near me
As the sweet Troilus. O you gods divine!
Make Cressid's name the very crown of falsehood,
If ever she leave Troilus! Time, force and death,
Do to this body what extremity you can;
105   But the strong base and building of my love
Is as the very centre of the earth,
Drawing all things to it. I will go in and weep.

PANDARUS   Do, do.

CRESSIDA   Tear my bright hair and scratch my praisèd cheeks,
110   Crack my clear voice with sobs and break my heart
With sounding Troilus. I will not go from Troy.   *Exeunt*

---

93 changed exchanged   **94 bane** poison/destruction/murder   **99 touch** feeling, hint
consanguinity kinship, blood relationship   **103 force** violence   **105 base** foundation
106 centre . . . it refers to the Elizabethan idea that all things were drawn toward the earth's
core; plays on architectural sense of **centre** as a "temporary framework supporting any
superstructure"   **111 sounding** crying out resoundingly

[Act 4 Scene 3]   *running scene 11*

Enter Paris, Troilus, Aeneas, Deiphobus, Antenor and Diomedes

PARIS   It is great morning, and the hour prefixed
Of her delivery to this valiant Greek
Comes fast upon. Good my brother Troilus,
Tell you the lady what she is to do,
5   And haste her to the purpose.
TROILUS   Walk into her house:
I'll bring her to the Grecian presently;
And to his hand when I deliver her,
Think it an altar, and thy brother Troilus
10   A priest there off'ring to it his heart.
PARIS   I know what 'tis to love,
And would, as I shall pity, I could help!
Please you walk in, my lords.   *Exeunt*

[Act 4 Scene 4]   *running scene 12*

Enter Pandarus and Cressida

PANDARUS   Be moderate, be moderate.
CRESSIDA   Why tell you me of moderation?
The grief is fine, full, perfect, that I taste,
And no less in a sense as strong
5   As that which causeth it. How can I moderate it?
If I could temporize with my affection,
Or brew it to a weak and colder palate,
The like allayment could I give my grief.
My love admits no qualifying dross.
Enter Troilus
10   No more my grief, in such a precious loss.

4.3   1 great morning broad daylight   **prefixed Of** prearranged for   **5 haste . . . purpose**
hurry her along, get her ready for it   **7 presently** immediately/soon   **12 would** I wish
as . . . pity as much as I pity   **4.4   3 fine** refined, pure   **6 temporize** negotiate, effect a
compromise   **7 brew** dilute, water down   **8 like allayment** same moderation, lessening
9 qualifying dross diluting impurity   **10 No more** no more does, neither can   **such . . . loss**
the loss of something so precious

PANDARUS	Here, here, here he comes, a sweet duck.
CRESSIDA	O Troilus! Troilus! *Embraces him*
PANDARUS	What a pair of spectacles is here! Let me embrace

too. 'O heart' as the goodly saying is,

15
    'O heart, heavy heart,
    Why sigh'st thou without breaking?'
Where he answers again,
    'Because thou canst not ease thy smart
    By friendship nor by speaking.'

20 There was never a truer rhyme. Let us cast away nothing, for
we may live to have need of such a verse: we see it, we see it.
How now, lambs?

TROILUS	Cressid, I love thee in so strange a purity,

That the blest gods, as angry with my fancy,
25 More bright in zeal than the devotion which
Cold lips blow to their deities, take thee from me.

CRESSIDA	Have the gods envy?
PANDARUS	Ay, ay, ay, ay: 'tis too plain a case.
CRESSIDA	And is it true that I must go from Troy?
TROILUS	A hateful truth.
CRESSIDA	What, and from Troilus too?
TROILUS	From Troy and Troilus.
CRESSIDA	Is't possible?
TROILUS	And suddenly, where injury of chance

30

35 Puts back leave-taking, jostles roughly by
All time of pause, rudely beguiles our lips
Of all rejoindure, forcibly prevents
Our locked embrasures, strangles our dear vows
Even in the birth of our own labouring breath.

---

11 duck term of endearment for a lover   **13 pair . . . here** sight the pair of you make (possibly **pair of spectacles** plays on the sense of "eyeglasses")   **17 he** i.e. the heart   **18 smart** pain   **21 we see it** i.e. we have seen how such words can console   **23 strange** rare, exceptional   **24 as** as if they are   **fancy** love   **25 More bright** which **fancy** is more bright   **26 Cold** chaste   **blow** breathe out (as they make their vows)   **27 envy** malice/jealousy   **34 where . . . chance** so that the cruelty of fate   **35 Puts back** prevents   **by** aside   **36 rudely** roughly, harshly, unkindly   **beguiles** cheats   **37 rejoindure** reunion (i.e. a kiss; also suggestive of "rejoinder," i.e. reply)   **38 embrasures** embraces   **dear** precious/heartfelt   **39 in . . . breath** as we struggle to give them voice (a grim image of infanticide)

40 We two, that with so many thousand sighs
 Did buy each other, must poorly sell ourselves
 With the rude brevity and discharge of one.
 Injurious time now with a robber's haste
 Crams his rich thiev'ry up, he knows not how:
45 As many farewells as be stars in heaven,
 With distinct breath and consigned kisses to them,
 He fumbles up into a loose adieu,
 And scants us with a single famished kiss,
 Distasting with the salt of broken tears.

50 **AENEAS** My lord, is the lady ready?   *Within*
 TROILUS Hark! You are called. Some say the genius so
 Cries 'Come' to him that instantly must die.
 Bid them have patience.— She shall come anon.

 PANDARUS Where are my tears? Rain, to lay this wind, or my
55 heart will be blown up by the root.   *[Exit]*

 CRESSIDA I must then to the Grecians?
 TROILUS No remedy.
 CRESSIDA A woeful Cressid 'mongst the merry Greeks!
 When shall we see again?

60 **TROILUS** Hear me, my love: be thou but true of heart—
 CRESSIDA I true? How now? What wicked deem is this?
 TROILUS Nay, we must use expostulation kindly,
 For it is parting from us.
 I speak not 'Be thou true' as fearing thee,
65 For I will throw my glove to Death himself,
 That there's no maculation in thy heart:
 But 'Be thou true', say I, to fashion in

---

42 discharge exhalation/payment **one** i.e. one sigh **43 Injurious** wounding, wrongful
44 thiev'ry booty, stolen valuables **46 distinct . . . kisses** individual words and ratifying kisses
to accompany each one **47 fumbles up** gathers clumsily together **48 scants** restricts,
supplies inadequately **49 Distasting** its sweetness destroyed **broken** interrupted (by sobs)
51 genius attendant spirit thought to accompany and influence a person throughout life
52 instantly at that moment, imminently **54 Rain . . . wind** i.e. I must cry to stop myself
sighing **lay** allay, calm **55 blown . . . root** uprooted (like a tree) **58 merry Greeks** a "merry
Greek" was a popular phrase for a jolly fellow **59 see** see each other **61 deem** thought,
notion, suspicion **62 use expostulation kindly** remonstrate gently with one another **63 it**
i.e. the opportunity to even talk **64 as fearing thee** as if I doubted you **65 throw my glove**
issue a challenge (to a duel) **66 maculation** stain **67 fashion in** introduce

My sequent protestation: be thou true,
And I will see thee.

70 CRESSIDA   O, you shall be exposed, my lord, to dangers
As infinite as imminent! But I'll be true.

TROILUS   And I'll grow friend with danger. Wear this sleeve.

CRESSIDA   And you this glove. When shall I see you?   *They*

TROILUS   I will corrupt the Grecian sentinels,   *exchange tokens*

75 To give thee nightly visitation.
But yet be true.

CRESSIDA   O heavens! 'Be true' again!

TROILUS   Hear why I speak it, love:
The Grecian youths are full of quality,

80 Their loving, well composed with gifts of nature,
Flowing and swelling o'er with arts and exercise.
How novelties may move, and parts with person,
Alas, a kind of godly jealousy —
Which, I beseech you, call a virtuous sin —

85 Makes me afraid.

CRESSIDA   O heavens, you love me not!

TROILUS   Die I a villain, then!
In this I do not call your faith in question
So mainly as my merit: I cannot sing,

90 Nor heel the high lavolt, nor sweeten talk,
Nor play at subtle games — fair virtues all,
To which the Grecians are most prompt and pregnant.
But I can tell that in each grace of these
There lurks a still and dumb-discoursive devil

95 That tempts most cunningly: but be not tempted.

---

68 sequent protestation following declaration   **72 sleeve** detachable sleeve, ornamented cuff
(given as a love token)   **74 corrupt** bribe   **79 quality** accomplishments/personal qualities
80 Their loving i.e. as lovers, in wooing   **composed** made up, put together   **81 arts and
exercise** well-practiced skills (**arts**)   **82 move** incite to love/arouse (sexually suggestive)
parts with person natural gifts together with the handsome man they belong to (possibly **parts**
plays on the sense of "genitals")   **83 godly** i.e. righteous   **89 mainly** much   **90 heel** dance
high lavolt a lively dance that involved leaping movements (from Italian *lavolta*, "the turn")
91 subtle cunning, involving strategy   **92 prompt and pregnant** readily disposed and
receptive   **94 still** continual/silent   **dumb-discoursive** silently persuasive, eloquent in
silence

CRESSIDA   Do you think I will?

TROILUS   No.
But something may be done that we will not:
And sometimes we are devils to ourselves,
100   When we will tempt the frailty of our powers,
Presuming on their changeful potency.

AENEAS   Nay, good my lord—   *Within*

TROILUS   Come, kiss, and let us part.

PARIS   Brother Troilus!   *Within*

105   TROILUS   Good brother, come you hither,
And bring Aeneas and the Grecian with you.

CRESSIDA   My lord, will you be true?

TROILUS   Who, I? Alas, it is my vice, my fault:
Whiles others fish with craft for great opinion,
110   I with great truth catch mere simplicity:
Whilst some with cunning gild their copper crowns,
With truth and plainness I do wear mine bare.

Enter the Greeks [Aeneas, Paris, Antenor, Deiphobus and Diomedes]
Fear not my truth: the moral of my wit
Is 'plain and true'; there's all the reach of it.—
115   Welcome, Sir Diomed! Here is the lady
Which for Antenor we deliver you.
At the port, lord, I'll give her to thy hand,
And by the way possess thee what she is.
Entreat her fair; and, by my soul, fair Greek,
120   If e'er thou stand at mercy of my sword,
Name Cressid and thy life shall be as safe
As Priam is in Ilium.

DIOMEDES   Fair Lady Cressid,
So please you, save the thanks this prince expects:
125   The lustre in your eye, heaven in your cheek,

---

98 will desire, wish   101 Presuming . . . potency relying too readily on a power that may in
fact prove changeable   109 craft cunning   for great opinion to secure great reputations
110 simplicity sincerity   111 crowns royal headgear (in the next line Troilus picks up on the
sense of "heads")   112 wear mine bare in its natural copper/go bareheaded   113 wit
thinking   114 all the reach the full extent   117 port city gate   118 by on   possess inform
119 Entreat her fair treat her courteously   fair noble   124 save keep, withhold

Pleads your fair usage, and to Diomed
You shall be mistress, and command him wholly.

TROILUS   Grecian, thou dost not use me courteously,
To shame the seal of my petition towards
130 I'praising her: I tell thee, lord of Greece,
She is as far high-soaring o'er thy praises
As thou unworthy to be called her servant.
I charge thee use her well, even for my charge,
For, by the dreadful Pluto, if thou dost not,
135 Though the great bulk Achilles be thy guard,
I'll cut thy throat.

DIOMEDES   O, be not moved, Prince Troilus.
Let me be privileged by my place and message,
To be a speaker free: when I am hence
140 I'll answer to my lust. And know, my lord,
I'll nothing do on charge. To her own worth
She shall be prized, but that you say 'Be't so',
I'll speak it in my spirit and honour, 'No.'

TROILUS   Come, to the port. I'll tell thee, Diomed,
145 This brave shall oft make thee to hide thy head.—
Lady, give me your hand, and, as we walk,
To our own selves bend we our needful talk.

[Exeunt Troilus, Cressida and Diomedes]

Sound trumpet

PARIS   Hark! Hector's trumpet.

AENEAS   How have we spent this morning!
150 The prince must think me tardy and remiss,
That swore to ride before him in the field.

---

126 Pleads makes the case for   **usage** treatment   **129 petition towards** request to you
132 thou you are   **servant** devotee, lover (like **mistress**, a term of courtly love)   **133 charge**
command   **even . . . charge** simply because I command it   **134 dreadful** inspiring dread,
fear-inducing   **Pluto** Greek god of the underworld   **137 moved** provoked, angered
138 place i.e. as a diplomat, negotiator   **message** mission   **139 hence** gone from here
140 answer . . . lust do as I please (e.g. respond to you in battle/seduce Cressida)   **lust**
will/sexual desire   **141 on charge** because it was commanded   **To** according to   **142 that**
insofar as, just because   **143 speak it** say   **145 brave** boast/defiance   **147 bend** we let us
direct   **150 tardy** reluctant, slow

PARIS	'Tis Troilus' fault: come, come, to field with him.
DEIPHOBUS	Let us make ready straight.
AENEAS	Yea, with a bridegroom's fresh alacrity,

155 Let us address to tend on Hector's heels:
The glory of our Troy doth this day lie
On his fair worth and single chivalry.   *Exeunt*

[Act 4 Scene 5]   *running scene 13*

Enter Ajax, armed, Achilles, Patroclus, Agamemnon, Menelaus,
Ulysses, Nestor, Calchas and others

AGAMEMNON   Here art thou in appointment fresh and fair,
Anticipating time. With starting courage,
Give with thy trumpet a loud note to Troy,
Thou dreadful Ajax, that the appallèd air
5   May pierce the head of the great combatant
And hale him hither.

AJAX   Thou, trumpet, there's my purse.
Now crack thy lungs, and split thy brazen pipe:
Blow, villain, till thy spherèd bias cheek
10   Outswell the colic of puffed Aquilon.
Come, stretch thy chest and let thy eyes spout blood.
Thou blowest for Hector.   *Trumpet sounds*

ULYSSES   No trumpet answers.

ACHILLES   'Tis but early days.

15   AGAMEMNON   Is not yond Diomed, with Calchas' daughter?

---

154 fresh eager   **155 address** prepare   **tend** attend, follow   **156 lie** depend   **157 single**
chivalry individual valor/valor in single combat   **4.5** *Location: near the Greek camp*
1 in appointment armed, equipped   **2 Anticipating** i.e. ahead of   **starting** energetic, eager
4 appallèd terrified, made pale   **6 hale** haul, drag   **7 trumpet** trumpeter   **8 brazen**
brass/audacious   **9 villain** wretch/servant   **spherèd** puffed out, rounded   **bias** i.e. puffed
out on one side, as if with a bias in it (i.e. the weight in a bowling ball that enabled it to be
rolled in a curve)   **10 colic** griping abdominal pain (here, attributed to excess wind)
Aquilon the north wind (often depicted with swollen cheeks)   **11 spout blood** i.e. due to burst
blood vessels from blowing so hard   **12 for** to summon   **14 early days** early on in the day
15 yond yonder, over there

ULYSSES   'Tis he, I ken the manner of his gait,
    He rises on the toe: that spirit of his
    In aspiration lifts him from the earth.
[*Enter Diomedes and Cressida*]

AGAMEMNON   Is this the lady Cressid?

20 DIOMEDES   Even she.

AGAMEMNON   Most dearly welcome to the Greeks,   *Kisses her*
    sweet lady.

NESTOR   Our general doth salute you with a kiss.

ULYSSES   Yet is the kindness but particular;
    'Twere better she were kissed in general.

25 NESTOR   And very courtly counsel: I'll begin.   *Kisses her*
    So much for Nestor.

ACHILLES   I'll take that winter from your lips, fair lady:
    Achilles bids you welcome.   *Kisses her*

MENELAUS   I had good argument for kissing once.

30 PATROCLUS   But that's no argument for kissing now;
    For thus popped Paris in his hardiment.   *Kisses her*

ULYSSES   O, deadly gall, and theme of all our scorns,
    For which we lose our heads to gild his horns.

PATROCLUS   The first was Menelaus' kiss, this, mine:

35 Patroclus kisses you.   *Kisses her again*

MENELAUS   O, this is trim!

PATROCLUS   Paris and I kiss evermore for him.

MENELAUS   I'll have my kiss, sir.— Lady, by your leave.

CRESSIDA   In kissing, do you render or receive?

---

16 ken know   **gait** walk, bearing   **18 aspiration** longing for something above one
21 dearly heartily (with suggestion of the expense incurred by the war that has brought her
there)   **23 Yet** as yet/however   **particular** individual/a single event   **24 in general** by
everyone/indiscriminately   **25 courtly** befitting court affairs and fashionable, elegant
behavior/befitting courtly love   **27 winter** i.e. Nestor's old age   **29 argument** subject
(Menelaus refers to Helen; may play on a sense of "vagina")   **30 argument** basis, reason
31 popped arrived unexpectedly/moved in suddenly   **hardiment** boldness/erect penis
32 theme . . . scorns reason for our being mocked/grounds of our contempt/cause for the
indignities of war   **33 lose our heads** lose our judgment/risk our lives   **gild his horns** add
false shine to Menelaus' cuckoldry (men with unfaithful wives were popularly supposed to
grow horns)   **36 trim** fine (sarcastic)   **37 for** instead of/in his place   **38 by your leave** with
your permission   **39 render** give

40 PATROCLUS   Both take and give.

   CRESSIDA   I'll make my match to live,
     The kiss you take is better than you give:
     Therefore no kiss.

   MENELAUS   I'll give you boot, I'll give you three for one.

45 CRESSIDA   You are an odd man: give even or give none.

   MENELAUS   An odd man, lady? Every man is odd.

   CRESSIDA   No, Paris is not; for you know 'tis true
     That you are odd and he is even with you.

   MENELAUS   You fillip me o'th'head.

50 CRESSIDA   No, I'll be sworn.

   ULYSSES   It were no match, your nail against his horn.
     May I, sweet lady, beg a kiss of you?

   CRESSIDA   You may.

   ULYSSES   I do desire it.

55 CRESSIDA   Why, beg then.

   ULYSSES   Why then for Venus' sake, give me a kiss,
     When Helen is a maid again, and his—

   CRESSIDA   I am your debtor, claim it when 'tis due.

   ULYSSES   Never's my day, and then a kiss of you.

60 DIOMEDES   Lady, a word: I'll bring you to your father.

   NESTOR   A woman of quick sense.

   ULYSSES   Fie, fie upon her!
     There's a language in her eye, her cheek, her lip;
     Nay, her foot speaks, her wanton spirits look out

65 At every joint and motive of her body.

---

41 I'll . . . live I'll stake my life on it, I'll bet   **42 take** i.e. receive from Cressida   **44 boot** something extra, an advantage, odds   **45 odd** peculiar/unique/single, i.e. wifeless (also plays on the notion of odd numbers and of odds in a betting game)   **even** an even number/equally/ straightforwardly   **46 odd** individual, unique   **48 odd** alone, wifeless   **is even** has settled his score (playing on the idea of being part of a couple)   **49 fillip me o'th'head** touch a sensitive spot, i.e. his cuckold's horns   **fillip** tap, strike smartly   **51 match** equal contest   **nail** fingernail   **horn** tough cuckold's horns   **54 desire** request (Cressida's response either points out a difference between this more formal request and begging, or picks up **desire**'s sense of "want, long for")   **57 maid** unmarried/a virgin (i.e. never)   **his** i.e. returned to Menelaus; alternatively, Ulysses breaks off without finishing   **58 when 'tis due** i.e. when that has happened   **59 a kiss** I'll claim a kiss   **61 quick sense** quick wit/lively sensibility/a ready sensuality   **62 Fie** expression of disgust or reproach   **64 wanton** lustful   **spirits** sentiments, character traits   **65 motive** moving limb, motion

O, these encounterers, so glib of tongue,
That give a coasting welcome ere it comes,
And wide unclasp the tables of their thoughts
To every tickling reader! Set them down
70   For sluttish spoils of opportunity
And daughters of the game.   *Exeunt [Diomedes and Cressida]*
Enter all of Troy: Hector, Paris, Aeneas, Helenus and Attendants.
Flourish

ALL   The Trojans' trumpet.

AGAMEMNON   Yonder comes the troop.

AENEAS   Hail, all you state of Greece. What shall be done
75   To him that victory commands? Or do you purpose
A victor shall be known? Will you the knights
Shall to the edge of all extremity
Pursue each other, or shall be divided
By any voice or order of the field?
80   Hector bade ask.

AGAMEMNON   Which way would Hector have it?

AENEAS   He cares not: he'll obey conditions.

ACHILLES   'Tis done like Hector, but securely done,
A little proudly, and great deal disprizing
85   The knight opposed.

AENEAS   If not Achilles, sir, what is your name?

ACHILLES   If not Achilles, nothing.

---

66 encounterers flirts, forward women   **67 give . . . comes** behave in a forward, overly welcoming manner before even being approached (**coasting**, i.e. accosting; may pun on "costing," i.e. costly to the man involved)   **68 wide unclasp** open wide   **tables** writing tablets, notebooks (often hinged; plays on the sense of "vaginas")   **69 tickling** lecherous/ engaged in sexual stimulation with the fingers   **Set them down** record, note them (plays on the sexual sense of "put them on their backs")   **70 spoils of opportunity** women who are sexually available on any occasion   **spoils** sexual plunder; plays on the idea of women sexually spoiled from overuse   **71 daughters . . . game** prostitutes   **74 state** men of rank **What** i.e. what honor, reward   **75 that victory commands** who wins   **purpose** intend that **76 known** acknowledged, declared   **Will you** do you wish that   **77 edge . . . extremity** point of death (without any interruption)   **78 be . . . field** they be separated by a marshal or by set rules in the field of combat   **80 bade** ordered me to   **82 conditions** agreed procedure **83 securely** overconfidently, carelessly   **84 disprizing** undervaluing, disdaining

AENEAS   Therefore Achilles. But whate'er know this:
In the extremity of great and little,
90   Valour and pride excel themselves in Hector;
The one almost as infinite as all,
The other blank as nothing. Weigh him well,
And that which looks like pride is courtesy.
This Ajax is half made of Hector's blood,
95   In love whereof, half Hector stays at home:
Half heart, half hand, half Hector comes to seek
This blended knight, half Trojan and half Greek.

ACHILLES   A maiden battle, then? O, I perceive you.

[*Enter Diomedes*]

AGAMEMNON   Here is Sir Diomed. Go, gentle knight,
100   Stand by our Ajax: as you and Lord Aeneas
Consent upon the order of their fight,
So be it, either to the uttermost,
Or else a breath. The combatants being kin
Half stints their strife before their strokes begin.   *Ajax and Hector*

105   ULYSSES   They are opposed already.   *enter the lists*

AGAMEMNON   What Trojan is that same that looks so heavy?

ULYSSES   The youngest son of Priam, a true knight,
// They call him Troilus: //
Not yet mature, yet matchless, firm of word,
110   Speaking in deeds and deedless in his tongue;
Not soon provoked nor being provoked soon calmed;
His heart and hand both open and both free,
For what he has he gives, what thinks he shows;
Yet gives he not till judgement guide his bounty,

---

89 In . . . Hector i.e. Hector's courage is as great as his vanity is nonexistent   **91 The one** i.e. valor   **all** the sum of everything   **92 The other** i.e. pride   **blank** i.e. absent   **Weigh** judge, assess the value of   **94 half . . . blood** Ajax's mother Hesione was Priam's sister, so he and Hector are cousins   **98 maiden** virginal, i.e. without bloodshed (with derogatory connotations of weakness)   **perceive** understand   **99 gentle** noble   **101 order** procedure, direction   **102 uttermost** point of death   **103 a breath** i.e. a series of more sporting bouts with pauses for breath   **104 stints** restrains   **strife** endeavors, strong exertions   **105 opposed** facing one another   *lists* designated combat area (literally, the barriers enclosing it)   **106 heavy** sad   **109 matchless** without equal   **firm of word** resolute in speech   **110 deedless . . . tongue** i.e. never boasting of his achievements   **112 free** generous   **114 bounty** generosity

115   Nor dignifies an impare thought with breath:
       Manly as Hector, but more dangerous,
       For Hector in his blaze of wrath subscribes
       To tender objects, but he in heat of action
       Is more vindicative than jealous love.
120   They call him Troilus, and on him erect
       A second hope as fairly built as Hector.
       Thus says Aeneas, one that knows the youth
       Even to his inches, and with private soul
       Did in great Ilium thus translate him to me.   *Alarum*

125   **AGAMEMNON**   They are in action.   *Hector and Ajax fight*

    NESTOR   Now, Ajax, hold thine own!

    TROILUS   Hector, thou sleep'st: awake thee!

    AGAMEMNON   His blows are well disposed. There, Ajax!

    DIOMEDES   You must no more.

  Trumpets cease

130   **AENEAS**   Princes, enough, so please you.

    AJAX   I am not warm yet: let us fight again.

    DIOMEDES   As Hector pleases.

    HECTOR   Why, then will I no more:
       Thou art, great lord, my father's sister's son,
135   A cousin-german to great Priam's seed.
       The obligation of our blood forbids
       A gory emulation 'twixt us twain:
       Were thy commixtion Greek and Trojan so
       That thou couldst say 'This hand is Grecian all,
140   And this is Trojan: the sinews of this leg
       All Greek, and this all Troy: my mother's blood
       Runs on the dexter cheek, and this sinister

---

115 impare uneven, unconsidered, unworthy   **117 subscribes** yields, grants mercy
118 tender objects pitiful sights, i.e. the defeated and defenseless   **119 vindicative** vindictive,
revengeful   **120 erect . . . Hector** i.e. he is expected to prove as worthy as Hector
123 Even . . . inches in every detail, from top to toe   **with private soul** confidentially, privately
and from the heart   **124 translate** interpret, explain, i.e. describe   *Alarum* call to battle
(usually trumpets or drums)   **125 in action** engaged in combat   **128 disposed** placed,
distributed   **129 no more** stop   **130 so** if it   **131 warm** warmed up   **135 cousin-german**
first cousin   **137 emulation** rivalry   **138 commixtion . . . Trojan** Trojan-Greek mixture
142 dexter right   **sinister** left

Bounds in my father's', by Jove multipotent,
Thou shouldst not bear from me a Greekish member
145   Wherein my sword had not impressure made
Of our rank feud. But the just gods gainsay
That any drop thou borrowed'st from thy mother,
My sacred aunt, should by my mortal sword
Be drained! Let me embrace thee, Ajax:
150   By him that thunders, thou hast lusty arms;
Hector would have them fall upon him thus.
Cousin, all honour to thee!   *Embraces him*

AJAX   I thank thee, Hector.
Thou art too gentle and too free a man:
155   I came to kill thee, cousin, and bear hence
A great addition earnèd in thy death.

HECTOR   Not Neoptolemus so mirable,
On whose bright crest Fame with her loud'st 'Oyez'
Cries 'This is he', couldst promise to himself
160   A thought of added honour torn from Hector.

AENEAS   There is expectance here from both the sides,
What further you will do.

HECTOR   We'll answer it:
The issue is embracement. Ajax, farewell.   *Embraces Ajax*

165   AJAX   If I might in entreaties find success —
As seld I have the chance — I would desire
My famous cousin to our Grecian tents.

DIOMEDES   'Tis Agamemnon's wish, and great Achilles
Doth long to see unarmed the valiant Hector.

---

143 Bounds in encloses   **multipotent** massively powerful   **144 bear** carry away   **member**
body part   **145 impressure** imprint   **146 rank** large/grievous/violent   **feud** i.e. the Trojan-
Greek war   **gainsay** forbid   **150 him that thunders** i.e. Jupiter/Jove, whose weapon was the
thunderbolt   **lusty** strong, vigorous   **154 gentle** noble   **free** generous   **156 addition** title
(i.e. honor, enhanced reputation)   **157 Neoptolemus** i.e. Achilles; in fact the name of his son,
Pyrrhus Neoptolemus   **mirable** admirable, marvelous   **158 crest** heraldic device on a coat of
arms/helmet, i.e. head   **'Oyez'** cries of "oyez," the shout a town crier used to summon
attention   **159 promise . . . Hector** assure himself of additional honor gained by defeating
Hector   **161 expectance** watchful anticipation, expectation   **164 issue** outcome   **166 seld**
seldom   **chance** i.e. to issue such an invitation   **desire** ask, invite

170   **HECTOR**   Aeneas, call my brother Troilus to me,
         And signify this loving interview
         To the expecters of our Trojan part:
         Desire them home.— Give me thy hand, my cousin,   *To Ajax*
         I will go eat with thee and see your knights.

Agamemnon and the rest [come forward]

175   **AJAX**   Great Agamemnon comes to meet us here.

     HECTOR   The worthiest of them tell me name by   *To Aeneas*
         name:
         But for Achilles, mine own searching eyes
         Shall find him by his large and portly size.

     AGAMEMNON   Worthy of arms, as welcome as to one
180   That would be rid of such an enemy —
         But that's no welcome: understand more clear,
         What's past and what's to come is strewed with husks
         And formless ruin of oblivion,
         But in this extant moment, faith and troth,
185   Strained purely from all hollow bias-drawing,
         Bids thee, with most divine integrity,
         From heart of very heart, great Hector, welcome.

     HECTOR   I thank thee, most imperious Agamemnon.

     AGAMEMNON   My well-famed lord of Troy, no less to you.   *To Troilus*

190   **MENELAUS**   Let me confirm my princely brother's greeting:
         You brace of warlike brothers, welcome hither.

     HECTOR   Who must we answer?

     AENEAS   The noble Menelaus.

     HECTOR   O, you, my lord? By Mars his gauntlet, thanks!
195   Mock not, that I affect th'untraded oath:

---

171 signify make known, report   **172 the . . . part** those Trojans who are awaiting news
173 Desire them ask them to go   **178 portly** stately, dignified   **179 Worthy of arms** you who
are so worthy to bear arms/receive embraces   **as . . . one** you are as welcome as you possibly
can be to one such as myself   **181 welcome** i.e. true, proper welcome   **184 extant** present,
existing   **troth** truth   **185 Strained purely** entirely purified   **hollow** false, insincere
bias-drawing deviation, crooked dealing (bowling metaphor: the bias causes swerving)
187 heart . . . heart the center of the heart   **188 imperious** majestic   **191 brace** pair
192 Who . . . answer? a polite way of asking Menelaus' name   **194 Mars his gauntlet** Mars'
armored glove   **195 affect** favor, assume, use   **th'untraded** the unconventional, unfamiliar

Your quondam wife swears still by Venus' glove.
She's well, but bade me not commend her to you.

MENELAUS   Name her not now, sir: she's a deadly theme.

HECTOR   O, pardon: I offend.

200   NESTOR   I have, thou gallant Trojan, seen thee oft,
Labouring for destiny, make cruel way
Through ranks of Greekish youth, and I have seen thee,
As hot as Perseus, spur thy Phrygian steed,
And seen thee scorning forfeits and subduements,

205   When thou hast hung thy advancèd sword i'th'air,
Not letting it decline on the declined,
That I have said unto my standers-by,
'Lo, Jupiter is yonder, dealing life!'
And I have seen thee pause and take thy breath,

210   When that a ring of Greeks have hemmed thee in,
Like an Olympian wrestling. This have I seen,
But this thy countenance, still locked in steel,
I never saw till now. I knew thy grandsire,
And once fought with him: he was a soldier good,

215   But, by great Mars, the captain of us all,
Never like thee. Let an old man embrace thee,
And, worthy warrior, welcome to our tents.

AENEAS   'Tis the old Nestor.

HECTOR   Let me embrace thee, good old chronicle,

220   That hast so long walked hand in hand with time:
Most reverend Nestor, I am glad to clasp thee.

---

196 quondam former   **Venus' glove** as Mars' lover Venus was unfaithful to her husband, Vulcan; the phrase plays on the sense of "vagina" (Latin for "sheath," "scabbard")   **197 bade me not** did not ask me to/asked me not to   **198 deadly theme** subject for mortal conflict/dire subject for discussion   **201 Labouring for destiny** doing the work of, employed by fate (in putting people to death)   **203 hot** hot-tempered/keen   **Perseus** killer of the snake-haired gorgon Medusa   **Phrygian steed** i.e. the winged horse Pegasus   **204 forfeits and subduements** the defeated, those near death (i.e. easy victims)   **205 hung** suspended, checked the swing of   **advancèd** outstretched, raised   **206 decline . . . declined** descend on the vanquished   **207 That** so that   **211 Olympian** god of Mount Olympus/wrestler at the Olympic games   **212 still** always   **locked in steel** i.e. covered by your helmet
219 chronicle historical record (Nestor's age makes him a storehouse of memories; perhaps suggests a penchant for lengthy stories)   **221 clasp** embrace

NESTOR   I would my arms could match thee in contention,
As they contend with thee in courtesy.
HECTOR   I would they could.
225 **NESTOR**   Ha?
By this white beard, I'd fight with thee tomorrow.
Well, welcome, welcome! I have seen the time.
ULYSSES   I wonder now how yonder city stands
When we have here her base and pillar by us.
230 **HECTOR**   I know your favour, Lord Ulysses, well.
Ah, sir, there's many a Greek and Trojan dead,
Since first I saw yourself and Diomed
In Ilium, on your Greekish embassy.
ULYSSES   Sir, I foretold you then what would ensue:
235 My prophecy is but half his journey yet;
For yonder walls, that pertly front your town,
Yond towers, whose wanton tops do buss the clouds,
Must kiss their own feet.
HECTOR   I must not believe you:
240 There they stand yet, and modestly I think,
The fall of every Phrygian stone will cost
A drop of Grecian blood: the end crowns all,
And that old common arbitrator, Time,
Will one day end it.
245 **ULYSSES**   So to him we leave it.
Most gentle and most valiant Hector, welcome:
After the general, I beseech you next
To feast with me and see me at my tent.
ACHILLES   I shall forestall thee, Lord Ulysses, thou!
250 Now, Hector, I have fed mine eyes on thee,

222 **arms** limbs/weapons   **contention** battle, strife   223 **contend** engage   227 **I . . . time** i.e.
I can remember the time when I could have fought you   229 **base and pillar** foundation and
support   230 **favour** appearance, face   233 **embassy** ambassadorial mission (i.e. an earlier
negotiation regarding reparations for the loss of Helen)   235 **half . . . yet** half-fulfilled
236 **pertly** audaciously, boldly   237 **wanton** insolent/playful/lascivious   **buss** kiss
240 **modestly** demurely, chastely (applies to the walls)/without exaggeration   241 **Phrygian**
i.e. Trojan; Phrygia, a region in Asia Minor (now Turkey), was the location of Troy
242 **the . . . all** i.e. the eventual outcome is all that matters, time decides all things (proverbial)
243 **arbitrator** one who decides and settles a matter between opposed parties (legal term)
245 **him** i.e. Time   249 **forestall** prevent

I have with exact view perused thee, Hector,
And quoted joint by joint.

HECTOR   Is this Achilles?

ACHILLES   I am Achilles.

255 HECTOR   Stand fair, I prithee: let me look on thee.

ACHILLES   Behold thy fill.

HECTOR   Nay, I have done already.

ACHILLES   Thou art too brief: I will the second time,
As I would buy thee, view thee limb by limb.

260 HECTOR   O, like a book of sport thou'lt read me o'er:
But there's more in me than thou understand'st.
Why dost thou so oppress me with thine eye?

ACHILLES   Tell me, you heavens, in which part of his body
Shall I destroy him? Whether there, or there, or there.   *Points*

265 That I may give the local wound a name
And make distinct the very breach whereout
Hector's great spirit flew. Answer me, heavens!

HECTOR   It would discredit the blest gods, proud man,
To answer such a question. Stand again;

270 Think'st thou to catch my life so pleasantly
As to prenominate in nice conjecture
Where thou wilt hit me dead?

ACHILLES   I tell thee, yea.

HECTOR   Wert thou the oracle to tell me so,

275 I'd not believe thee. Henceforth guard thee well,
For I'll not kill thee there, nor there, nor there,
But, by the forge that stithied Mars his helm,
I'll kill thee everywhere, yea, o'er and o'er.
You wisest Grecians, pardon me this brag:

---

251 exact detailed, precise   **perused** inspected, examined   **252 quoted** scrutinized   **joint**
limb, body part (probably, picking up on **fed** and continued in **fill**, with connotations of a
butcher's joint of meat)   **255 fair** in full view   **259 As** as if   **260 book of sport** hunting
manual   **262 oppress** (seek to) dominate   **265 local** individual, specific   **266 make distinct**
mark out/differentiate   **267 spirit** soul/life-giving essence (thought to be carried in the blood)
flew took flight/flowed   **269 Stand again** stand up (implying Achilles has knelt to the
gods)/stand still/stand forward   **270 catch** capture, seize   **pleasantly** easily/mockingly
271 prenominate specify in advance   **nice** precise, detailed   **conjecture** prediction
277 stithied . . . helm forged Mars' helmet

280   His insolence draws folly from my lips,
       But I'll endeavour deeds to match these words,
       Or may I never—

    AJAX   Do not chafe thee, cousin:
       And you, Achilles, let these threats alone,
285   Till accident or purpose bring you to't.
       You may every day enough of Hector
       If you have stomach. The general state, I fear,
       Can scarce entreat you to be odd with him.

    HECTOR   I pray you let us see you in the field:
290   We have had pelting wars, since you refused
       The Grecians' cause.

    ACHILLES   Dost thou entreat me, Hector?
       Tomorrow do I meet thee, fell as death:
       Tonight all friends.

295   HECTOR   Thy hand upon that match.

    AGAMEMNON   First, all you peers of Greece, go to my tent:
       There in the full convive you. Afterwards,
       As Hector's leisure and your bounties shall
       Concur together, severally entreat him.
300   Beat loud the taborins, let the trumpets blow,
       That this great soldier may his welcome know.

                       Exeunt. [*Troilus and Ulysses remain*]

    TROILUS   My lord Ulysses, tell me, I beseech you,
       In what place of the field doth Calchas keep?

    ULYSSES   At Menelaus' tent, most princely Troilus:
305   There Diomed doth feast with him tonight,
       Who neither looks on heaven nor on earth,
       But gives all gaze and bent of amorous view
       On the fair Cressid.

---

283 chafe thee anger yourself   **285 accident** chance event   **to't** i.e. to fight Hector
287 stomach appetite   **general state** Greek generals, council/whole Greek cause
288 entreat prevail upon, persuade   **odd** at odds, at variance   **290 pelting** paltry, petty
refused spurned, cast off   **293 fell** fierce, cruel   **295 match** agreement, contract (plays on
the sense of "contest")   **296 peers** nobles/companions   **297 in** to   **convive you** feast, be
convivial   **298 bounties** generosity, kindness   **299 severally** individually   **entreat** invite
300 taborins drums   **303 keep** lodge, dwell   **307 bent** direction

TROILUS   Shall I, sweet lord, be bound to thee so much,
310   After we part from Agamemnon's tent,
To bring me thither?

ULYSSES   You shall command me, sir.
As gentle tell me, of what honour was
This Cressida in Troy? Had she no lover there
315   That wails her absence?

TROILUS   O, sir, to such as boasting show their scars
A mock is due. Will you walk on, my lord?
She was beloved, she loved; she is, and doth:
But still sweet love is food for fortune's tooth.   *Exeunt*

[Act 5 Scene 1]   *running scene 14*

Enter Achilles and Patroclus

ACHILLES   I'll heat his blood with Greekish wine tonight,
Which with my scimitar I'll cool tomorrow.
Patroclus, let us feast him to the height.

PATROCLUS   Here comes Thersites.

Enter Thersites

5   ACHILLES   How now, thou core of envy!
Thou crusty batch of nature, what's the news?

THERSITES   Why, thou picture of what thou seem'st, and idol of
idiot worshippers, here's a letter for thee.   *Gives a letter*

ACHILLES   From whence, fragment?

10   THERSITES   Why, thou full dish of fool, from Troy.

---

309 bound obliged, indebted   **313 As gentle** i.e. be so courteous as to   **honour** reputation,
good name   **316 such as** those who   **scars** i.e. wounds of love   **317 A mock** mockery (i.e.
for boasting, but the further implication is that Diomedes' flirtation with Cressida would make
her former lover the object of ridicule)   **318 is, and doth** is still beloved and still loves
319 still always   **food . . . tooth** subject to being preyed on by fortune (playing on the idea of
fortune having a **sweet** tooth)   **5.1   *Location: the Greek camp*   2 scimitar** short curved
sword   **cool** i.e. by exposing it to the air (with connotations of chilling with fear)   **5 core**
essence/center (as in the hard center of a boil)   **6 crusty** scabby/ill-tempered (plays on the
sense of "with a baked crust")   **batch** product/baker's batch (plays on "botch," i.e. boil)
nature conceivably plays on the sense of "semen"   **7 picture** mere image   **9 fragment**
insignificant or incomplete being/leftover, scrap of food   **10 fool** idiocy (plays on the sense of
"cream and stewed fruit pudding")

PATROCLUS   Who keeps the tent now?

THERSITES   The surgeon's box or the patient's wound.

PATROCLUS   Well said, adversity, and what need these tricks?

THERSITES   Prithee be silent, boy: I profit not by thy talk: thou
15   art thought to be Achilles' male varlet.

PATROCLUS   Male varlet, you rogue? What's that?

THERSITES   Why, his masculine whore. Now, the rotten diseases
of the south, guts-griping, ruptures, catarrhs, loads o'gravel
i'th'back, lethargies, cold palsies and the like, take and take
20   again such preposterous discoveries.

PATROCLUS   Why thou damnable box of envy, thou, what
mean'st thou to curse thus?

THERSITES   Do I curse thee?

PATROCLUS   Why no, you ruinous butt, you whoreson
25   indistinguishable cur.

THERSITES   No? Why art thou then exasperate, thou idle
immaterial skein of sleaved silk, thou green sarcenet flap for
a sore eye, thou tassel of a prodigal's purse, thou? Ah, how
the poor world is pestered with such waterflies, diminutives
30   of nature!

---

11 keeps the tent is looking after Achilles' tent/is guilty of keeping to their tent
12 surgeon's box surgeon's instrument case (Thersites responds to **tent**'s meaning of "surgical
implement for cleaning a **wound**")   **13 adversity** perversity (because Thersites deliberately
misunderstands words)   **need** is the point of   **15 varlet** knave, rogue/attendant, servant
(hence "prostitute")   **17 diseases . . . south** i.e. venereal disease, popularly perceived as
coming from Italy, especially the southern city of Naples, which had high rates of syphilis;
also suggests the south wind, thought to convey disease, and perhaps the lower half of the
body   **18 guts-griping** colic or similar illness causing intestinal spasms   **ruptures** hernias
catarrhs colds, phlegm-producing illnesses   **loads o'gravel i'th'back** kidney stones
19 palsies fever characterized by trembling; the Quarto text has a longer list at this point (see
appended list of "Quarto passages that do not appear in the Folio," p. 138)   **take** strike, infect
20 preposterous discoveries revelations of perversity (**preposterous** literally means "back to
front," suggesting anal sex)   **21 box** plays on the sense of "vagina"   **24 ruinous** ruined, i.e.
rotten (also suggesting "diseased")   **butt** cask (plays on the sense of "buttocks")
25 indistinguishable shapeless, misshapen   **26 exasperate** exasperated, enraged
27 immaterial insubstantial, flimsy   **skein . . . silk** reel of fine silk thread   **sleaved** separated
into filaments, plays on "sleeved"   **sarcenet** fine silken cloth; green suggests immaturity
or girlish weakness   **flap** patch   **28 tassel** dangling fringed decoration (possible phallic
connotations)   **prodigal** lavish, wasteful spender (perhaps suggestive of sexual exhaustion)
purse may play on the sense of "scrotum"   **29 pestered** infested/irritated   **waterflies** i.e.
buzzing insects

PATROCLUS   Out, gall!

THERSITES   Finch-egg!

ACHILLES   My sweet Patroclus, I am thwarted quite
From my great purpose in tomorrow's battle.

35   Here is a letter from Queen Hecuba,
A token from her daughter, my fair love,
Both taxing me and gaging me to keep
An oath that I have sworn. I will not break it:
Fall Greeks, fail fame, honour or go or stay,

40   My major vow lies here, this I'll obey.
Come, come, Thersites, help to trim my tent:
This night in banqueting must all be spent.
Away, Patroclus!   *Exeunt [Achilles and Patroclus]*

THERSITES   With too much blood and too little brain, these two

45   may run mad: but if with too much brain and too little blood
they do, I'll be a curer of madmen. Here's Agamemnon, an
honest fellow enough and one that loves quails, but he has
not so much brain as earwax; and the goodly transformation
of Jupiter there, his brother, the bull — the primitive statue

50   and oblique memorial of cuckolds, a thrifty shoeing-horn in
a chain, hanging at his brother's leg — to what form but that
he is should wit larded with malice and malice forced with
wit turn him to? To an ass, were nothing: he is both ass and
ox. To an ox, were nothing: he is both ox and ass. To be a dog,

---

31 Out expression of dismissive irritation   **gall** bitterness/poison/irritating sore or painful
pustule   **32 Finch-egg!** i.e. small/insignificant thing   **36 daughter . . . love** i.e. Polyxena
37 taxing imposing duty on/calling to account/reproving   **gaging** binding, committing
39 Fall Greeks should the Greeks be defeated   or either   **41 trim** tidy, deck out   **44 blood**
temper, hot-headedness/passion/sexual desire   **47 fellow** usually used for servants, lower-
class or worthless men, so a dismissive term for Agamemnon   **quails** birds eaten as
delicacies/prostitutes   **49 Jupiter . . . bull** i.e. Menelaus, the horned cuckold, here compared
to Jupiter who transformed himself into a bull in order to abduct Europa   **primitive statue**
original, archetypal image   **50 oblique memorial** indirect reminder   **thrifty** useful/ordinary,
not elaborate   **shoeing-horn** again alluding to the cuckold's horns; plays on the sexual senses
of "shoe" (vagina) and "horn" (penis)   **in on**   **51 hanging . . . leg** i.e. Menelaus is a hanger-
on, dependent on Agamemnon   **that he is** his current one   **52 wit** i.e. Thersites' wit
larded mixed, saturated/stuffed (culinary term for the insertion of bacon strips into chicken)
forced strengthened/stuffed (in a culinary sense)   **53 To** i.e. to transform him into   **ass and
ox** suggesting fool and cuckold

55 a mule, a cat, a fitchew, a toad, a lizard, an owl, a puttock, or a herring without a roe, I would not care: but to be Menelaus, I would conspire against destiny. Ask me not what I would be if I were not Thersites, for I care not to be the louse of a lazar, so I were not Menelaus. Hoy-day, spirits and fires!

Enter Hector, Ajax, Agamemnon, Ulysses, Nestor, Diomedes, [Troilus and Menelaus,] with lights

60 AGAMEMNON   We go wrong, we go wrong.

AJAX   No, yonder 'tis: there, where we see the light.

HECTOR   I trouble you.

AJAX   No, not a whit.

Enter Achilles

ULYSSES   Here comes himself to guide you.

65 ACHILLES   Welcome, brave Hector. Welcome, princes all.

AGAMEMNON   So now, fair prince of Troy, I bid goodnight.
Ajax commands the guard to tend on you.

HECTOR   Thanks and goodnight to the Greeks' general.

MENELAUS   Goodnight, my lord.

70 HECTOR   Goodnight, sweet lord Menelaus.

THERSITES   Sweet draught. 'Sweet' quoth a? Sweet sink,   *Aside*
sweet sewer.

ACHILLES   Goodnight and welcome, both at once, to those
That go or tarry.

AGAMEMNON   Goodnight.   [*Exeunt Agamemnon and Menelaus*]

75 ACHILLES   Old Nestor tarries, and you too, Diomed,
Keep Hector company an hour or two.

DIOMEDES   I cannot, lord. I have important business,
The tide whereof is now.— Goodnight, great Hector.

HECTOR   Give me your hand.

80 ULYSSES   Follow his torch; he goes to Calchas'
tent: *Aside to Troilus*
I'll keep you company.

---

55 fitchew polecat/prostitute   **puttock** scavenging bird of prey, buzzard   **56 but to be** faced with the prospect of being/were I to be   **58 care . . . be** wouldn't mind being   **59 lazar** leper   **so** so long as   **Hoy-day** expression of surprise   **67 tend on** escort, protect   **71 draught** cesspool, sewer   **quoth a** did he say   **sink** cesspool, sewer   **78 tide whereof** time for which

TROILUS	Sweet sir, you honour me.
HECTOR	And so, goodnight.

[Exit Diomedes, with Ulysses and Troilus following]

ACHILLES   Come, come, enter my tent.

Exeunt [Achilles, Hector, Ajax and Nestor]

85   THERSITES   That same Diomed's a false-hearted rogue, a most unjust knave; I will no more trust him when he leers than I will a serpent when he hisses: he will spend his mouth and promise like Brabbler the hound; but when he performs, astronomers foretell it: that it is prodigious, there will come
90   some change. The sun borrows of the moon when Diomed keeps his word. I will rather leave to see Hector than not to dog him. They say he keeps a Trojan drab, and uses the traitor Calchas his tent. I'll after. Nothing but lechery! All incontinent varlets!   *Exit*

[Act 5 Scene 2]   *running scene 15*

Enter Diomedes

DIOMEDES	What, are you up here, ho? Speak.	
CALCHAS	Who calls?	*Within*
DIOMEDES	Calchas, I think. Where's your daughter?	
CALCHAS	She comes to you.	*Within*

Enter Troilus and Ulysses [at a distance, with Thersites following]

Troilus and Ulysses speak aside throughout the scene

5   ULYSSES   Stand where the torch may not discover us.

Enter Cressida

TROILUS	Cressid comes forth to him.
DIOMEDES	How now, my charge?

---

86 **unjust** dishonest, untrustworthy   **leers** looks sideways/smiles disarmingly/glances seductively   87 **spend his mouth** bay, bark loudly (hunting term)   88 **Brabbler** a boastful liar, a brawler   **performs** keeps his word, follows his words with deeds   89 **astronomers fortell it** i.e. like a rare and significant event in the heavens   **prodigious** ominous
90 **borrows of** i.e. dims, reflects the light of (an unnatural event)   91 **leave to see** abandon seeing   92 **dog him** follow Diomedes   **drab** whore   **uses** regularly visits   94 **incontinent** sexually unrestrained   **5.2** *Location: the Greek camp (outside Calchas' tent)*
5 **discover** reveal   7 **charge** responsibility, one entrusted to my care

CRESSIDA   Now, my sweet guardian! Hark, a word with you.

They whisper

TROILUS   Yea, so familiar?

10   ULYSSES   She will sing any man at first sight.

THERSITES   And any man may sing her, if he can take   *Aside*
her clef: she's noted.

DIOMEDES   Will you remember?

CRESSIDA   Remember? Yes.

15   DIOMEDES   Nay, but do, then;
And let your mind be coupled with your words.

TROILUS   What should she remember?

ULYSSES   List!

CRESSIDA   Sweet honey Greek, tempt me no more to folly.

20   THERSITES   Roguery!

DIOMEDES   Nay, then—

CRESSIDA   I'll tell you what—

DIOMEDES   Foh, foh! Come, tell a pin: you are a
forsworn – – – – .

CRESSIDA   In faith, I cannot. What would you have me do?

25   THERSITES   A juggling trick — to be secretly open.   *Aside*

DIOMEDES   What did you swear you would bestow on me?

CRESSIDA   I prithee do not hold me to mine oath:
Bid me do anything but that, sweet Greek.

DIOMEDES   Goodnight.

30   TROILUS   Hold, patience!

ULYSSES   How now, Trojan?

CRESSIDA   Diomed—

DIOMEDES   No, no, goodnight: I'll be your fool no more.

---

10 sing . . . sight sing to/get to know instantly, as if sight-reading music/have sex with any man quickly as if he were music to be sight-read (possible allusion to the sirens' song) **11 take her clef** find the right musical key (clef)/possess her sexually (punning on **cleft**, i.e. "vagina") **12 noted** marked, observed/notorious/set down in musical notation **18 List!** Listen! **19 folly** foolishness/lechery **23 tell a pin** i.e. don't talk to me of trifles (**pin** may play on the sense of "(small) penis," a derogatory reference to Troilus) **forsworn – – – –** perjured, oath-breaking (dashes in original text indicate an omitted obscenity) **25 juggling trick** magic trick/deceitful ruse/sexual intercourse **secretly open** frank in private/sexually available in secret/modest and bold simultaneously/sexually accessible (playing on sense of **secret** meaning genitals) **33 fool** plaything/dupe

	TROILUS	Thy better must.
35	CRESSIDA	Hark, one word in your ear.
	TROILUS	O, plague and madness!
	ULYSSES	You are moved, prince. Let us depart, I pray you,

Lest your displeasure should enlarge itself
To wrathful terms: this place is dangerous;
40   The time right deadly. I beseech you go.

TROILUS   Behold, I pray you!

ULYSSES   Nay, good my lord, go off:
You flow to great distraction. Come, my lord!

TROILUS   I pray thee, stay.

45   ULYSSES   You have not patience. Come.

TROILUS   I pray you, stay. By hell and hell-torments
I will not speak a word!

DIOMEDES   And so, goodnight.

CRESSIDA   Nay, but you part in anger.

50   TROILUS   Doth that grieve thee? O withered truth!

ULYSSES   Why, how now, lord?

TROILUS   By Jove, I will be patient.

CRESSIDA   Guardian! Why, Greek!

DIOMEDES   Foh, foh! Adieu: you palter.

55   CRESSIDA   In faith, I do not: come hither once again.

ULYSSES   You shake, my lord, at something; will you go?
You will break out.

TROILUS   She strokes his cheek!

ULYSSES   Come, come.

60   TROILUS   Nay, stay. By Jove, I will not speak a word:
There is between my will and all offences
A guard of patience; stay a little while.

---

34 Thy better i.e. Troilus himself   **37 moved** agitated, upset, angry   **39 wrathful terms** i.e. a
fight   **42 go off** leave   **43 flow . . . distraction** are becoming increasingly agitated, frenzied
(alludes to a swelling river)   **50 grieve** distress, upset   **truth** fidelity   **54 palter** equivocate/
haggle/trifle/mumble   **57 break out** explode in anger/leap out from concealment   **61 will** i.e.
desire to confront Cressida and Diomedes   **all offences** the actions Troilus might take/
Cressida's wrongdoing to him

THERSITES	How the devil Luxury, with his fat rump	*Aside*

and potato-finger, tickles these together! Fry, lechery, fry!

65 DIOMEDES But will you, then?

CRESSIDA In faith, I will, lo! Never trust me else.

DIOMEDES Give me some token for the surety of it.

CRESSIDA I'll fetch you one. *Exit*

ULYSSES You have sworn patience.

70 TROILUS Fear me not, sweet lord.

I will not be myself, nor have cognition

Of what I feel: I am all patience.

Enter Cressida [with Troilus' sleeve]

THERSITES Now the pledge: now, now, now!

CRESSIDA Here, Diomed, keep this sleeve. *She may give him the sleeve*

75 TROILUS O beauty! Where is thy faith?

ULYSSES My lord—

TROILUS I will be patient: outwardly I will.

CRESSIDA You look upon that sleeve? Behold it well.

He loved me — O false wench! — Give't me again.

80 DIOMEDES Whose was't? *She may take back the sleeve*

CRESSIDA It is no matter, now I have't again.

I will not meet with you tomorrow night:

I prithee, Diomed, visit me no more.

THERSITES Now she sharpens: well said, whetstone! *Aside*

85 DIOMEDES I shall have it.

CRESSIDA What, this?

DIOMEDES Ay, that. *He may take the sleeve*

CRESSIDA O, all you gods! O pretty, pretty pledge!

Thy master now lies thinking in his bed

90 Of thee and me, and sighs, and takes my glove,

---

63 Luxury lechery   **64 potato-finger** large penis/fat finger (also sexually suggestive as a digit that **tickles** sexually)   **Fry** burn with lust (with connotations of the burning symptoms of venereal disease)/burn in hell   **66 lo** used to add emphasis   **else** otherwise   **67 token** item used as a pledge   **surety** assurance   **71 be myself** i.e. allow myself to act on my feelings   **cognition** recognition, knowledge   **84 sharpens** toughens her resistance/sharpens Diomedes' desire (with erectile connotations)   **whetstone** stone used for sharpening swords (plays on the senses of vagina/woman/whore)

And gives memorial dainty kisses to it,
As I kiss thee.   *She may attempt to take back the sleeve*

DIOMEDES   Nay, do not snatch it from me.

CRESSIDA   He that takes that takes my heart withal.

95   DIOMEDES   I had your heart before, this follows it.

TROILUS   I did swear patience.

CRESSIDA   You shall not have it, Diomed — faith, you shall not:
I'll give you something else.

DIOMEDES   I will have this. Whose was it?

100   CRESSIDA   It is no matter.

DIOMEDES   Come, tell me whose it was.

CRESSIDA   'Twas one that loved me better than you will.
But, now you have it, take it.

DIOMEDES   Whose was it?

105   CRESSIDA   By all Diana's waiting-women yond,
And by herself, I will not tell you whose.

DIOMEDES   Tomorrow will I wear it on my helm,
And grieve his spirit that dares not challenge it.

TROILUS   Wert thou the devil, and wor'st it on thy horn,

110   It should be challenged.

CRESSIDA   Well, well, 'tis done, 'tis past. And yet it is not:
I will not keep my word.

DIOMEDES   Why then, farewell:
Thou never shalt mock Diomed again.

115   CRESSIDA   You shall not go: one cannot speak a word,
But it straight starts you.

DIOMEDES   I do not like this fooling.

THERSITES   Nor I, by Pluto: but that that likes not me   *Aside*
pleases me best.

120   DIOMEDES   What, shall I come? The hour?

---

91 **memorial** bestowed in remembrance   92 **thee** refers to the sleeve; various stagings are
possible in this sequence, and some editors have suggested that the ensuing line ("do not
snatch it") should be spoken by Cressida, not Diomedes   94 **withal** with it, as well
105 **Diana's waiting-women** i.e. the stars (**Diana** was the Roman goddess of chastity and the
moon)   **yond** up there   108 **grieve** hurt, distress   **his spirit** i.e. the spirit of whoever owns
the sleeve   109 **wor'st** wore   116 **starts you** provokes a sudden reaction in you, makes you
swerve off in another direction   118 **likes** pleases

CRESSIDA	Ay, come — O Jove! — do come — I shall be plagued.	
DIOMEDES	Farewell till then.	*Exit*
CRESSIDA	Goodnight: I prithee come.	

CRESSIDA Troilus, farewell! One eye yet looks on thee,

125 But with my heart the other eye doth see.

Ah, poor our sex! This fault in us I find,

The error of our eye directs our mind:

What error leads must err. O, then conclude

Minds swayed by eyes are full of turpitude.   *Exit*

130 THERSITES A proof of strength she could not publish more,

Unless she say 'My mind is now turned whore.'

ULYSSES All's done, my lord.

TROILUS It is.

ULYSSES Why stay we then?

135 TROILUS To make a recordation to my soul

Of every syllable that here was spoke.

But if I tell how these two did co-act,

Shall I not lie in publishing a truth?

Sith yet there is a credence in my heart,

140 An esperance so obstinately strong,

That doth invert that test of eyes and ears,

As if those organs had deceptious functions,

Created only to calumniate.

Was Cressid here?

145 ULYSSES I cannot conjure, Trojan.

TROILUS She was not, sure.

ULYSSES Most sure she was.

TROILUS Why, my negation hath no taste of madness.

---

121 be plagued suffer, be tormented/be afflicted with divine punishment   **125 with . . . see**
i.e. my other eye, representative of my true feelings, focuses on Diomedes (**eye** puns on "I")
126 poor our our poor   **127 error** mistake/deception/wandering, straying   **128 What**
whatever   **129 swayed** ruled, directed   **turpitude** wickedness, depravity   **130 proof . . .**
more she could not state a stronger proof (i.e. tried and tested truth)   **132 All's done** i.e. it's
over, there is no more to see   **135 recordation** record, commemorative account   **137 co-act**
behave together   **139 Sith** since   **credence** faith, belief, trust   **140 esperance** hope
141 test evidence, testimony (most editors prefer Quarto's "th'attest")   **142 deceptious**
deceptive, misleading   **143 calumniate** slander   **145 conjure** i.e. magically produce a vision
of Cressida   **148 negation** denial   **hath . . . of** does not seem like

ULYSSES   Nor mine, my lord: Cressid was here but now.

150 TROILUS   Let it not be believed for womanhood!
Think, we had mothers; do not give advantage
To stubborn critics, apt, without a theme
For depravation, to square the general sex
By Cressid's rule: rather think this not Cressid.

155 ULYSSES   What hath she done, prince, that can soil our
mothers?

TROILUS   Nothing at all, unless that this were she.

THERSITES   Will he swagger himself out on's own eyes?   *Aside*

TROILUS   This she? No, this is Diomed's Cressida.
If beauty have a soul, this is not she:
160 If souls guide vows, if vows are sanctimony,
If sanctimony be the gods' delight,
If there be rule in unity itself,
This is not she: O madness of discourse,
That cause sets up with and against thyself
165 By foul authority, where reason can revolt
Without perdition, and loss assume all reason
Without revolt! This is and is not Cressid.
Within my soul there doth conduce a fight
Of this strange nature, that a thing inseparate
170 Divides more wider than the sky and earth,
And yet the spacious breadth of this division
Admits no orifex for a point as subtle
As Ariachne's broken woof to enter.

---

149 but now only a moment ago   **150 for** for the sake of   **151 advantage** opportunity
152 a . . . depravation grounds on which to base all women's depravity/grounds for vilification
155 soil stain, dishonor · **157 swagger . . . eyes** blusteringly talk himself out of believing the
evidence of his own eyes   **160 sanctimony** holy, holiness   **162 there . . . itself** unity cannot
be divided   **163 discourse** rationality   **164 That . . . thyself** that sets up arguments (**cause**)
for and against itself   **165 By** abiding by, employing   **foul** false/corrupt, flawed/illegible,
incomprehensible   **revolt** i.e. against itself   **166 perdition** destroying itself   **loss** loss of
reason, i.e. madness (also recalls loss of Cressida)   **reason** appearance of reason   **167 revolt**
contradiction   **168 conduce** take place   **169 a thing** i.e. Cressida   **inseparate** indivisible
170 Divides more wider is more widely divided   **172 Admits** allows   **orifex** orifice, opening
subtle finely spun   **173 Ariachne** i.e. Arachne, a weaver turned into a spider by Minerva;
alternatively a conflation of Arachne and Ariadne, who gave Theseus thread to use in finding
his way out of the labyrinth of the Minotaur   **woof** cross-threads in weaving (hence the
strand of a spider's web)

Instance, O instance, strong as Pluto's gates,
175 Cressid is mine, tied with the bonds of heaven:
Instance, O instance, strong as heaven itself,
The bonds of heaven are slipped, dissolved and loosed,
And with another knot, five-finger-tied,
The fractions of her faith, orts of her love,
180 The fragments, scraps, the bits and greasy relics
Of her o'er-eaten faith, are bound to Diomed.

ULYSSES   May worthy Troilus be half attached
With that which here his passion doth express?

TROILUS   Ay, Greek, and that shall be divulgèd well
185 In characters as red as Mars his heart
Inflamed with Venus. Never did young man fancy
With so eternal and so fixed a soul.
Hark, Greek: as much as I do Cressid love,
So much by weight hate I her Diomed.
190 That sleeve is mine that he'll bear in his helm:
Were it a casque composed by Vulcan's skill
My sword should bite it. Not the dreadful spout
Which shipmen do the hurricano call,
Constringed in mass by the almighty Fenne,
195 Shall dizzy with more clamour Neptune's ear
In his descent than shall my prompted sword
Falling on Diomed.

THERSITES   He'll tickle it for his concupy.   *Aside*

---

174 Instance evidence   **Pluto's gates** the gates of the underworld   **177 slipped** unloosed,
let go (with connotations of moral failure)   **178 five-finger-tied** i.e. bound by human hands
179 fractions fragments, shreds   **orts** scraps, leftovers (culinary term)   **181 o'er-eaten**
gnawed at all over, eaten away (the sense of "surfeited" is possible but less likely)
182 May . . . express? Can worthy Troilus be half as seized by the emotion of events as his
passionate words suggest?   **185 red** passionate/bloody (captures sense of sexual desire and
the consequences of warfare)   **Mars his heart** Mars' heart   **186 fancy** love   **189 by weight**
in equal proportion   **191 casque** helmet   **192 spout** waterspout, or the hurricane that
produces it/heavy downpour   **194 Constringed** compressed, drawn together   **Fenne** dragon
of classical myth   **196 his** i.e. the spout's   **prompted** ready/provoked   **198 He'll . . .**
concupy Troilus will be provoked to violence on account of his own (or Diomedes') lust/
Diomedes will receive blows (or fight it out) for his (or Troilus') lust   **tickle** beat, chastise (or
Thersites may mockingly employ the milder sense of "titillate, assault gently"; sexual
connotations are probable)   **concupy** concupiscence, lust/concubine, mistress

TROILUS   O Cressid! O false Cressid! False, false, false!
200   Let all untruths stand by thy stainèd name,
And they'll seem glorious.

ULYSSES   O, contain yourself:
Your passion draws ears hither.

Enter Aeneas

AENEAS   I have been seeking you this hour, my lord.
205   Hector, by this, is arming him in Troy.
Ajax, your guard, stays to conduct you home.

TROILUS   Have with you, prince.— My courteous lord, adieu.
Farewell, revolted fair! And, Diomed,
Stand fast, and wear a castle on thy head!

210   ULYSSES   I'll bring you to the gates.

TROILUS   Accept distracted thanks.

Exeunt Troilus, Aeneas and Ulysses

THERSITES   Would I could meet that rogue Diomed! I would
croak like a raven: I would bode, I would bode. Patroclus will
give me anything for the intelligence of this whore. The parrot
215   will not do more for an almond than he for a commodious
drab. Lechery, lechery, still wars and lechery: nothing else
holds fashion. A burning devil take them!   [*Exit*]

[Act 5 Scene 3]   *running scene 16*

Enter Hector and Andromache

ANDROMACHE   When was my lord so much ungently tempered,
To stop his ears against admonishment?
Unarm, unarm, and do not fight today.

HECTOR   You train me to offend you: get you gone.
5   By all the everlasting gods, I'll go!

---

200 **by** next to   205 **this** this time   206 **stays** waits   207 **Have with you** I'll come with you,
let's go   **lord** i.e. Ulysses   208 **revolted fair** faithless beauty   209 **Stand fast** be prepared
castle type of close helmet   211 **distracted** agitated, troubled, confused   213 **raven** a bird of
ill omen, often associated with death   **bode** prophesy   214 **the intelligence of** information
about   **parrot** proverbially fond of almonds   215 **commodious drab** accommodating whore
5.3   *Location: Troy*   1 ungently tempered unkindly, roughly disposed   4 **train** induce
offend pain, hurt/sin against, wrong

ANDROMACHE   My dreams will, sure, prove ominous to the day.

HECTOR   No more, I say.

Enter Cassandra

CASSANDRA   Where is my brother Hector?

ANDROMACHE   Here, sister, armed and bloody in intent.

10   Consort with me in loud and dear petition,
Pursue we him on knees: for I have dreamt
Of bloody turbulence, and this whole night
Hath nothing been but shapes and forms of slaughter.

CASSANDRA   O, 'tis true.

15   HECTOR   Ho! Bid my trumpet sound!

CASSANDRA   No notes of sally, for the heavens, sweet brother.

HECTOR   Be gone, I say: the gods have heard me swear.

CASSANDRA   The gods are deaf to hot and peevish vows:
They are polluted off'rings, more abhorred
20   Than spotted livers in the sacrifice.

ANDROMACHE   O, be persuaded! Do not count it holy
To hurt by being just: it is as lawful,
For we would give much, to use violent thefts,
And rob in the behalf of charity.

25   CASSANDRA   It is the purpose that makes strong the vow;
But vows to every purpose must not hold:
Unarm, sweet Hector.

HECTOR   Hold you still, I say;
Mine honour keeps the weather of my fate:
30   Life every man holds dear, but the dear man
Holds honour far more precious, dear, than life.—

Enter Troilus

How now, young man? Mean'st thou to fight today?

---

6 to with regard to   9 bloody bloodthirsty   10 Consort join   dear heartfelt, earnest
15 trumpet trumpeter   16 sally sudden attack   18 peevish foolish/headstrong, obstinate
20 spotted tainted, discolored, diseased   22 just faithful to an oath   is i.e. would be
23 For . . . much because we wish to be generous   use engage in/make a habit of
25 purpose intention (i.e. cause for which the vow was taken)   26 every purpose any
intention (i.e. unworthy, spurious reasons)   hold be binding   29 keeps . . . of maintains the
advantage over (literally, keeps to the windward side of)   30 Life . . . man every man considers
life precious, but the honorable man   31 dear addressed to Cassandra? alternatively
"precious-dear"

ANDROMACHE   Cassandra, call my father to persuade.

Exit Cassandra

HECTOR   No, faith, young Troilus; doff thy harness, youth:

35   I am today i'th'vein of chivalry.
Let grow thy sinews till their knots be strong,
And tempt not yet the brushes of the war.
Unarm thee, go, and doubt thou not, brave boy,
I'll stand today for thee and me and Troy.

40   TROILUS   Brother, you have a vice of mercy in you,
Which better fits a lion than a man.

HECTOR   What vice is that? Good Troilus, chide me for it.

TROILUS   When many times the captive Grecian falls,
Even in the fan and wind of your fair sword,

45   You bid them rise and live.

HECTOR   O, 'tis fair play.

TROILUS   Fool's play, by heaven, Hector.

HECTOR   How now? How now?

TROILUS   For th'love of all the gods,

50   Let's leave the hermit pity with our mothers,
And when we have our armours buckled on,
The venomed vengeance ride upon our swords,
Spur them to ruthful work, rein them from ruth.

HECTOR   Fie, savage, fie!

55   TROILUS   Hector, then 'tis wars.

HECTOR   Troilus, I would not have you fight today.

TROILUS   Who should withhold me?
Not fate, obedience, nor the hand of Mars
Beck'ning with fiery truncheon my retire;

60   Not Priamus and Hecuba on knees,

---

33 **father** father-in-law, i.e. Priam   34 **doff** take off   **harness** armor   35 **i'th'vein of** in the mood for   37 **tempt** risk   **brushes** collisions, hostile encounters   41 **lion** as the noblest of beasts, the lion was proverbially said to spare the defenseless   43 **captive** defeated, with no escape   44 **fan and wind** i.e. as he brandishes it, without even needing to strike   **fair** noble, fine/even-handed, just   47 **Fool's play** perhaps puns on "foul play" (to oppose **fair play**)   53 **ruthful** piteous, lamentable, causing woe   **ruth** pity, compassion   55 **then 'tis wars** that (the abandonment of pity) is true war   59 **truncheon** thick staff (such as that used by a marshal to control procedure in an official duel)   **retire** retreat

Their eyes o'ergallèd with recourse of tears;
Nor you, my brother, with your true sword drawn,
Opposed to hinder me, should stop my way,
But by my ruin.

Enter Priam and Cassandra

65   CASSANDRA   Lay hold upon him, Priam, hold him fast:
He is thy crutch; now if thou loose thy stay,
Thou on him leaning, and all Troy on thee,
Fall all together.

PRIAM   Come, Hector, come, go back:
70   Thy wife hath dreamt, thy mother hath had visions,
Cassandra doth foresee, and I myself
Am like a prophet suddenly enrapt
To tell thee that this day is ominous:
Therefore come back.

75   HECTOR   Aeneas is afield,
And I do stand engaged to many Greeks,
Even in the faith of valour, to appear
This morning to them.

PRIAM   Ay, but thou shalt not go.

80   HECTOR   I must not break my faith.
You know me dutiful: therefore, dear sir,
Let me not shame respect; but give me leave
To take that course by your consent and voice,
Which you do here forbid me, royal Priam.

85   CASSANDRA   O Priam, yield not to him!

ANDROMACHE   Do not, dear father.

HECTOR   Andromache, I am offended with you:
Upon the love you bear me, get you in.   *Exit Andromache*

TROILUS   This foolish, dreaming, superstitious girl
90   Makes all these bodements.

---

61 o'ergallèd heavily inflamed   **recourse** repeated flowing   **64 But . . . ruin** except by killing
me   **66 loose thy stay** release your support, prop; **loose** plays on "lose"—the two words were
not always distinguished   **72 enrapt** carried away by prophetic inspiration   **75 afield** on the
battlefield   **76 engaged** pledged   **77 the . . . valour** a warrior's honorable pledge
82 shame respect i.e. violate my duty to respect your wishes   **89 This . . . girl** i.e. Cassandra
90 bodements prophecies, forebodings

CASSANDRA   O, farewell, dear Hector!
Look, how thou diest! Look, how thy eye turns pale!
Look, how thy wounds do bleed at many vents!
Hark, how Troy roars, how Hecuba cries out,
95   How poor Andromache shrills her dolour forth!
Behold, distraction, frenzy and amazement,
Like witless antics, one another meet,
And all cry, 'Hector! Hector's dead! O Hector!'
TROILUS   Away! Away!
100   CASSANDRA   Farewell. Yes, soft: Hector, I take my leave;
Thou dost thyself and all our Troy deceive.   *Exit*
HECTOR   You are amazed, my liege, at her exclaim.
Go in and cheer the town: we'll forth and fight,
Do deeds of praise and tell you them at night.
105   PRIAM   Farewell. The gods with safety stand about thee!
                    [*Exeunt Priam and Hector, separately.*] *Alarum*
TROILUS   They are at it, hark! Proud Diomed, believe,
I come to lose my arm, or win my sleeve.
Enter Pandarus
PANDARUS   Do you hear, my lord? Do you hear?
TROILUS   What now?
110   PANDARUS   Here's a letter come from yond poor girl.   *Gives a letter*
TROILUS   Let me read.
PANDARUS   A whoreson tisick, a whoreson rascally tisick so
troubles me, and the foolish fortune of this girl, and what
one thing, what another, that I shall leave you one o'th's
115   days: and I have a rheum in mine eyes too, and such an ache
in my bones that, unless a man were cursed, I cannot tell
what to think on't. What says she there?

---

95 shrills . . . forth shrieks out her grief   96 distraction madness   amazement alarm,
bewilderment   97 antics grotesque buffoons   100 soft wait a moment   101 deceive
delude/betray   102 amazed stunned/confused/dismayed   exclaim outcry   103 cheer
encourage, urge on   105 with . . . about i.e. protect   112 tisick consumptive cough,
infection of lungs and throat   114 o'th's of these   115 rheum watery discharge (the eyes are
affected by syphilis)   ache . . . bones suggestive of syphilis, which causes bone decay
117 on't of it

TROILUS   Words, words, mere words, no matter from the heart;
Th'effect doth operate another way.   *Tears the letter*

120   Go, wind to wind, there turn and change together.
My love with words and errors still she feeds;
But edifies another with her deeds.

// PANDARUS   Why, but hear you? //

// TROILUS   Hence, brother lackey! Ignomy and shame //

125   // Pursue thy life, and live aye with thy name! //

Alarum.   *Exeunt*

[Act 5 Scene 4]   *running scene 17*

Enter Thersites in [the midst of an] excursion

THERSITES   Now they are clapper-clawing one another, I'll go
look on. That dissembling abominable varlet, Diomed, has
got that same scurvy, doting, foolish young knave's sleeve of
Troy there in his helm. I would fain see them meet, that that
5   same young Trojan ass, that loves the whore there, might
send that Greekish whore-masterly villain with the sleeve
back to the dissembling luxurious drab, of a sleeveless
errand. O'th't'other side, the policy of those crafty swearing
rascals — that stale old mouse-eaten dry cheese, Nestor,
10   and that same dog-fox, Ulysses — is not proved worth a
blackberry. They set me up in policy that mongrel cur, Ajax,
against that dog of as bad a kind, Achilles. And now is the
cur Ajax prouder than the cur Achilles, and will not arm

---

119 Th'effect . . . way i.e. the effect of the letter goes quite against its aim/her actions
contradict her words   **120 wind** empty, insubstantial words (sense then shifts to "gusts of
air")   **turn and change** flutter, intermingle (**turn** plays on the senses of "deceive/alter/desert"
and **change** on the sense of "alter, change loyalty")   **121 errors** lies, deceit   **still** yet/
constantly   **122 edifies** builds up (plays on the idea of causing penile erection)   **deeds**
actions/sexual acts   **124 Hence** get away   **Ignomy** ignominy, shame, dishonor
5.4   *Location: the battlefield, between Troy and the Greek camp   excursion* bout of
fighting (moving across the stage)   **1 clapper-clawing** beating up, thrashing   **2 dissembling**
deceitful   **4 fain** gladly   **6 whore-masterly** lecherous, whore-using   **7 luxurious drab** lustful
whore   **of on   sleeveless** fruitless, futile (plays on the literal sense of "without Troilus'
sleeve")   **8 policy** strategy/cunning   **swearing** i.e. uttering (grand or false) pledges and
claims   **10 dog-fox** male fox (proverbially cunning)   **11 set me** set (**me** is used for emphasis)

today, whereupon the Grecians begin to proclaim barbarism,
15   and policy grows into an ill opinion.

Enter Diomedes and Troilus

Soft! Here comes sleeve, and th'other.

TROILUS   Fly not, for shouldst thou take the river Styx,
I would swim after.

DIOMEDES   Thou dost miscall retire:
20   I do not fly, but advantageous care
Withdrew me from the odds of multitude.
Have at thee!

THERSITES   Hold thy whore, Grecian! Now for thy whore,
Trojan! Now the sleeve, now the sleeve!

                    [*Exeunt Troilus and Diomedes, fighting*]

Enter Hector

25   HECTOR   What art thou, Greek? Art thou for Hector's match?
Art thou of blood and honour?

THERSITES   No, no. I am a rascal, a scurvy railing knave, a very
filthy rogue.

HECTOR   I do believe thee: live.   [*Exit*]

30   THERSITES   God-a-mercy, that thou wilt believe me; but a plague
break thy neck for frighting me! What's become of the
wenching rogues? I think they have swallowed one another: I
would laugh at that miracle — yet, in a sort, lechery eats
itself. I'll seek them.   *Exit*

---

14 proclaim barbarism declare a preference for lawlessness, ignorance (as opposed to **policy**, i.e. authoritative strategy)   **15 grows . . . opinion** becomes poorly regarded   **17 take** take to **Styx** river that departed souls had to cross in order to reach the classical underworld (i.e. Troilus would pursue Diomedes beyond death itself)   **19 miscall retire** wrongly term this withdrawal a retreat   **20 advantageous care** concern for my advantage   **21 of multitude** i.e. that were stacked against me   **22 Have at thee!** i.e. here I come (standard utterance at the opening of a fight)   **23 Hold** hold on to/defend   **for** i.e. fight for   **25 for Hector's match** a match for Hector   **26 blood** noble blood/spirit, passion   **28 filthy** low, scurvy, contemptible   **30 God-a-mercy** God have mercy on you   **plague** blow/affliction   **32 wenching** whoring   **33 sort** way, manner   **eats itself** is self-destructive; perhaps alludes to the corrosive effects of syphilis, which decays the bones

[Act 5 Scene 5]

Enter Diomedes and Servants

DIOMEDES   Go, go, my servant, take thou Troilus' horse;
Present the fair steed to my lady Cressid.
Fellow, commend my service to her beauty;
Tell her I have chastised the amorous Trojan,
5   And am her knight by proof.
SERVANT   I go, my lord.   [*Exit*]

Enter Agamemnon

AGAMEMNON   Renew, renew! The fierce Polydamas
Hath beat down Menon: bastard Margarelon
Hath Doreus prisoner,
10   And stands colossus-wise, waving his beam,
Upon the pashèd corpses of the kings
Epistrophus and Cedius: Polyxenes is slain,
Amphimachus and Thoas deadly hurt,
Patroclus ta'en or slain, and Palamedes
15   Sore hurt and bruisèd. The dreadful sagittary
Appals our numbers: haste we, Diomed,
To reinforcement, or we perish all.

Enter Nestor [and Soldiers]

NESTOR   Go, bear Patroclus' body to Achilles,
And bid the snail-paced Ajax arm for shame.
20   There is a thousand Hectors in the field:
Now here he fights on Galathe his horse,
And there lacks work: anon he's there afoot,
And there they fly or die, like scalèd sculls
Before the belching whale; then is he yonder,

5.5   **3 commend** convey, present   **5 proof** trial in combat/evidence/the result   **7 Renew**
i.e. renew the assault   **8 bastard Margarelon** illegitimate son of Priam (Margareton in the
sources)   **10 colossus-wise** like the Colossus of Rhodes, a gigantic statue of Apollo that
supposedly stood astride the entrance to the harbor   **beam** staff/lance   **11 pashèd** smashed,
battered   **14 ta'en** captured   **15 dreadful** fear-inducing   **sagittary** centaur (half-man, half-
horse) who supposedly fought for the Trojans; famed for his archery   **16 Appals** terrifies,
makes pale   **17 To reinforcement** i.e. to reinforce our struggling troops/to renew our attack
22 anon shortly/at another time   **afoot** on foot   **23 scalèd sculls** schools of scaly fish
24 belching spouting

25   And there the straying Greeks, ripe for his edge,
Fall down before him, like the mower's swathe.
Here, there, and everywhere, he leaves and takes,
Dexterity so obeying appetite
That what he will he does, and does so much
30   That proof is called impossibility.

Enter Ulysses

ULYSSES   O, courage, courage, princes! Great Achilles
Is arming, weeping, cursing, vowing vengeance:
Patroclus' wounds have roused his drowsy blood,
Together with his manglèd Myrmidons,
35   That noseless, handless, hacked and chipped, come to him,
Crying on Hector. Ajax hath lost a friend
And foams at mouth, and he is armed and at it,
Roaring for Troilus, who hath done today
Mad and fantastic execution,
40   Engaging and redeeming of himself
With such a careless force and forceless care
As if that luck, in very spite of cunning,
Bade him win all.

Enter Ajax

AJAX   Troilus, thou coward Troilus!   *Exit*
45 DIOMEDES   Ay, there, there.

NESTOR   So, so, we draw together.   *Exit*

Enter Achilles

ACHILLES   Where is this Hector?
Come, come, thou boy-queller, show thy face:

---

25 edge sword edge   **26 mower** reaper   **swathe** row of scythed crops   **27 leaves and takes** leaves one dead as he cuts down another/spares one man and kills another
28 appetite desire, will   **30 proof . . . impossibility** the deeds he carries out seem impossible
34 Myrmidons band of warriors from Thessaly, led by Achilles   **36 Crying on** crying out in complaint/calling for vengeance against   **39 Mad** furious   **fantastic** extraordinary
execution actions/slaughter   **40 Engaging . . . himself** entering into combat and emerging alive (financial language; to engage was to mortgage, to redeem to buy back)   **41 careless . . . care** casual attacking strength and effortless self-defense   **42 luck** fortune   **in . . . cunning** i.e. in defiance of his enemy's skills   **46 draw together** grow united, pull together (in contrast to the previous factional state)   **48 boy-queller** boy-killer (referring to the death of Patroclus)

Know what it is to meet Achilles angry.

50   Hector? Where's Hector? I will none but Hector.   *Exit*

[Act 5 Scene 6]   *running scene 17 continues*

Enter Ajax

AJAX   Troilus, thou coward Troilus, show thy head!

Enter Diomedes

DIOMEDES   Troilus, I say! Where's Troilus?

AJAX   What wouldst thou?

DIOMEDES   I would correct him.

5   AJAX   Were I the general, thou shouldst have my office

Ere that correction.— Troilus, I say! What, Troilus!

Enter Troilus

TROILUS   O traitor Diomed! Turn thy false face, thou traitor,

And pay thy life thou owest me for my horse!

DIOMEDES   Ha, art thou there?

10   AJAX   I'll fight with him alone: stand, Diomed.

DIOMEDES   He is my prize: I will not look upon.

TROILUS   Come, both you cogging Greeks, have at you both!

Exeunt Troilus [fighting Diomedes and Ajax]

Enter Hector

HECTOR   Yea, Troilus? O, well fought, my youngest brother!

Enter Achilles   *Pursuing Hector*

ACHILLES   Now do I see thee! Have at thee, Hector!   *They fight*

15   HECTOR   Pause, if thou wilt.

ACHILLES   I do disdain thy courtesy, proud Trojan;

Be happy that my arms are out of use:

My rest and negligence befriends thee now,

---

50 none have nobody   **5.6   4 correct** punish, deliver retribution   **5 office** position, role
6 Ere that correction i.e. before I'd let you (rather than me) punish Troilus   **10 stand** stay put
11 prize reward, trophy/captive of war/booty seized in war   **look upon** be an onlooker
12 cogging deceitful, cheating   **Greeks** plays on the sense of "cunning people"   **15 wilt**
would like to, need to (an honorable offer of **pause** to the presumably battle-weary Achilles)
17 arms limbs/weapons   **out of use** not working, out of action (due to exhaustion)   **18 rest
and negligence** i.e. need for rest and abandonment of the fight

But thou anon shalt hear of me again:
20   Till when, go seek thy fortune.   *Exit*

HECTOR   Fare thee well:
I would have been much more a fresher man,
Had I expected thee.— How now, my brother!

Enter Troilus

TROILUS   Ajax hath ta'en Aeneas. Shall it be?
25   No, by the flame of yonder glorious heaven,
He shall not carry him: I'll be ta'en too,
Or bring him off. Fate, hear me what I say:
I reck not though thou end my life today.   *Exit*

Enter one in armour

HECTOR   Stand, stand, thou Greek: thou art a goodly mark.
30   No? Wilt thou not? I like thy armour well:
I'll frush it and unlock the rivets all,
But I'll be master of it. Wilt thou not, beast, abide?
Why then fly on, I'll hunt thee for thy hide.   *Exeunt*

[Act 5 Scene 7]   *running scene 17 continues*

Enter Achilles with Myrmidons

ACHILLES   Come here about me, you my Myrmidons.
Mark what I say: attend me where I wheel,
Strike not a stroke, but keep yourselves in breath,
And when I have the bloody Hector found,
5   Empale him with your weapons round about,
In fellest manner execute your arm.
Follow me, sirs, and my proceedings eye:
It is decreed Hector the great must die.   *Exeunt*

---

19 anon shortly   **25 flame** i.e. sun   **26 carry** capture/prevail over   **27 bring him off** rescue
him   **28 reck** care   **29 mark** target/notable sight   **31 frush** smash, bruise   **33 hide**
(animal) skin, i.e. armor   **5.7   2 attend** follow/pay attention   **wheel** range around/turn
around, change direction (military term applying to the movement of troops)   **3 in breath** i.e.
fit and ready   **5 Empale** enclose, fence (may pun on "impale" and possibly plays on the sense
of "make pale")   **6 fellest** cruelest, fiercest   **execute your arm** use your weapons
7 proceedings actions

[Act 5 Scene 8]

running scene 17 continues

Enter Thersites [at a distance], Menelaus and Paris, [fighting]

THERSITES   The cuckold and the cuckold-maker are at it. Now,
bull! Now, dog! 'Loo, Paris, 'loo! Now my double-henned
sparrow! 'Loo, Paris, 'loo! The bull has the game: 'ware
horns, ho!   *Exeunt Paris and Menelaus*

Enter Bastard [Margarelon]

5   MARGARELON   Turn, slave, and fight.

THERSITES   What art thou?

MARGARELON   A bastard son of Priam's.

THERSITES   I am a bastard too: I love bastards. I am a bastard
begot, bastard instructed, bastard in mind, bastard in valour,
10 in everything illegitimate. One bear will not bite another,
and wherefore should one bastard? Take heed, the quarrel's
most ominous to us: if the son of a whore fight for a whore,
he tempts judgement. Farewell, bastard.   *[Exit]*

MARGARELON   The devil take thee, coward!   *Exit*

[Act 5 Scene 9]

running scene 17 continues

Enter Hector

HECTOR   Most putrefied core, so fair without,
Thy goodly armour thus hath cost thy life.
Now is my day's work done; I'll take good breath.
Rest, sword, thou hast thy fill of blood and death.   *Takes off his*

Enter Achilles and his Myrmidons   *helmet and hangs his*

5   ACHILLES   Look, Hector, how the sun begins to set;   *shield behind him*
How ugly night comes breathing at his heels:

5.8   2 bull i.e. Menelaus (who has a cuckold's horns)   **dog** i.e. Paris; dogs were used in
bull-baiting, a popular pastime; as an insult, "dog" implies base qualities   **'Loo** a call of
encouragement to a dog   **double-henned sparrow** i.e. Paris, as he has two women (Helen and
his first wife, Oenone); the **sparrow** was associated with lechery and a "hen" is a derogatory
term for a woman/whore   **3 has the game** is winning (ironically playing on the sense of
game as "sexual quarry")   **'ware** beware of   **5 slave** villain, wretch   **6 What** who
9 begot conceived   **11 wherefore** why   **quarrel** cause of the war   **13 judgement** divine
retribution   **5.9   1 core** body   **without** on the outside (refers to the armor Hector admired
in Act 5 Scene 6)

Even with the vail and darking of the sun,
To close the day up, Hector's life is done.

HECTOR   I am unarmed: forgo this vantage, Greek.

10   ACHILLES   Strike, fellows, strike: this is the man I seek.   *They attack*
So, Ilium, fall thou! Now, Troy, sink down!   *and Hector falls*
Here lies thy heart, thy sinews and thy bone.
On, Myrmidons, cry you all amain,
'Achilles hath the mighty Hector slain.'   *Retreat [sounded]*

15   Hark! A retreat upon our Grecian part.

A MYRMIDON   The Trojan trumpet sounds the like, my lord.

ACHILLES   The dragon wing of night o'erspreads the earth,
And, stickler-like, the armies separates.
My half-supped sword, that frankly would have fed,

20   Pleased with this dainty bait, thus goes to bed.   *Sheathes his*
Come, tie his body to my horse's tail;   *sword*
Along the field I will the Trojan trail.   *Exeunt*

[Act 5 Scene 10]

running scene 17 continues

*Sound retreat. Shout. Enter Agamemnon, Ajax, Menelaus, Nestor,
Diomedes and the rest, marching*

AGAMEMNON   Hark, hark! What shout is that?

NESTOR   Peace, drums!

SOLDIER   Achilles! Achilles! Hector's slain! Achilles!   *Within?*

DIOMEDES   The bruit is, Hector's slain, and by Achilles.

5   AJAX   If it be so, yet bragless let it be:
Great Hector was a man as good as he.

AGAMEMNON   March patiently along. Let one be sent
To pray Achilles see us at our tent.

---

7 vail going down (literally, lowering a flag or weapons in submission; puns on "veil")
darking darkening   **9 vantage** advantage   **Greek** again recalls the proverbial association
between Greeks and cheats   **13 amain** loudly, with might   **18 stickler-like** like a tournament
umpire   **19 frankly** freely, without restraint (perhaps with connotations of porcine greed; a
"frank" was a sty, as well as a term for the process of fattening pigs)   **20 dainty bait** tasty
morsel, fine snack   **5.10   4 bruit** news   **5 bragless** without boasting   **7 patiently** calmly,
with quiet expectation

If in his death the gods have us befriended,

10   Great Troy is ours, and our sharp wars are ended.   *Exeunt*

[Act 5 Scene 11]   *running scene 17 continues*

Enter Aeneas, Paris, Antenor and Deiphobus

AENEAS   Stand, ho! Yet are we masters of the field:
Never go home; here starve we out the night.
Enter Troilus
TROILUS   Hector is slain.
ALL   Hector? The gods forbid!
5   **TROILUS**   He's dead, and at the murderer's horse's tail,
In beastly sort, dragged through the shameful field.
Frown on, you heavens, effect your rage with speed!
Sit, gods, upon your thrones, and smile at Troy!
I say, at once let your brief plagues be mercy,
10   And linger not our sure destructions on!
AENEAS   My lord, you do discomfort all the host!
TROILUS   You understand me not that tell me so:
I do not speak of flight, of fear, of death,
But dare all imminence that gods and men
15   Address their dangers in. Hector is gone:
Who shall tell Priam so? Or Hecuba?
Let him that will a screech-owl aye be called
Go in to Troy and say there 'Hector's dead.'
There is a word will Priam turn to stone;
20   Make wells and Niobes of the maids and wives,
Cool statues of the youth, and, in a word,

---

9 his i.e. Hector's   10 sharp harsh, vicious, merciless   5.11   1 Yet still   2 starve we out
let us endure   6 sort manner   8 smile at smile in mocking scorn at/be kind to (i.e. by meting
out swift destruction)   9 at . . . mercy be merciful by making our afflictions immediate and
brief   11 discomfort discourage   host army   14 dare . . . in dare to face all impending evils
that gods and men can prepare to endanger me   17 screech-owl thought to be birds of ill
omen, their cry believed to herald death   aye forever   19 will Priam turn that will turn
Priam   20 Niobes Niobe boasted that having numerous children made her superior to
Latona/Leto, mother to Apollo and Diana; as a punishment for her blasphemy, Niobe's children
were killed and she turned into a rock that forever shed tears   21 Cool statues i.e. struck
dumb and frozen in grief

Scare Troy out of itself. But, march away:
Hector is dead, there is no more to say.
Stay yet. You vile abominable tents,
25   Thus proudly pight upon our Phrygian plains,
Let Titan rise as early as he dare,
I'll through and through you! And, thou great-sized
    coward,
No space of earth shall sunder our two hates:
I'll haunt thee like a wicked conscience still,
30   That mouldeth goblins swift as frenzy's thoughts.
Strike a free march to Troy! With comfort go:
Hope of revenge shall hide our inward woe.

Enter Pandarus

PANDARUS   But hear you, hear you!

TROILUS   Hence, broker-lackey! Ignomy and shame
35   Pursue thy life, and live aye with thy name!

Exeunt. [Pandarus remains]

PANDARUS   A goodly med'cine for mine aching bones! O world,
world, world! Thus is the poor agent despised! O traitors and
bawds, how earnestly are you set a-work, and how ill requited!
Why should our endeavour be so desired and the performance
40   so loathed? What verse for it? What instance for it? Let me see:
Full merrily the humble-bee doth sing,
Till he hath lost his honey and his sting.
And being once subdued in armèd tail,
Sweet honey and sweet notes together fail.

---

25 **pight** pitched   26 **Titan** Roman sun god   27 **through and through** i.e. rampage through
wreaking havoc (perhaps with suggestion of running through with a sword)   **great-sized
coward** i.e. Achilles   28 **sunder** divide, part   **two hates** mutual hatred   29 **haunt** frequent,
hang around/pursue, molest in the manner of troubling thoughts/visit in the manner of a
spirit   **still** constantly   30 **goblins** demons   **frenzy's thoughts** the frenzied thoughts of
madness   31 **free** unregimented, in no formal marching order (i.e. hasty)/unimpeded, direct
comfort courage   34 **broker-lackey** pander, lowly go-between   **Ignomy** ignominy, dishonor
36 **aching bones** suggestive of syphilis, which decays the bones   38 **requited** rewarded
39 **endeavour** efforts   **performance** fulfillment, achievement   40 **verse** rhyme, song/biblical
text   **instance** illustrative example   41 **humble-bee** bumblebee   42 **honey** plays on the
senses of "sexual joy/semen"   **sting** plays on the sense of "erect penis"   43 **subdued . . . tail**
having lost his sting/having lost his erection/having been infected by a diseased vagina

45   Good traders in the flesh, set this in your painted cloths:
            As many as be here of panders' hall,
            Your eyes, half out, weep out at Pandar's fall;
            Or if you cannot weep, yet give some groans,
            Though not for me, yet for your aching bones.
50   Brethren and sisters of the hold-door trade,
            Some two months hence my will shall here be made:
            It should be now, but that my fear is this,
            Some gallèd goose of Winchester would hiss.
            Till then I'll sweat and seek about for eases,
55   And at that time bequeath you my diseases.   *Exit*

---

45 traders . . . flesh pimps/whores/fornicators   **painted cloths** wall-hangings decorated with morally instructive scenes or mottos   **46 hall** guild, profession   **47 out** blind from either weeping or syphilis   **49 aching bones** symptom of syphilis   **50 hold-door** brothel-keeping **53 gallèd** vexed, angered/inflamed and sore with venereal disease   **goose of Winchester** prostitute, so called because of the many brothels of Southwark, which was under the jurisdiction of the Bishop of Winchester   **54 sweat** the conventional treatment for syphilis involved inducing sweating   **eases** treatments, means of easing symptoms

TEXTUAL NOTES

Q = First Quarto text of 1609
F = First Folio text of 1623
F2 = a correction introduced in the Second Folio text of 1632
F3 = a correction introduced in the Third Folio text of 1663/64
F4 = a correction introduced in the Fourth Folio text of 1685
Ed = a correction introduced by a later editor
SD = stage direction
SH = speech heading (i.e. speaker's name)

List of parts = Ed

Prologue 12 barks = F2. F = *Barke* **17 Antenorides** = Ed. F = Antenonidus
1.1.29 when . . . thence = Ed. F = then she comes, when she is thence
   42 her = Q. F = it **76 SH PANDARUS** = F *(uncorrected)*. F *(corrected)* =
   Troy.
1.2.2 SH ALEXANDER = Ed. F = *Man.* **35 disdain** = Q. F = disdaind
   67 nor = Q. F = not **81 wit** = Ed. F = will **112 he so** = Q. F = he is so
   129 marvellous *spelled* maruel's *in* F **160 for it** = Q. F = for is **162 do** =
   Q. F = does **176 tell** = Q. *Not in* F **194 there's** = Q. *Not in* F **195 will** = Q.
   F = ill **203 shall see** = Q. F = shall **216 note** = Q. F = not
1.3.2 jaundice *spelled* Iaundies *in* F **119 their** = Q. F = her **157 scaffoldage**
   spelled Scaffolage *in* F **203 calls** = Q. F = call **243 Trojan** *spelled* Troyan
   throughout F **245 the praised** = Q. F = he prais'd
2.1.2 boils *spelled* Biles *and* Byles *in* F **19 o'thy** = F3. F = o'th thy
   25 porcupine *spelled* Porpentine *in* F **86 bade the** = Q. F = bade thee
   tenor = Q. F = tenure **100 your** = Ed. F = their **107 peace** = Q. *Not in* F
   108 brach = Ed. F = Brooch
2.2.46–47 And . . . reason = Q. *Line 47 printed after line 48 in* F **58 mad** = Q
   *(*madde*)*. F = made **73 sieve** = Q. F = same **112 Ilium** = Ed. F = Illion
   (throughout)
2.3.7 engineer *spelled* Enginer *in* F **67 serpigo** *spelled* Suppeago *in* F
   72 shent = Ed. F = sent **81 if you** = Q. F = if **95 knits not,** = Q. F =
   knits, not **99 his legs** = Q. F = his legge **125 lunes** = Ed. F = lines
   166 worth = Q. F = wroth **215 SH NESTOR** = Ed. *Printed after* "warm"
   in F
3.1.148 SH PARIS = Q. *Not in* F
3.2.20 repurèd = Q. F = reputed **21 Swooning** *spelled* Sounding *in* F
   22 tuned = Q. F = and **61 fears** = Ed. F = teares **63 safer** = Q. F = safe

68 Nor = Q. F = Not **109 grown** = Q. F = grow **119 Cunning** = Ed. F = Comming **194 with a bed** = Ed. *Not in* F *or* Q

3.3.4 come = F4. F = loue **117 man** = Q. F = may **139 fasting** = Q. F = feasting **164 rear** = Ed. F = neere **171 farewell** = Q. F = farewels **180 give** = Ed. F = goe **215 our** = Q. F = her **260 this** = Q. F = his

4.1.71 the = Q. F = which

4.2.13 joys = Ed. F = eyes **78 SD** *Enter Cressida* = Ed. F = *Enter Pandarus and Cressid* **103 force** = Q. F = orce

4.4.9 dross = Q. F = crosse **42 one** = Q. F = our **50 SD** *Within* F *also prints "Enter AEneas" here, possibly reflecting alternative stagings* **80 gifts** = Ed. F = guift **81 Flowing** = Ed. F = Flawing **107 true?** F *mistakenly prints an Exit for Cressida here* **126 usage** = Q. F = visage **157 SD** *Exeunt placed at line 151 in* F

4.5.15 yond = Q. F = yong **103 breath** = Q. F = breach **158 'Oyez'** = Ed. F = (O yes)

5.1.27 sleaved *spelled* Sleyd *in* F **71 sewer** = Ed. F = sure

5.2.11 sing = Q. F = finde **12 clef** = Q (Cliff). F = life **28 do** = Q. F = do not **94 takes** = Ed. F = rakes **188 much as** = F2. F = much

5.3.5 By all the = Q. F = By the **23 give . . . use** = Ed. F = count giue much to as **93 do** = Q. F = doth

5.4.8 errand *spelled* errant *in* F **9 stale** = Q. F = stole

5.8.2 'Loo = F4. F = lowe *(throughout speech)* **5 SH MARGARELON** = Ed. F = *Bast.*

5.9.16 SH A MYRMIDON = Ed. F = *Gree.* **trumpet** = Q. F = Trumpets **20 bait** = Q. F = bed

QUARTO PASSAGES THAT DO NOT APPEAR IN THE FOLIO

Following 3.3.108:
> To others' eyes; nor doth the eye itself,
> That most pure spirit of sense, behold itself,

Following 4.5.31:
> And parted thus you and your argument.

Following 5.1.19 (after "cold palsies"):
> raw eyes, dirt-rotten livers, wheezing lungs, bladders full of
> impostume, sciaticas, limekilns i'the palm, incurable bone-
> ache, and the rivelled fee-simple of the tetter,

Some copies of the 1609 Quarto have the following prefatory epistle:

> A neuer writer, to an euer reader. Newes.
> **E**Ternall reader, you haue heere a new play, neuer stal'd with the Stage,
> neuer clapper-clawd with the palmes of the vulger, and yet passing full of
> the palme comicall; for it is a birth of your braine, that neuer vnder-
> tooke any thing commicall, vainely: And were but the vaine names of
> commedies changde for the titles of Commodities, or of Playes for Pleas;
> you should see all those grand censors, that now stile them such vanities,
> flock to them for the maine grace of their grauities: especially this
> authors Commedies, that are so fram'd to the life, that they serue for the
> most common Commentaries, of all the actions of our liues, shewing

---

pure . . . sense most refined, exquisite of the senses   **parted . . . argument** separated you and
the object of your love/put an end to your claim/penetrated the vagina that had been yours
raw inflamed   **impostume** abscesses   **limekilns** white deposits (perhaps suggesting psoriasis)
bone-ache i.e. syphilis, which causes the bones to decay   **rivelled** shriveled   **fee-simple**
permanence (legal term for absolute possession of land or property)   **tetter** scaly skin
eruptions

such a dexteritie, and power of witte, that the most displeased with Playes, are pleasd with his Commedies. And all such dull and heauy-witted worldlings, as were neuer capable of the witte of a Commedie, comming by report of them to his representations, haue found that witte there, that they neuer found in them-selues, and haue parted better wit-tied then they came: feeling an edge of witte set vpon them, more then euer they dreamd they had braine to grinde it on. So much and such sauored salt of witte is in his Commedies, that they seeme (for their height of pleasure) to be borne in that sea that brought forth Venus. Amongst all there is none more witty then this: And had I time I would comment vpon it, though I know it needs not, (for so much as will make you thinke your testerne well bestowd) but for so much worth, as euen poore I know to be stuft in it. It deserues such a labour, as well as the best Commedy in Terence *or* Plautus. *And beleeue this, that when hee is gone, and his Commedies out of sale, you will scramble for them, and set vp a new English Inquisition. Take this for a warning, and at the perrill of your pleasures losse, and Iudgements, refuse not, nor like this the lesse, for not being sullied, with the smoaky breath of the multitude; but thanke fortune for the scape it hath made amongst you. Since by the grand possessors wills I beleeue you should haue prayd for them rather then beene prayd. And so I leaue all such to bee prayd for (for the states of their wits healths) that will not praise it.   Vale.*

SCENE-BY-SCENE ANALYSIS

PROLOGUE

The Prologue establishes the Trojan wars as the setting and conflict as the play's central theme. The Greeks are camped outside of Troy, fighting for the return of Helen, wife of Menelaus, who was abducted by "wanton Paris." This lengthy and bloody conflict has its basis in personal relationships, highlighting the tensions between the concerns of the individual and the state and between duty and desire. In a moment of meta-theater, the Prologue informs the "fair beholders" of the play that it begins "in the middle" of the war for dramatic purposes, drawing our attention to the themes of time and performance.

ACT 1 SCENE 1

Lines 1–84: Inside Troy, Troilus laments that he has no will to fight because of the "cruel battle" "within" his heart over Cressida, again emphasizing the tensions between individual and state, but also the close relationship between love and conflict. Pandarus argues that Troilus must be patient, adding that he has had "small thanks" for his attempts to bring the two together. His overtly sexual language provides a contrast to Troilus' more traditionally poeticized declarations of love. Pandarus declares that he will advise Cressida to join her father, who has defected to the Greeks, and, despite Troilus' protests, he leaves.

Lines 85–114: As a call to battle sounds, Troilus laments that the only way he can woo Cressida is through Pandarus, who is "tetchy," and that Cressida herself is "stubborn, chaste" and "against all suit." He is interrupted by Aeneas, who asks why he is not fighting, and they leave to join the battle.

ACT 1 SCENE 2

Cressida questions Alexander about recent events. We learn that Hector is angry and shamed, having been "struck down" in battle by a Greek warrior, Ajax, raising the themes of honor and heroism. Alexander amuses Cressida with his description of Ajax, whose heroic qualities, such as being "valiant as the lion," are undermined by his lack of intelligence and wit: he is also as "slow as the elephant." Pandarus arrives and immediately begins to talk of Troilus, comparing him to Hector and saying that he is "the better man." Cressida's responses reveal her quick wit and strength of character. As they banter, a retreat is sounded, and Pandarus suggests that they watch the warriors return. Pandarus identifies each man for Cressida, commenting on their virtues and comparing each one unfavorably to Troilus. The effect is undermined by Cressida, whose clever, noncommittal responses foil Pandarus' attempts to praise Troilus. Her responses also show her awareness of her own sexual worth and vulnerability. A messenger arrives, calling Pandarus to Troilus. Alone, Cressida comments that her uncle is no more than a pimp, before revealing that she is, in fact, attracted to Troilus. She explains that she is "hold[ing] . . . off" because she is enjoying his pursuit of her, observing that "Men prize the thing ungained more than it is," establishing the idea of a woman's value/worth.

ACT 1 SCENE 3

Lines 1–215: The focus shifts from personal to military/political matters. In the Greek camp, Agamemnon argues that although the Greeks have made little progress in the wars (Troy has held out against their siege for seven years), such conflicts are "But the protractive trials of great Jove" that will reveal their true strengths. Ulysses argues that the problem lies in the lack of leadership in the Greek camp. He demonstrates his cunning and political abilities as he makes his argument, suggesting that all systems and hierarchies need order, implemented by their leaders. He compares a badly led army to an infected human body in "an envious fever," one of many images of disease and sickness throughout. Agamemnon asks Ulysses for the "remedy." Ulysses lays much of the blame with Achilles, who "Grows dainty of his worth" (he has become too full of himself, reinforcing Cressida's attribution of worth or value to people at the end of the previous scene). Ulysses suggests that Achilles is neglecting his military duties to lie "upon a lazy bed" with his lover, Patroclus. He describes how Patroclus amuses Achilles by impersonating the other princes "like a strutting player," emphasizing the theme of performance. They are interrupted by Aeneas with a message from Hector.

Lines 216–314: With great ceremony, Aeneas announces that Hector challenges any "Grecian that is true in love" to single combat. Agamemnon agrees that a challenger shall be found, and offers Aeneas their hospitality.

Lines 315–398: Ulysses tells Nestor of his plan. He argues that the challenge "Relates in purpose only to Achilles." Nestor points out that whoever meets with Hector represents Greece; he will be "a man distilled / Out of [their] virtues" and that their reputation is dependent on the outcome of the fight. Ulysses argues that they should not let Achilles meet Hector: if he wins they will have to suffer his "pride and salt scorn," and if he loses then the Trojans will have witnessed the defeat of their "best man." He suggests instead a rigged "lottery," which "blockish" Ajax wins, with the leaders publicly agreeing that he is "the worthier man." If Ajax defeats Hector, they can claim to have backed the right man, and if he loses, they can say that they have better men than him. Either way, Achilles will be annoyed at having his "plumes" plucked and given to Ajax. Nestor says that he will put the plan to Agamemnon.

ACT 2 SCENE 1

Ajax calls Thersites, who ignores him and continues to criticize Agamemnon in typically scurrilous language. When he does arrive, Thersites insults Ajax, calling him a "fool" and "sodden-witted," revealing his own unpleasant character and emphasizing Ulysses' argument about the lack of order in the Greek camp. Ajax questions

Thersites about the recent proclamation, but Thersites continues to insult him. Ajax is beating Thersites when Achilles and Patroclus arrive. Thersites continues to bait Ajax, who beats him again. Achilles also argues with Thersites, reinforcing the sense of disorder and ill-discipline. Thersites leaves, and Achilles informs Ajax of Hector's challenge, claiming that if it was not being put to a lottery, the challenger would be himself. Ajax is scornful, and goes to find out more.

ACT 2 SCENE 2

Lines 1–98: In Troy, Priam relays a message from the Greeks, containing a repetition of their demand that the Trojans "Deliver Helen" and thus end the war. Hector suggests that they do so, arguing that many Trojan souls have been lost over "a thing not ours nor worth to us." Troilus argues that Hector should not weigh "the honour and worth" of so great a king as their father, but Helenus backs Hector, pointing out that Troilus' arguments lack reason. They continue to argue, sustaining the theme of "worth," with Troilus asking a question that is pertinent to the whole play: "What's aught but as 'tis valued?" He points out that Helen is now Paris' wife and they must "stand firm by honour." He reminds them that they praised Paris for his capture of Helen and cannot now "Beggar the estimation which [they] prized / Richer than sea and land."

Lines 99–219: They are interrupted by Cassandra, who wildly declaims a prophecy: they must return Helen or Troy will burn. Hector is impressed by this "divination," but Troilus says she is "mad" and that her prophecy is a "brainsick rapture." Paris declares that he would continue to fight alone for Helen. Priam reminds him that he has "the honey" of Helen as a reward, his brothers have only "the gall" that his actions have resulted in, but Paris echoes Troilus' arguments concerning honor: his "ransacking" of Helen is only wiped out in his "honourable keeping" of her. If they were to give her up it would be a disgrace to their "great worths" and "shame" to him. Hector claims that Troilus and Paris argue with the "hot passion" of youth rather than reason. Nonetheless, he agrees to continue to fight for Helen, as it is a matter of honor.

ACT 2 SCENE 3

Lines 1–83: Thersites contemplates his "fury" at "the elephant Ajax" and calls on Mercury to wreak "vengeance" on the whole Greek camp. Patroclus, hearing him talking, emerges from Achilles' tent and calls out, but Thersites ignores him. Achilles then appears and they all trade insults, with Thersites branding everyone from Agamemnon to Patroclus "a fool." They are interrupted by the approach of Agamemnon and several others, at which Achilles returns to his tent, saying that he will "speak with nobody." He calls Thersites, leaving Patroclus to speak with Agamemnon. Patroclus explains that Achilles is sick and cannot leave his tent, but Agamemnon tells him to inform Achilles that they are there. When Patroclus has gone, Ulysses says that Achilles cannot be sick, they have just seen him "at the opening of his tent." Ajax declares that Achilles is sick with "pride," and asks to speak to Agamemnon. They step aside.

Lines 84–151: Nestor and Ulysses speculate on Ajax's reasons for speaking to Agamemnon, but are pleased that they appear to have provoked a rift between Ajax and Achilles. Patroclus returns, bringing an impudent message from Achilles. Displeased, Agamemnon sends Patroclus back with the message that they think Achilles "over-proud / And under-honest," and that if he continues they will have "none of him." He also sends Ulysses to hear Achilles' answer. Ajax asks Agamemnon if he thinks that Achilles is a "better man" than him, but Agamemnon, in accordance with Ulysses' earlier plan, fulsomely praises Ajax. Ajax observes that he hates "a proud man," and Nestor points out the irony of this statement in an aside (the first of many in this scene that serve to highlight the divided nature of the Greek camp).

Lines 152–261: Ulysses brings the news that Achilles will not go into battle the next day, although he cannot give any good reason, being apparently consumed by his own "self-worth." Agamemnon recommends that Ajax speak with Achilles, but Ulysses delivers a careful speech, flattering Ajax and suggesting that this would be insulting to such a "thrice-worthy and right valiant lord." The Greek leaders continue to praise Ajax, secretly observing the effects of this on his inflated pride and revealing their scorn. They advise Agamemnon to forget Achilles, and then suggest Ajax as the best man to fight Hector.

ACT 3 SCENE 1

In Troy, Pandarus speaks with a servant as he waits for Paris. The servant describes Helen as "the mortal Venus, the heart-blood of beauty," reinforcing her reputation and creating audience anticipation. Paris arrives with Helen, and the audience can finally view the character that is at the center of the play's events, in a scene that emphasizes the potential disparity between reputation and reality (also witnessed in the explorations of "heroism" so far). Pandarus flatters them both and asks to speak with Paris alone. Helen mocks Pandarus' obsequious flattery, and remains, interrupting the conversation as Pandarus asks Paris to excuse Troilus' absence from supper that evening. Despite Pandarus' denials, Paris and Helen guess that Troilus will be with Cressida. The bawdy tone of the conversation is sustained by Pandarus' song.

ACT 3 SCENE 2

Troilus is waiting to see Cressida. His language is conventionally poetic and lover-like as he asks Pandarus to pluck Cupid's "painted wings" and fly him to Cressida, but it is undermined by Pandarus' prosaic response. Pandarus goes to fetch Cressida. As he waits, Troilus anticipates their meeting in language that, while poetic, has clear sexual overtones, reinforcing the essentially physical basis for Troilus and Cressida's relationship. Pandarus returns with Cressida, and, after several bawdy speeches, leaves them alone. Their brief exchange is romantic, but both characters show an awareness of a sexual undercurrent. They are interrupted by Pandarus, who wishes to know why they have "not done talking," hurrying them toward the consummation of their relationship and emphasizing the tensions between romance and physical passion. Cressida declares her love for Troilus, but shows uncertainty. Troilus reassures her of his constancy, and his "integrity and truth." He promises that in the future people will talk of being "As true as Troilus." Moved, Cressida promises that if she is ever unfaithful, people will talk of being "As false as Cressid." Pandarus impatiently interrupts and urges them away to "a chamber with a bed," a direct and unsentimental end to their romantic declarations.

ACT 3 SCENE 3

Lines 1–70: In the Greek camp, Calchas reminds the Greek leaders that he has "abandoned Troy" and "Incurred a traitor's name" on their behalf. He asks for "a little benefit" in return, requesting that a recently captured Trojan be used in exchange for his daughter, Cressida. His argument that this exchange shall be used to "buy" his daughter emphasizes concerns with human "worth," and Cressida's increasing role as a commodity. Agamemnon agrees and sends Diomedes to make the exchange, and to tell the Trojans that Ajax is ready to meet Hector's challenge. Ulysses observes Achilles and Patroclus at the entrance to their tent. He suggests to Agamemnon that the leaders walk past Achilles "As if he were forgot." Ulysses will go last, and if Achilles questions him, he will show him that it is his pride that is causing the "strangeness" of the others. Agamemnon says that he will "lead the way," and the others follow his example as he walks past Achilles with barely a word.

Lines 71–220: Achilles is indignant at this treatment. Seeing Ulysses, who is apparently reading, he decides to interrupt and ask his opinion. Ulysses tells him that he is reading an argument by someone who suggests that, however many good qualities a man may have, he cannot boast of these "virtues," but instead can only know of them insofar as they are reflected back by the good opinions of others. He gives Ajax as his example, commenting how he seems unaware of the strengths he has, but is already being praised by the "Grecian lords" for his forthcoming fight with Hector "As if his foot were on brave Hector's breast / And great Troy shrinking." Achilles asks if his own deeds are "forgot." Ulysses suggests that the past is easily forgotten, and that only "perseverance . . . Keeps honour bright," and that a man has only to stop behaving with honor for "a thousand" ambitious men to rush for his place. He points out that if Achilles continues to "entomb" himself in his tent, his past deeds and reputation will be forgotten. Achilles tries to argue that he has reasons for wanting his privacy, but Ulysses has a final point of persuasion. He tells Achilles that everyone knows that he is "in love" with one of Priam's daughters, but that he might prefer that his reputation was for the defeat of Hector than the seduction of Polyxena.

Lines 221–312: Once Ulysses has left, Patroclus claims that it is his fault that Achilles has neglected his duties. He urges Achilles to "rouse" himself and restore his reputation. Achilles asks Patroclus to find Thersites and outlines his intention to invite the Trojan lords "unarmed" to meet him at his tent after the combat. As he talks, Thersites arrives and describes Ajax as proud, "like a peacock." When Achilles asks him to take a message to Ajax, Thersites says that Ajax will not listen, and invites Patroclus to try to speak to him while he demonstrates how Ajax will behave. They begin their "pageant of Ajax," furthering the theme of performance, and Thersites shows how Ajax ignores all questions that are put to him. Achilles decides that Thersites will deliver a letter to Ajax, and goes to write it, musing on his own "troubled" mind.

ACT 4 SCENE 1

Lines 1–54: In Troy, Aeneas greets Paris, who is accompanied by several other Trojan leaders and Diomedes, the Greek emissary. Aeneas and Diomedes exchange lengthy courtesies, combining fulsome praises with the desire that they will meet each other in battle soon. Paris comments on the irony of this "despiteful'st gentle greeting," full of "noblest hateful love," emphasizing again the close relationship between love and conflict. Aeneas questions why Priam has sent for him, and Paris explains that Aeneas is to take

Diomedes to Calchas' house, where Cressida will be exchanged for Antenor. He tells Aeneas in an aside that he believes Troilus to be with Cressida, and asks him to warn his brother of their approach. Aeneas comments that Troilus had rather give up Troy to Greece than give up Cressida, but Paris comments that the "bitter disposition of the time" means that it cannot be helped. Aeneas goes to find Troilus and Cressida.

Lines 55–84: Paris asks Diomedes who "merits fair Helen most": himself or Menelaus. Diomedes answers that they both deserve her, as neither seems to care for her "soilure" and both are willing to allow "a costly loss of wealth and friends" in order to keep her. He describes Menelaus as a "cuckold" and Paris as a "lecher" who are equal in their desire for "a whore," a speech that undermines the romantic/epic qualities of the legend. Paris suggests that Diomedes is "too bitter," but Diomedes does not believe that Helen is worth the suffering endured by both sides. Paris refuses to be drawn, and they go to find Calchas' house.

ACT 4 SCENE 2

Troilus and Cressida say good-bye after their night together. Their parting is romantic, but this atmosphere is interrupted by the arrival of Pandarus, who coarsely inquires after Cressida's "maidenhead." There is a knock at the door, and Cressida sends Pandarus while she takes Troilus to hide. Pandarus denies that Troilus is in the house, but Aeneas insists on speaking to him. Troilus emerges, and Aeneas hurriedly breaks the news that Paris is approaching, and that Cressida is to be exchanged for Antenor. Dismayed, Troilus goes to meet the others, leaving Pandarus to break the news to Cressida, pitying Troilus and cursing Antenor as he does so. Cressida insists that she will not go, claiming that she has forgotten her father and that her only love is for Troilus.

ACT 4 SCENE 3

Paris tells Troilus that he must prepare Cressida for the exchange.

ACT 4 SCENE 4

Pandarus urges Cressida to "be moderate," but she argues that her grief is "full" and she cannot lessen it. Troilus arrives and the lovers embrace. Even Pandarus is moved beyond his usual coarseness as Troilus reiterates his love for Cressida and blames the gods for taking her from him. Aeneas calls and Troilus sends Pandarus to stall him, promising to bring Cressida "anon." Troilus tells Cressida that there is "no remedy": she must go. He urges her to be "true of heart" and they exchange tokens; she gives him a glove, and he gives her a sleeve. Troilus promises to bribe the Greek guards and visit her at night, and once again asks her to "be true." Cressida feels that he doubts her fidelity, but Troilus claims that he is just jealous of the "Grecian youths." Aeneas and Paris call once more, and arrive as Troilus assures Cressida of his own fidelity. Troilus urges Diomedes to "Entreat her fair" and "use her well," an ambiguous statement that foreshadows future events and emphasizes Cressida's role as a sexual commodity. Troilus accompanies Diomedes and Cressida to the city gate. As they leave, a trumpet sounds to announce Hector's challenge to Ajax, and Paris and Aeneas hurry to watch.

ACT 4 SCENE 5

Lines 1–71: At the Greek camp, Ajax prepares for combat. As the trumpet sounds again, Diomedes approaches with Cressida. The Greek leaders take it in turns to kiss Cressida (ostensibly in welcome, but the episode has sexual overtones and Cressida's recognizably direct and witty approach could be perceived as flirtatious). Menelaus sadly comments that he "had a good argument for kissing once," reminding us again of the events that began the whole conflict, and creating a possible parallel between Helen (who has been represented ambiguously as both victim and "whore") and Cressida. As Diomedes takes Cressida to her father, Nestor praises her as "a woman of quick sense," while Ulysses describes her as "wanton" and "sluttish."

Lines 72–174: The Trojan leaders arrive with great ceremony. Aeneas tries to establish the terms of combat, and points out that Hector and Ajax are related, so Hector will be more lenient. Diomedes returns and Agamemnon instructs him to agree upon terms with Aeneas. As Hector and Ajax prepare to fight, Agamemnon observes Troilus, who "looks so heavy," and Ulysses tells him of Troilus' great reputation. Hector and Ajax fight, then break away. Ajax offers to fight again, but Hector refuses on the grounds of their kinship. In a somewhat anticlimactic conclusion to the long-awaited fight, they embrace instead, and Ajax, backed by the Greek leaders, invites Hector back to the Grecian camp. Hector accepts, sending Aeneas to fetch Troilus.

Lines 175–319: In contrast to their reception of Cressida, the Greek generals greet Hector with admiration and courtesy. They exchange civilities, praising each other's heroism and temporarily setting aside their differences. Only Achilles behaves with hostility, threatening to "destroy" Hector. Ajax intervenes and Hector and Achilles agree to be "calm" until they meet on the battlefield the next day and Agamemnon invites them all to a feast. Troilus asks Ulysses where he might find Calchas. Ulysses replies that Calchas is dining with Diomedes in Menelaus' tent that night, adding that Diomedes "gives all gaze and bent of amorous view / On the fair Cressid." Troilus asks to be taken there after the feast.

ACT 5 SCENE 1

Thersites brings Achilles a letter from Troy. Patroclus and Thersites trade insults as Achilles reads his letter. Achilles reveals that it is from Hecuba, containing a token from Polyxena reminding him of his oath not to fight. Reluctantly, he declares that he will keep his vow. He leaves with Patroclus, calling Thersites to follow to prepare his tent for the feasting. Thersites begins another lengthy curse against them both, as well as Agamemnon and Menelaus, when the party of Greeks, with Hector, arrive looking for Achilles' tent. Achilles himself comes out to greet them. Agamemnon and Menelaus excuse themselves, as does Diomedes. As Achilles, Hector, Ajax, and Nestor go with Achilles, Ulysses quietly tells Troilus to follow Diomedes, offering to accompany him. Thersites, who has been watching all this time, decides to follow them.

ACT 5 SCENE 2

Lines 1–131: Diomedes arrives at Calchas' tent and asks for Cressida. Troilus and Ulysses arrive and conceal themselves to watch the meeting, as does Thersites. Cressida greets Diomedes as her "sweet guardian," and, as he whispers to her, says that he is a "Sweet honey Greek" who "tempts" her. Troilus' asides reveal his despair at her familiarity, while Thersites' comments are more directly damning of Cressida's morality. Ulysses tries to persuade Troilus to leave, but he remains. As they watch, Cressida agrees to become Diomedes' lover. He asks for a token in "surety of it," and she goes to fetch one, returning with Troilus' sleeve. Diomedes asks who it belonged to, and Cressida has a change of heart, telling Diomedes that she will not meet with him, and asking him not to visit her again. Diomedes asks again whose sleeve it is, and when Cressida will not tell, he declares that he will wear it in battle the next day. As he goes to leave, she capitulates, telling him that he can come to her again. Once Diomedes has left, Cressida, unaware that Troilus can hear her, bids him "farewell," blaming her defection on the weakness of her sex. Thersites comments that Cressida has now proved that she is a "whore."

Lines 132–217: Ulysses tries to persuade Troilus to leave, but he is stunned, refusing to believe what he has just seen. He declares that he will kill Diomedes in battle and cries out against "false Cressid!" As Ulysses urges him to be calm, Aeneas arrives with the news that Hector has already returned to Troy and that Troilus must also leave. Ulysses accompanies him to the gate, leaving Thersites to comment that there is nothing but "wars and lechery," an apposite reflection of the events of the play.

ACT 5 SCENE 3

Andromache urges Hector not to go into battle, claiming that she has had "ominous" dreams of "bloody turbulence." They are joined by Cassandra, who agrees with Andromache, but Hector insists on fighting for the sake of honor. As Troilus enters, Andromache sends Cassandra to fetch Priam. Hector urges his younger brother not to fight, promising to stand for both of them, but Troilus criticizes Hector for his "vice of mercy" and the compassion he shows to his opponents. He declares that they should go to war without pity and declares his intention to fight. Cassandra returns with Priam, who adds his pleas to those of Andromache and Cassandra, reiterating that both women have had dreams and visions about the day's potential tragedy. Hector insists that he will fight, despite Cassandra's prophecies, and goes to join the battle. Alone, Troilus declares bitterly that he will retrieve his sleeve from Diomedes. Pandarus brings a letter from Cressida, which Troilus dismisses as "mere words, no matter from the heart."

ACT 5 SCENE 4

The remainder of the play comprises brief, frantic scenes, highlighting the pace and confusion of the battle.

Still cursing everything, Thersites watches as Troilus and Diomedes meet. They exit, fighting, as Hector enters. He challenges Thersites, demanding to know if he is "of blood and honour," but Thersites insists that he is merely a "knave" and Hector leaves him. Thersites, continuing in his role of observer, declares that he will find Diomedes and Troilus, "the wenching rogues," and watch their fight.

ACT 5 SCENE 5

Diomedes sends his servant to Cressida with Troilus' horse, and the message that he has "chastised the amorous Trojan" and is now her knight by "proof" of combat. Agamemnon enters, calling for reinforcements and listing the dead and wounded, which include Patroclus. Nestor tells some soldiers to take Patroclus' body to Achilles. He describes how there seem to be "a thousand Hectors in the field" as the Trojan is everywhere, fighting hard. Ulysses enters, bringing the news that Patroclus' death has "roused" Achilles' "drowsy blood," and that Ajax is fiercely "Roaring for Troilus." Ajax enters briefly, looking for Troilus, followed by Achilles, furiously searching for Hector.

ACT 5 SCENE 6

Ajax and Diomedes meet, both looking for Troilus, who arrives looking for Diomedes. As Ajax and Diomedes argue about who will fight
him, Troilus attacks them both and all three exit, fighting. Hector
enters in time to see them leave and praises Troilus' skills. Achilles
approaches Hector and they fight, until Hector, with the honorable
"mercy" that Troilus mentioned earlier, offers Achilles the opportunity to "pause." Battle-weary Achilles has no choice, although he
"distain[s]" Hector's "courtesy" and promises that they shall meet
again. Troilus returns with the news that "Ajax hath ta'en Aeneas,"
and vows to rescue him if he dies in the attempt.

ACT 5 SCENE 7

Achilles instructs the Myrmidons to follow him and, when they have
found Hector, to kill him.

ACT 5 SCENE 8

Thersites watches Menelaus and Paris, "the cuckold and the cuckold-
maker," as they fight. As they exit, Margarelon challenges Thersites
to fight, but he runs away.

ACT 5 SCENE 9

Hector rests briefly, removing his helmet and shield. As he does so,
Achilles approaches with the Myrmidons. Despite Hector's protest
that he is "unarmed," Achilles urges his warriors to "strike," showing none of the honor and mercy that Hector himself shows. The
Greeks sound a retreat, and Achilles drags Hector's body back to the
camp behind his horse.

ACT 5 SCENE 10

A soldier brings the news that Achilles has slain Hector. In contrast
to his earlier pride, Ajax comments that Hector was a good man, and

that his death should be "bragless." Agamemnon sends someone to fetch Achilles, observing that if Hector is really dead, then the battle is won. Despite this, the mood of the Greeks is subdued rather than triumphant.

ACT 5 SCENE 11

Aeneas is defiant until Troilus brings the news that Hector is dead. He reports that Hector's corpse has been dragged "at the murderer's horse's tail" round the battlefield, emphasizing Achilles' brutality and lack of heroism. Wearily, Troilus calls on the gods to be mercifully quick in their destruction of Troy, telling Aeneas that he does not speak of the war, but of the whole human condition. He says that they must march back to Troy with the news of Hector's death, and, in doing so, they will turn Priam "to stone" and "Scare Troy out of itself." He then swears his revenge on Achilles, acknowledging that this threat is merely to hide his "inward woe." As he leaves, Pandarus tries to speak with him, but Troilus insults the "broker-lackey" and leaves. The last words are spoken by Pandarus, who complains of his ill-treatment, and his diseased body (a final image of decay), the last in a series of anticlimaxes and unfinished narratives that characterize this play.

TROILUS AND CRESSIDA IN PERFORMANCE: THE RSC AND BEYOND

The best way to understand a Shakespeare play is to see it or ideally to participate in it. By examining a range of productions, we may gain a sense of the extraordinary variety of approaches and interpretations that are possible—a variety that gives Shakespeare his unique capacity to be reinvented and made "our contemporary" four centuries after his death.

We begin with a brief overview of the play's theatrical and cinematic life, offering historical perspectives on how it has been performed. We then analyze in more detail a series of productions staged over the last half-century by the Royal Shakespeare Company. The sense of dialogue between productions that can only occur when a company is dedicated to the revival and investigation of the Shakespeare canon over a long period, together with the uniquely comprehensive archival resource of promptbooks, program notes, reviews, and interviews held on behalf of the RSC at the Shakespeare Birthplace Trust in Stratford-upon-Avon, allows an "RSC stage history" to become a crucible in which the chemistry of the play can be explored.

We then go to the horse's mouth. Modern theater is dominated by the figure of the director. He or she must hold together the whole play, whereas the actor must concentrate on his or her part. The director's viewpoint is therefore especially valuable. Shakespeare's plasticity is wonderfully revealed when we hear the directors of two highly successful productions answering the same questions in very different ways.

FOUR CENTURIES OF *TROILUS AND CRESSIDA*: AN OVERVIEW

The circumstances of the early performances of *Troilus and Cressida* are not simply unknown, but obscured by conflicting evidence. The original title page of the 1609 Quarto of the play tells us it is printed "as it was acted by the Kings Maiesties seruants at the Globe,"[17] but another printing the same year removes this claim and adds a note to the reader telling us the play was "neuer stal'd with the Stage, neuer clapper-clawd with the palmes of the vulgar."[18] Scholars have puzzled over the implications of these mutually contradictory claims: was the play unsuccessful? Was it the victim of censorship? Was it ever performed in Shakespeare's theater?

Claims that the play was written with the Globe in mind are supported by the play's scale and use of multiple playing levels, as in Act 1 Scene 2. The pillars of the theater may have been used to "conceal" the eavesdroppers in Act 5 Scene 2, and the wit of Thersites (almost certainly a role for the company fool, Robert Armin) may certainly have appealed to the "vulgar" groundlings. However, other scholars have argued that the play was instead written for a private, academic audience at the Inns of Court. The fact that the play was almost excluded from the First Folio of Shakespeare's works may go further to suggest that the play, for reasons lost to history, never received a public showing in its original form until the twentieth century.

Not until 1679, when John Dryden adapted the play as *Troilus and Cressida; or, Truth Found Too Late*, is there a firm record of performance. The play's Prologue apologizes for adapting the original by having Thomas Betterton play the ghost of Shakespeare himself, brought on stage to admit that he was "Untaught, unpractis'd, in a barbarous Age,"[19] and that his "rough-drawn Play" required improvement. While praising Shakespeare, the emphasis on the roughness of the play licenses adaptation to the taste of the times. Most significant is an entirely new fifth act, turning the play into a more conventional tragedy. In Dryden's version, Cressida remains true to Troilus, with her father telling her "You must dissemble love to Diomede still" (Act 4 Scene 2) in order to conceal their escape plan, but Troilus believes her to be genuinely unfaithful. During the later fighting, she attempts to prevent Troilus from killing Diomedes as it would undo their plans. As she protests her fidelity to the furious Troilus, however, Diomedes presents Cressida's ring and claims he had taken "full possession" (Act 5 Scene 2). As Troilus calls down curses on Cressida, she kills herself. In a bleak final battle, a repentant and vengeful Troilus kills Diomedes before being slain by Achilles.

The adaptation was first performed by the Duke's Company at Dorset Garden in 1679 with Betterton as Troilus, and was revived in 1697 and again in 1709, with Betterton now playing Thersites. Between 1720 and 1723 there were a few further revivals, with Lacy Ryan as Troilus and James Quin as Hector and then Thersites. The attraction of leading actors to multiple roles is perhaps an indicator that the play was already seen as an ensemble drama, whose lack of clear star roles may partially account for its lack of popularity during the actor-manager years of the eighteenth and nineteenth centuries.

Troilus and Cressida was not entirely forgotten, however, during its absence from the stage. Although neither was performed, John Philip Kemble began creating a promptbook toward the end of the eighteenth century, and in 1852 G. H. Davidson published an acting edition, probably prepared by Thomas Hailes Lacy. This version adheres relatively closely to the original text, although the more indecorous aspects of Cressida's role are not shown onstage. An interest in spectacle pervades the text, most notably in a conclusion which omits the Epilogue, the curtain instead descending on a tableau featuring Achilles in his chariot dragging Hector's body. The opportunities for grand spectacle, such as costume designs taken from Homer, undoubtedly appealed to Victorian tastes for historical re-creation, but the cynicism and dubious morality of the play continued to render it unstageable. George Daniel's remarks in the introduction to the Lacy text make clear his feelings that "Cressida is throughout a hypocrite and a wanton,"[20] a prejudicial judgment of the character that continued to color attitudes toward the play into the twentieth century.

"[Shakespeare] seems wilfully and maliciously to have attempted to dethrone the idols of ancient Greece, and to show them to us in a light at once distorted and disagreeable."[21] Critics and directors at the beginning of the twentieth century showed renewed interest in *Troilus and Cressida* as satire, now understanding the play to be deliberately unpleasant. A British theater newly interested in the original conditions of presentation was open to fresh exploration of the play, even if the press were not quite so prepared. William Poel's 1913 production for the Elizabethan Stage Society confused reviewers with its combination of Elizabethan dress for the Greeks and classical costumes for the Trojans, and the casting of female actors in several male roles was criticized for being at odds with Poel's experiments in Elizabethan practices. However, Edith Evans "was superlative at Cressida, and must have made fervent Chaucerians weep";[22] she "enacted this subtle part with abundant individuality, the affectation of her sing-song voice, when shamming indifference or coyness, being only one among many ingenious touches."[23] The reviewers were less enthused by a clownish Ajax and a general burlesque spirit, though it was noted that this was less Poel's fault than Shakespeare's.

Poel's production was preceded by that of Charles Fry in 1907 at Great Queen Street, who revived the play for what the *Evening Standard* declared was "the first time since Shakespeare's death." This production was "chiefly valuable from the elocutionary point of view,"[24] providing a showcase for Fry's reciting talents against a simple green curtain. These two productions reclaimed *Troilus and Cressida* as a play for the new century, free from expectations of a Victorian spectacular. The divorce from attitudes toward propriety and decorum would take longer, and Cressida, Helen, Pandarus, and Thersites in particular continued to offend the tastes of Edwardian reviewers—the women for their sexual frankness and the men for the vulgarity of their language.

It was not until after the First World War that the play finally received professional English-language productions. Robert Atkins' 1923 production for the Old Vic marked the conclusion of producer Lilian Baylis' project to stage all of Shakespeare's known works, and the *Morning Post* was more interested in the presence of Princess Mary than the "vagaries"[25] of the performance itself. Henry Herbert's 1932 production at the Broadway Theater in New York, however, demonstrated increasing critical interest in the play. Here, "Cressida was played from Troilus' point of view,"[26] with her potential for treachery obvious from the start.

With the onset of war, the play took on a new urgency. One newspaper, under the headline "Shakespeare's Anti-War Play," informed prospective audiences that "the play is essentially anti-war in its bias and implications. This, doubtless, was the basis of its popularity in Germany during the years of disillusionment prior to the advent of the Nazi regime."[27]

German theater makers had seen value in the play long before Fry, resurrecting it in Munich in 1898 and Berlin in 1899 and 1904. Ernst von Wolzogen's 1898 production anticipated Poel in its attempt to recreate Elizabethan playing conditions, including the representation of Elizabethan spectators "presented as brutishly stupid,"[28] but performed the play as farce and was a disaster, and Paul Lindau's 1904 production at the Deutsches Theater was greeted with walkouts by an uncomprehending audience. In the wake of the First World War, however, the play took on a more political edge. Otto Falckenberg played Thersites in his own productions of 1925 and 1936 in Munich, undercutting traditional representations of the character as a simple clown by making him "a man utterly disillusioned,"[29] providing scathing comment on the current political state of Germany.

B. Iden Payne's 1936 production at Stratford-upon-Avon was performed in the same political shadow, with one newspaper remarking on the "definite interest this parodied heroism holds for our day, when the shattering of reputations is not so much a sport as a habit."[30] Payne, following Poel, used Elizabethan costume and simple staging. Most praise was reserved for Pamela Brown's Cressida, who "gave the giddy jilt a lisp, through which she contrived to convey a suggestion of levity and insincerity from the very beginning of her performance,"[31] and for a Ulysses who "succeeded admirably in displaying the cynicism, the eloquence and the time-serving diplomacy of the character."[32] While not hugely successful, it was these cynical and unsentimental aspects of the play that increasingly captured attention, the play reflecting a growing public disillusionment. Two years later, contemporary resonances were further emphasized by Michael Macowan's production at the Westminster Theatre. Utilizing modern dress, weaponry, and barbed wire in a direct confrontation of the national mood, the production occasioned a lengthy debate in *The Times* letter pages as academics argued that it was the first to truly demonstrate that "if ever there was a play for the times it is this."[33] It was a growing feeling that led to frequent postwar revivals of the play.

Anthony Quayle's 1948 Stratford production displayed a common trend to contrast "on the one side the licentious luxury of the Trojans and on the other the stern and serious soldiery of the Greeks."[34] Paul Scofield's "delicate," "sensitive," and "emotional"[35] Troilus, a role which has continually challenged actors, was singled out for praise, and the curtain fell on the image of him mourning Hector's body.

Pandarus' epilogue, while having enjoyed a resurgence in the late twentieth and early twenty-first centuries, was long felt to be an inappropriate and weak ending to the play and often cut or, as here, moved to an earlier point, allowing the play to close on an emotional rather than a satiric note. Quayle returned to play Pandarus for Glen Byam Shaw in a 1954 production that "never allows the piece to seem too bitter . . . rightly emphasising that rather sad detachment which allows the ridiculous, the comic and the tragic to co-exist side by side."[36] With weak performances in the central roles, however, critics were unable to anchor their readings of the play in the sympathetic lovers, and it was the ugliness of Pandarus that left the biggest impression, Quayle "mincing, lisping, and gloating over the passions of his 'Twoilus and Cwessida.' "[37]

Tyrone Guthrie's influential 1956 Old Vic production situated the play in the 1920s, where "soldiers' fancy uniforms came straight from an Ivor Novello musical" and "the mighty Achilles wandered on in a dressing-gown, toying with a brandy balloon glass and a cigarette."[38] Guthrie's satirical reading of the play targeted prevailing attitudes regarding war as heroic, recreating a prewar Britain which allowed him to draw "a parallel in the death of the Archduke and the theft of Helen as excuses for action."[39] Downplaying the physical and sexual elements of the play, Guthrie's production recreated *Troilus and Cressida* in a world of socialites and superficiality that underscored the "military stupidity" of its leaders.

Peter Hall and John Barton's 1960 Stratford production (discussed in more detail below) reacted directly against the recent modern-dress productions, instead placing its classically costumed actors in an octagonal "sand pit," allowing for an abstract and timeless repre-

1. Anthony Quayle's 1948 production: a "sensitive" and "emotional" Paul Scofield as Troilus, with Heather Stannard as Cressida.

sentation of battlegrounds. Critics found Dorothy Tutin's Cressida "a wisp of ripping carnality that is almost unbearably alluring," while Max Adrian's Pandarus' "immense, dirty, quivering gusto"[40] stole the show so successfully that reviewers questioned the function of Peter O'Toole's more subdued Thersites. Hall revisited the play in

2001 with New York's Theater for a New Audience, this time with a twelve-sided sandpit, in an unsuccessful production that needed "bold direction to point it one way or another."[41]

The Stratford Ontario Shakespeare Festival debuted *Troilus* in a 1963 production directed by Michael Langham which, despite poor audiences, featured strong performances and Martha Henry who "recognized that the key to Cressida's character is that she has none, a point magnificently etched by an expression of frightening vacuity on her final exit."[42] The festival's next version, directed by David Williams in 1987, attempted to mesh commentary on sexual politics (fetish gear, drag queens, and orgies) with commentary on colonial politics (an evocation of the British Raj, imagining the Trojans as Indians and the Grecians as empire-builders), but failed to satisfactorily address either.

The play struggled on English-speaking stages through the 1970s and 1980s. Elijah Moshinsky's 1976 National Theatre production at the Young Vic was pronounced "a maladroit failure."[43] In an intimate setting, the play struggled to find its focus amid an ensemble of strong performances: "emphasis goes to whoever has the power to secure it,"[44] and reviewers looked in vain for coherence. Richard Cottrell's 1979 production for the Bristol Old Vic was criticized for the same fault, and reviewers were not persuaded by the deliberate casting of actors rather less heroically statured than expected. John Wood's production at Ottawa's National Arts Centre in 1984 was visually striking with metallic sets evoking the Bronze Age, but sacrificed story to design. On television, Jonathan Miller's 1981 adaptation for the BBC was a faithful retelling of the play, enlivened by some cheeky design references: the *M*A*S*H*-inspired Grecian camp, pin-ups of Lucas Cranach's nudes in Ajax's tent, and the incomplete wooden leg of the Trojan Horse in the background. Charles Gray's Pandarus was weary rather than malicious, delivering his epilogue "with a terrifying, self-absorbed madness,"[45] while Anton Lesser took advantage of the intimacy of the camera to present a more reflective Troilus than usual. The play was having more success in translation: Jeffrey Leavis and Deguchi Norio codirected a 1972 production for the Bungaku-ze Company set in ancient Japan, and the indeterminate setting of Dieter Dorn's 1986 Munich production gave the impression of "something archaic and passionate, of eruptive ferocity barely restrained, of a primitive culture in its harsh exoticism."[46] For a play that battled to find a "voice" in performance, translation seemed to liberate its deeper, rawer aspects.

Trevor Nunn's 1999 production at the National Theatre marked a revival in the play's fortunes on the cusp of the twenty-first century. He emphasized a cultural divide, casting white actors as the Grecians and black actors as Trojans. The sight of Sophie Okonedo's delicate Cressida being "positively mauled" by the Grecian commanders upon her arrival in their camp was deliberately uncomfortable, and the play closed with "an image of her in grieving isolation,"[47] finding its emotional core in this character's devastation. However, it was strong ensemble performances that captured the imagination of reviewers, with "the big ideals of honour and love . . . filtered through a wide variety of wartime lives."[48]

The subsequent decade saw four major productions in the UK, as well as growing interest internationally: Michael Bogdanov's graphically sexual *Troilus + Cressida* provided Australia's Bell Shakespeare Company's biggest ever financial success in its 2000 run at Sydney Opera House's Playhouse.[49] Peter Stein directed a spectacular version for the Edinburgh International Festival in 2006 that was criticized for length and dullness, the lumbering set arguably more animated than the cast. Critics referred to Stein's interpretation as "Romeo and Juliet in times of conflict,"[50] an impression partially owing to the interpolation of a tragic death for Troilus at the end of the play: Pandarus brought Cressida in to beg forgiveness, a forgiveness that Troilus expressly denied her, instead turning and running into the spears of the waiting Myrmidons.

Interest in the sexuality of the play has been increasingly apparent. In Andrew Hilton's 2003 Tobacco Factory production,

Ian Barritt's majestically louche Pandarus is the central character of the play. Pale, fleshy, imperious and prurient, he's a self-important old fruit who exists through the erotic and heroic life of others. He is, indeed, a "trader of the flesh," and the phrase is a metaphor for the whole play. What is war but a trade in human flesh, where the profits are as monstrous and futile as the losses?[51]

In 1954, one reviewer had asked of Shaw's production "whether [Achilles'] unhealthy relationship with the effeminate Patroclus need have been quite so flagrantly and emphatically stressed by the producer."[52] By contrast, the "blatantly camp displays" of Richard Monette's 2003 production at Stratford Ontario "failed to shock . . . and at the same time seemed pointlessly overdone."[53] By 2008 (Cheek by Jowl on tour) and 2009 (Shakespeare's Globe), an openly gay Achilles was standard; both productions using the character to explore issues of sexual identity through his dual loves for the feminized Patroclus and the testosterone-fueled world of war. The Cheek by Jowl production, directed by Declan Donnellan, also featured a glamorous Helen "posing for photographs with the new man in her life, Paris, as if for a spread in *Hello!* Magazine,"[54] epitomizing the emptiness of "love" in a world where true affection no longer had a place. Richard Cant's Thersites, meanwhile, was "a drag-queen who enjoys nothing more than skittering around in high heels,"[55] entertaining the Grecian troops with his cabaret act. This Thersites was reminiscent of the BBC's casting of camp icon "The Incredible Orlando" in the role, who described his performance as "a scurvy railing bitch—a bit of a cow, really . . . she owns herself and doesn't answer to anyone."[56]

In Matthew Dunster's Globe production, the warlike Greeks contrasted with the comfort-oriented world of the Trojans, in which "semi-nude, doe-eyed servant boys pad about, risking a goosing from Matthew Kelly's lecherously camp Pandarus."[57] Interestingly, and reminiscent of the focus of early twentieth-century reviewers, it was Laura Pyper's Cressida who once again attracted the most attention. This purple-haired teenager's combination of cynicism and naivety chimed with contemporary teenage attitudes; as she gave Diomedes Troilus' sleeve, girls of a similar age in the auditorium gasped in shock, the sleeve being read as a modern "promise bracelet" whose attendant significance reverberated across the centuries. As the play continues to find new audiences and new resonances, it will no doubt continue to cement its claim as Shakespeare's "play for the times."

AT THE RSC

John Barton

The RSC's first three productions, in 1960, 1968, and 1976, were all directed by John Barton; the first in conjunction with Peter Hall and the last with Barry Kyle. They were very different, reflecting Barton's developing ideas, and dividing critical opinion about a play still regarded as controversial.

In 1960 *Troilus and Cressida* was fifth in a series of six plays that, according to the program notes, aimed to trace "the range, development and paradox of Shakespearean comedy." Many critics quibbled with this classification and were taken aback by the set and effects:

> In years to come, no doubt, we shall look back and say, " 'Troilus and Cressida'? Ah, yes—that's the one they did in sand and fog." For all of the play . . . is performed on a circular arena of sand—a cockpit or a no man's land for the interminable Greek-Trojan war—and the long battle scenes are wrapped in property smoke which swirls out into the auditorium.[58]

Despite misgivings, the majority recognized how effective the set was: "Extraordinarily difficult to stage, it gets now as imaginative projection, as I remember, set upon a low octagonal platform covered with sand . . . and with a background device, by Leslie Hurry, that is the colour of dried blood."[59] Costumes were "traditional": "armour and oiled bodies, sombre tones [gold and russet] assisting . . . in . . . contrasting of the opposing armies,"[60] but the directors' approach was not. After describing the play's discrepancy between noble words and ignoble deeds, one reviewer suggested that "Shakespeare probably never even noticed the discrepancy," before going on to analyze how the directors (still frequently referred to as "producers") had made a play out of what he saw as Shakespeare's failure:

> The producers have found the shape which Shakespeare himself missed; they have built upon a feeling that the universe is corrupt, and that worms triumph over nobility, a logical theatrical structure. The play contemplates lust and betrayal destroying grandeur. In the first part of the production, the spectacle is watched through the eyes of Max Adrian's clever and repulsive Pandarus with a lecherous, lip-licking lascivious delight. In the second part Pandarus almost vanishes, and his place is taken by the ragged and filthy Thersites, in whom the continuation of the story, as well as his own degraded nature, inspires a spiritually vomiting disgust. We begin by finding the world and the sins that Shakespeare sees in it titillating; and in the end they make us spew.[61]

The critic's visceral response to the production captures the mind-set of the time, postwar, post-Suez debacle, post the theatrical revolution of the late 1950s' "angry young men": a society on the brink of the social revolution of the 1960s.

John Barton's next production in 1968—the year of student unrest in Europe and America—was even more uncompromisingly radical. His company notes, reprinted in the program, set out his reading of the play:

> The play is to some extent an attack on our cosy habit of generalising. We use abstract words like Honour, Fame, Beauty and Truth to sanction what we do and give ourselves a sense of order and meaning. We need these to smooth over the confusion of life, and to avoid acknowledging the chaos within ourselves . . . the Greeks are basically in touch with reality, and destructive, while the Trojans are self-destructive, romantic and blind.[62]

Barton employed a totally bare set: "Apart from military standards and the intermittent couch, the players—servants, or soldiers masked in bronze—themselves institute the only settings we see."[63]

Response to his vision was a mixture of outrage and confused admiration; even those critics who admired it had reservations:

> Perhaps because Shakespeare labelled him a scurrilous Gre-
> cian, no one has trusted Thersites's view of Troilus and Cres-
> sida as all wars and lechery. John Barton has now done so, and
> the result is the most coherent and impassioned version of the
> play I have yet seen.
>
> The other elements—honor, dignity, love—are there only to
> be poisoned. For once, Troilus and Cressida seems an uncom-
> plicated, almost schematic work. It takes place under the
> emblem of a golden bull, symbolizing at once the Guernica-like
> carnage and the cuckolding of Menelaus that gives the war its
> pretext. And what the production shows is that all the Trojans
> and Greeks need is a pretext. There is no attempt—as in Mr.
> Barton's 1960 production—to give the two sides separate
> characteristics. Off duty they were rogues of rough matting;
> on the battlefield they are almost naked. The encounter is
> voluptuous and both sides desire it.
>
> At first the production draws you into this infected atmos-
> phere by glamorizing it—both in the balletic collisions of oiled
> bodies and at the very centre of the war on Helen's vast bed.
> The Helen-Pandarus scene is usually played satirically but
> here Sheila Allen gives it an erotic charge that makes other
> matters seem unimportant compared with a shimmering
> golden robe and a hand exploring cheek.[64]

Benedict Nightingale, like Irving Wardle, had reservations, despite what he describes as Barton's "striking and daring aperçu that this war is a sort of lechery itself. War is sex and sex is war."[65] Most crit-ics reacted unfavorably to the overt homosexuality of the relation-ship between Achilles and Patroclus: "Achilles (Alan Howard) has been turned into a raging old queen in a gold wig and an embroi-dered fur coat."[66]

Herbert Kretzmer suggested that the production "echoes some of the weighty splendours of this company's 'Wars of the Roses,'" but he, too, had misgivings:

The lovers of the title played with fire and charm by Michael Williams and newcomer Helen Mirren are so swamped by magnificently staged battles, generous with gore and what seemed to me an overstressed concern with homosexuality in the warring camps of Greeks and Trojans.

Costumes and armour are frequently and literally dropped to reveal men in a state of semi-nudity, roaring lustily at each other like Rugby players sharing a shower. I am not sure that all this rough stuff makes the play any more coherent. But it certainly provided rich opportunities for bravura performances by Alan Howard (Achilles), Patrick Stewart (Hector), Bernard Lloyd (Paris), Richard Moore (Ajax) and Norman Rodway as a hideous clown barnacled with boils, running sores and phallic symbols.

Troilus and Cressida runs for something like 3½ hours and could with advantage lose 45 minutes of talk and five pints of artificial blood. But it remains a most impressive thing to see.[67]

For his third attempt, in 1976, this time with Barry Kyle, Barton again recorded his thoughts in the program notes. His ideas about the play have moved on and his condemnation seems less outright:

In *Troilus and Cressida*, Shakespeare invites tragic, comic, satiric, intellectual and compassionate responses almost at the same time. This shiftingness of view is also embodied in the play's presentation of character. There is a very remarkable difference between the declared intentions of the characters and the actual deeds done by them. Again and again a character enunciates certain intentions and beliefs which are confounded by his actions . . . Again and again, a character who seems to be foolish or cruel or stupid turns up with something completely the opposite to one's first view of him, and that seems to me to be not a chaotic view of human nature but a truthful and realistic one.[68]

Many critics remembered his previous production—some only too well—and on the whole compared this one favorably with the last:

"In his celebrated, and lamentably influential, production some years ago, John Barton reduced its various moods to garish nihilism. His new version (co-directed with Barry Kyle) goes some way towards making amends."[69] Michael Billington agreed that this production "trusts the play to yield up its own dark ambiguities. Last time round Barton seemed almost to be reading us a lecture on Shakespeare's sexual disgust: this time the tone is saner, cooler, more balanced."[70]

The fixed wooden set comprising a jutting hexagonal stage and vertical beams was universally disliked. Billington was one of many to point out its limitations: "Visually the production is not much helped by the cramping timbered structure that this year hogs the Stratford stage."[71] The two sides on this occasion were carefully distinguished, though: the Greeks represented as "a bunch of arrogant greybeards," the Trojans as "romantic young men who regard the war like a prolonged Test Match but display courage rather than heroism."[72]

Barton reprised certain elements from his previous production to no greater critical approval:

> Mr Barton carried over several features from his controversial 1968 version: the Trojans were virtually naked when they went into battle, and so were the Myrmidons throughout; Achilles was showily effeminate; Thersites was covered with bleeding sores and wore a grotesque mouth-shaped codpiece with a dangling red tongue/penis; Thersites and Pandarus had a song-and-dance routine for the epilogue. My objection to these things was not that they were offensive, as some found them, but that they distracted one from concentrating on that complicated language, without being closely enough related to the text to act as visual symbols of it.[73]

J. W. Lambert also compared the two productions, and attempted to analyze the differences between them, although the representation of Achilles induced a queasy simile:

> When Mr Barton last directed "Troilus and Cressida" in 1968, he did so with due, not to say excessive regard for the fashion of the day—smoke, strobe-lighting, slow motion, barricades of

2. John Barton's 1976 production, with several features carried over "from his controversial 1968 version: the Trojans were virtually naked when they went into battle."

buttocks, Achilles in drag and a fleeting glimpse of Helen Mirren in the nude. Sensationalism was all the go, hysteria the passport to paradise. Eight years on, though we still have smoke and slow motion for the battle scenes, the overall tone of this sardonic commentary on senseless war and the weakness of the flesh is very different. Shock tactics have been replaced by ironic invention, comic and otherwise.

Oriental, solemn, ceremonious Trojans confront Greeks who are all bemused or crafty old shepherds in funny straw hats, except oafish Ajax, a Diomed played by Paul Shelley as a sharp career officer—and of course Achilles, the unscrupulous aristocrat among the yeomanry: far more effeminate than

Paul Moriarty as his catamite Patroclus, Robin Ellis's sulking prince is a degenerate echo of Alan Howard's tortured assumption in 1968, a writhing, fleshly bully who nibbles and sucks at his words like a fish caressing some putrescent morsel at the mouth of a sewer.

His Trojan rival Hector, on the other hand, is played by Michael Pennington with a blade-straight vocal and physical line which nevertheless easily encompasses his inconsistent, unkind chivalry.[74]

Roger Warren concludes that, despite his reservations, "it was a consistently interesting and absorbing occasion . . . Whatever Mr Barton's over-emphasis or over-ingenuity, he enabled his cast to bring out the 'shifting' ambiguous quality of much, at least, of the play, and certainly much more than in his previous version."[75]

After Barton

In 1981 Terry Hands staged the play at the Aldwych. Irving Wardle suggested that the fundamental difference was Hands' rejection of Barton's intellectualized approach to play and characters:

What Mr Hands has done is to release them from any binding directorial concept and give them the chance to live to the full on their own terms—apparently in the hope that if a pattern does emerge it will be Shakespeare's.[76]

This ad hoc approach to the text produced inconsistent results:

Strong performances and interesting interpretation alternated with excess and confusion. Farrah's designs were equally typical, a hotchpotch of the modern, the medieval, and (occasionally) the Greek: barbed wire, greatcoats and harmonica music of the trenches clashed against helmets with elaborate hinged visors, armour and sabres.[77]

Michael Billington thought that "If one can deduce any message from Mr Hands' production, it is that the play is about the moral chaos induced by exhaustion."[78] Playing for comedy, the play's satirical edge was missing.

Howard Davies' production at the Royal Shakespeare Theatre in 1985 offered politics and history with comic and tragic overtones. Setting was crucial:

> Ralph Koltai has designed a single set, consisting of the white interior of a nineteenth-century mansion three quarters smashed by war. Peeling pictures, broken shutters, a chandelier and some fallen curtains hung crazily above a grandiose staircase. By turns Trojan and Greek, public and private, conference chamber and troops' taverna, it placed us on the shores of the Black Sea in the 1850s. This context had, of course, more than merely geographical appropriateness to recommend it. It invoked the Crimean War in order to make us think, simultaneously, of the heroic idealism of the Charge of the Light Brigade and the brutal reality of the wards at Scutari.[79]

John Peter argued that the decision to update the play had a sound rationale:

> The Crimean War was one of the last armed conflicts in which old-fashioned individual gallantry still had some meaning; and this sense, of personal courage and honest chivalry at their last gasp in the roar of impersonal and disillusioned warfare, fits perfectly the mood of this complex, questioning and angry play.[80]

Dubbed a "feminist" production, the most controversial aspect was Juliet Stevenson's performance as Cressida (discussed below). Irving Wardle argued that "The prevailing tone was comic, going much beyond the bitterly sardonic into the region of gags and belly-laughs." He saw the key performance in this interpretation as Alun Armstrong's Thersites, "a Geordie clown in thick-pebble glasses, characteristically seen parading up and down as Agamemnon wearing a saucepan helmet which he then cannot get off."[81]

The 1990 production in the Swan theater marked the RSC directorial debut of the twenty-four-year-old Sam Mendes and established his reputation. The uniformly strong playing of his ensemble cast enabled Mendes to create "a bleakly comic version of the play"[82] in

a temporal no man's land where Greek helmets, khaki, and anglepoise lamps can co-exist. As in *The Wasteland*, the horror is not passed off here as a little local unpleasantness, but is felt to be happening in all ages at once, Thermopylae contemporary with Passchaendale. The eclecticism of design also provides ideal conditions for satiric deflation.[83]

Cressida (Amanda Root) dabbled her feet in a paddling pool, in which the Trojan soldiers ceremoniously washed their swords and faces after the day's fighting. Pandarus framed the play:

The prologue was given to the blazered Pandarus of Norman Rodway ("armed" in a medal to which he pointed with a challenging twinkle), and spoken with a crisp intelligence and wit that marked much of the evening. Pandarus' helpful remarks to "all tongue-tied maidens here" ended the first half of the play before the intermission, so that, with the epilogue too, he framed the evening, his jaunty, dressy start, medial salaciousness, and final diseased decrepitude marking the progress of the play.[84]

The direction was critically acclaimed:

There were scenes of brilliantly directed theatricality too: the Greek generals scruffy and murky in council behind their long upstage table contrasted with the brilliantly lit elegance of the Trojans, seated round the perimeter of the playing space, the theatre become debating chamber, under the chairmanship of the patriarchal figure of Griffith Jones's Priam, in octogenarian splendour in white naval uniform.[85]

Mendes employed small, original directing touches to clarify the narrative and the significance of the individuals caught up in it:

3. Sam Mendes' 1990 production, with Amanda Root as Cressida and a blazered Norman Rodway as Pandarus, dabbling their feet in a paddling pool "in which the Trojan soldiers ceremoniously washed their swords and faces after the day's fighting."

time and again Mendes worked with remarkable economy. The addition of the moment of the exchange of Antenor for Cressida, for instance, became another ritual, familiar from spy-films perhaps but still powerful, particularly in the warm welcome Antenor received, defining neatly the unimportance of Cressida for the Trojans.[86]

Very much a company play, it was the extraordinary performance of Simon Russell Beale, who confesses that he "didn't have a great deal of enthusiasm for Thersites to begin with,"[87] which was singled out:

> The chief glory of the evening is Simon Russell Beale's hilariously repulsive performance as Thersites . . . Hunchbacked, rheumy-eyed and limping, and wearing a greasy raincoat, Russell Beale savours every syllable of his character's scabrous sneers and jibes persuading the audience to laugh the possibility of human decency to scorn.[88]

Ian Judge was, as many critics pointed out, an unlikely choice of director for the next RSC production in 1996:

> Ian Judge openly rejoices in his richly deserved reputation as a director of popular (possibly populist) productions of Shakespeare's comedies; so his choice as a director of *Troilus and Cressida* caused a good deal of speculation, some of it hostile in anticipation. In the event, this was an earnest, somewhat old-fashioned evening in the theatre, replicating many of the devices that have attached themselves to the play in successive RSC stagings (men in tight leather, clouds of smoke, campy performances as Pandarus, Achilles, and Patroclus).[89]

In the program notes, Judge argued that the play is "a complete one-off. It's a comedy, but the nature of that comedy is to do with how we keep ourselves alive in a world so intolerable and bleak."[90] Critics were not entirely convinced by the nudity, bare buttocks, and humor, but felt that the tragedy of the second half worked better:

> The scene-setting Prologue was delivered by Richard McCabe as if he were a TV warm-up man. Clive Francis plays the ringleted Pandarus as if he were Frankie Howerd in a camp sitcom called Up Phrygia. And the great scenes of debate among the Greeks and Trojans were relentlessly busy in a way that obscured the density of their arguments about military tactics and moral honour.

But when it gets to the heart of the matter, Judge's production calms down; and what it brings out, with growing assurance, is the destructiveness of time which is the noun which reverberates through the play.[91]

Michael Boyd's 1998 production, which opened at the Barbican Pit before transferring to the Swan, updated the play's setting but left many critics confused about its exact whereabouts:

Boyd's powerful but perplexing staging opens with sepia photographs of soldiers, suggesting that we are on the Western Front during the First World War. Then you notice that a lot of the characters have Irish accents. The Irish Civil War perhaps? Then it becomes clear that while the Trojans are Irish, the Greeks are British. The IRA versus the Black and Tans? The shelled Roman Catholic chapel which dominates Tom Piper's spare but highly atmospheric set, seems to confirm this impression, but why, then, does Achilles look like a present-day Serbian war-crimes thug, and Ajax resemble a particularly dim heavy-metal rock star?
What Boyd is presumably trying to suggest is any war-torn territory in which fine words cover vile actions.[92]

Boyd added a number of directorial touches: Patroclus (Elaine Pyke) was killed by the Greeks, not Hector, Cassandra carried around a black shawl wrapped up to suggest a dead child, and Thersites was played as a "filthy cross between a war photographer and a bowler-hatted music-hall clown."[93]

For the Complete Works Festival, the distinguished German director Peter Stein's production in association with the RSC opened at the Edinburgh festival in 2006. His first ever English-language production, described as "huge, beautiful and stately,"[94] was dedicated to Barton's 1968 production from which it took inspiration.

"As False as Cressid" (3.2.184)

Like *Romeo and Juliet*, the play tells the story of a love affair doomed by a hostile environment. But Troilus is more like an early narcissistic Romeo, and Cressida doesn't die but is handed over to the enemy and is unfaithful. Her name becomes, as Pandarus prophesies, a byword for infidelity. The part represents a challenge for any actor, especially Act 4 Scene 5 when Cressida arrives in the Greek camp. Edith Evans made her debut in the role in William Poel's 1912 production and established her distinguished professional career. It is notable how frequently the actor playing the role has been singled out for her performance, often against the critics' better judgment and by playing against contemporary ideas about the character.

Many critics were surprised by the sexiness of Dorothy Tutin's interpretation in 1960, but even more that she played Cressida sympathetically:

> Thersites comes near to the truth about Cressida when he calls her a "commodious drab." Hazlitt speaks of her as "a giddy girl, an unpractised jilt," and Agate put it on record that he thought Cressida "an impossible part, requiring a personality to launch whole navies and burn the topless towers of a hundred cities."
>
> Dorothy Tutin's personality could launch atomic navies; and if she has not the power to burn whole cities, then she is certainly capable of giving them a good singeing. Her Cressida is a performance of smouldering voluptuousness, physical in essence with sensuous walk, heaving breast and passionate eyes. Emotionally there are moments of eloquence, yet there is a niceness about this Cressida which jars on the amoral picture of Shakespeare's wanton. Miss Tutin seems to wish us to believe that this travesty of virtue has some real moral conscience. It is to her great credit that she almost succeeds.[95]

Reviews of Barton's 1968 production are mainly too obsessed and/or incensed by Alan Howard's Achilles to worry much about Helen Mirren's Cressida. Benedict Nightingale objects that "Miss Mirren has nothing to do with the Cressida described by Ulysses, the only voice in the play we can trust." He tells us that "Her wanton spirits look out at every joint and motion of her body" before objecting that Mirren just isn't "wanton" enough in "the joints, not to

4. Dorothy Tutin as Cressida with David Buck as Diomedes, 1960: "Her Cressida is a performance of smouldering voluptuousness, physical in essence with sensual walk, heaving breast and passionate eyes."

mention the motions."[96] W. A. Darlington offers a more thoughtful response:

> In John Barton's present production at Stratford-on-Avon
> Helen Mirren has a very clear and to me original reading. She
> makes the girl shallow-pated rather than wicked and estab-

lishes this in her first scene with Pandarus. During her love-scenes with Troilus she convinces herself of her own sincerity and is all the more vehement in its defence because she really knows how little depth she has.

Arrived in the Greek camp, she gives herself away to the wise Ulysses by the increasing pleasure with which she responds to her new host's very warm welcome and it is easy to see that her devotion to Troilus will not last.[97]

Francesca Annis' performance in 1968 drew much favorable comment, although critics were disconcerted by the "stock courtesan mask, fitted to the back of her head-dress, which she suddenly revealed as she walked off at the end of the betrayal scene." Roger Warren goes on to suggest:

This gross schematic ostentation flatly contradicted both the ambiguity of Cressida's feeling, and Francesca Annis's subtle presentation of it . . . certainly Troilus and Cressida for the first time in my experience held the center of their play. Francesca Annis perfectly caught the "slipper" changeability of Cressida, sophisticated one moment, the next giving intense value to the haunting solemnity with which Cressida swears truth,

When time is old and hath forgot itself,
When waterdrops have worn the stones of Troy.

This scene, with its magnificent juxtaposition of present and future, and of passionate seriousness and bawdy wit, was the high point of the play, superbly realized by Miss Annis, David Waller's expert Pandarus, and Mike Gwilym's coherent and un-mannered Troilus.[98]

Carol Royle, fresh from TV soap opera, was an unusual choice for Cressida in Hands' 1981 production but was nevertheless widely praised for the "intelligence and fire"[99] she brought to Cressida. In an interview with Linda Christmas, Royle discussed her approach to the role:

On first reading, I didn't find her a calculating woman, though I can see an element of that in her. But on the whole I'm still inclined to see her as a victim. She is a lady full of doubts, and she behaves the way she does because of the situation she is in and the society in which she lives.

Troilus seems to be giving her away to the Grecian camp. He doesn't want her to go but he lets her go because it gives him tactical military advantage. And then she falls in lust, not love, with Diomedes and has to admit that fidelity is not part of her make-up at all.[100]

Juliet Stevenson's performance in Davies' 1985 production was controversial, and she has herself explained how hard it can be to interpret Shakespeare's women onstage and the desire to "react against the way tradition and prejudice have stigmatised them."[101] The updating of the play, however, allowed Stevenson scope to rein-terpret the role: "Cressida, more interestingly, was re-read as a seri-ous nineteenth-century New Woman whose infidelity reflected, not moral weakness, but her status as the victim of an aggressively mas-culine culture."[102] The staging of her arrival in the Greek camp was much commented upon:

When she arrived at the Greek camp, the generals subjected her to brutally violent kisses that amounted to assault. At first appalled, she soon began to play their game, a point brilliantly made when Ulysses asked for his kiss: "Why, beg then," she replied tartly, snapping her fingers to indicate that he should kneel. She had become a love-object after all.[103]

Amanda Root's Cressida in 1990 was seen by Benedict Nightin-gale as "too knowing, too calculating, too Greek,"[104] but Martin Hoyle argued that

Amanda Root's Cressida has the ambiguity of youth. She can turn and swivel without losing sympathy, especially as Sam Mendes' production subscribes to the current theory of the

5. Juliet Stevenson as Cressida, 1985: "When she arrived at the Greek camp, the generals subjected her to brutally violent kisses that amounted to assault."

helpless girl responding to Diomedes through sheer panic. Her welcome by the appreciative Greek camp is heavy with the threat of rape, however much at odds this is with the self-possessed pertness of her lines at this point.[105]

In 1996 Victoria Hamilton's performance was recognized by many critics as the production's "triumph. Her girlish Cressida is not the usual inconstant flirt with both eyes on the main chance, but a serious, self-possessed girl, delighted by first love":[106]

The evening's secret weapon is Victoria Hamilton's Cressida, whose steamy affair with Troilus . . . strikes a lipsmacking note of opportunism, desperation and lust.[107]

In Michael Boyd's 1998 production,

Jayne Ashbourne looking like a delightfully plump and flirta-tious barmaid in a rural Irish pub, touchingly captures Cressida's awareness of her own shop-soiled morality, while the effectively choreographed scene in which she is forcibly kissed by the Greek generals is almost as shocking as a gang rape.[108]

This scene was striking and effective, although a number of critics felt that the "exaggeratedly expressionistic artifice" of the tango was at odds with the "naturalistic acting" style.[109]

Two women, Cressida and Helen, are at the heart of this play about love and war. Ideas about the play and interpretations of these roles have changed with ideas about women's place in culture and society. Young women actors have succeeded with Cressida, going beyond the shallow stereotype to suggest how her life is defined by social positioning and determined by gender. The added sympathy and complexity of their interpretations has fundamentally changed critical perceptions of Cressida, the role of women, and the play itself.

THE DIRECTOR'S CUT: INTERVIEWS WITH MICHAEL BOYD AND TREVOR NUNN

Michael Boyd was born in Belfast in 1955, educated in London and Edinburgh, and completed his MA in English literature at Edinburgh University. He trained as a director at the Malaya Bronnaya Theatre in Moscow. He then went on to work at the Belgrade Theatre in Coventry, joining the Sheffield Crucible as associate director in 1982. In 1985 Boyd became founding artistic director of the Tron theater in Glasgow, becoming equally acclaimed for staging new writing and innovative productions of the classics. He was drama director of the New Beginnings Festival of Soviet Arts in Glasgow in 1999. He joined the RSC as an associate director in 1996 and has since directed numerous productions of Shakespeare's plays. He won the Laurence Olivier Award for Best Director for his version of the *Henry VI* plays in the RSC's "This England: The Histories" in 2001. He took over as artistic director of the RSC in 2003 and oversaw the extraordinarily successful Complete Works Festival in 2006–07. His own contribution to this, and the company's subsequent season, was a cycle of all eight history plays, from *Richard II* through to *Richard III*, with the same company of actors. This transferred to London's Roundhouse Theatre in 2008 and won multiple awards. Here he answers questions about his production of *Troilus and Cressida* for the RSC in 1998.

Sir Trevor Nunn is the most successful and one of the most highly regarded of modern British theater directors. Born in 1940, he was a brilliant student at Cambridge, strongly influenced by the literary close reading of Dr. F. R. Leavis. At the age of just twenty-eight he succeeded Peter Hall as artistic director of the RSC, where he remained until 1978. He greatly expanded the range of the company's work and its ambition in terms of venues and touring. He also achieved huge success in musical theater and subsequently became artistic director of the National Theatre in London. His productions are always full of textual insights, while being clean and elegant in design. Among his most admired Shakespearean work has been a series of tragedies with Ian McKellen in leading roles: *Macbeth* (1976, with Judi Dench, in the dark, intimate space of The Other Place), *Othello* (1989, with McKellen as Iago and Imogen Stubbs as Desdemona), and *King Lear* (2007, in the Stratford Complete Works Festival, on world tour, and then in London). Here he reflects upon his production of *Troilus and Cressida* for the National Theatre in London in 1999.

Did you and your designer go for an evocation of the Trojan War or of some other particular war—or the suggestion that this could be any war?

MB: We wanted to suggest a war where cynical expediency and realpolitik could credibly clash with dynastic family loyalty and heroism. Our world suggested both the Spanish Civil War and the conflict between the Irish and the British in the early twentieth century.

TN: *Troilus and Cressida* is categorized by scholarly opinion as a "problem play" along with *Measure for Measure* and *All's Well That Ends Well*. Practitioners in the theater can be forgiven for asking, "What's the problem?" *Troilus and Cressida* is thrillingly complex in both structure and language, but we know from many contemporary productions that it can work devastatingly in the theater, and that the intricacies and convolutions of its verse need not lessen its emotional and philosophical impact.

I have long believed—but I cannot prove it—that at the time of writing *Troilus*, Shakespeare and his actors had started to perform at the smaller indoor theater in Blackfriars, as well as maintaining their repertoire at The Globe. Performing to a smaller, more focused audience, in a space lit by candlepower, and with the acoustics of a roofed enclosed room, would have encouraged Shakespeare to experiment with ever more naturalistic effects in his verse, and indeed to raise the bar of complex thought in his writing, liberated by a new sense of intimacy and the luxury of total audibility.

When I was a student I saw a superbly successful production of *Troilus and Cressida*, directed by Peter Hall, with Dorothy Tutin as an extraordinarily voluptuous Cressida, surrounded by a wonderfully diverse company, including Peter O'Toole as Thersites, Max Adrian as Pandarus, and Eric Porter as Ulysses. The action of the play took place in a sand pit. Partly as "homage" to this brilliant evocation of the play, and partly to try to develop the idea a stage further, I created a production at the National Theatre in 1999, designed by Rob Howell, which featured a much bigger sand pit, of reddish-orange sand, that appeared almost miraculously to be able to change color between one scene and another. With the addition of tent-like shapes, we were able to move with cinematic continuous flow between Troy and the Greek camp.

There is, in my view, no value whatsoever in updating *Troilus and Cressida* to a later century, with implications of the horrors of more modern mechanical warfare. Many plays of Shakespeare benefit immensely from being seen through the prism of a modern setting, but Troilus is not one of them. The play relies on concepts of honor, nobility, and the existence of mythic heroic figures, one of them the son of a goddess, that have no real equivalents in the modern world, and its plot moves toward confrontations of single combat; indeed highly symbolic single combat, to the point when—by foul means— Achilles destroys Hector and the war itself seems thereby to have been decided.

And the movement between city and camp, domestic settings and battlefield: how did you convey that visually?

MB: For our small-scale touring production, Tom Piper designed a burned-out, war-torn chapel-cum-kitchen which could move from Priam's family dinner-table to the battlefield with ease. A red velvet curtain could be drawn across to suggest a tent or a press conference backdrop, and to conceal the damage wrought by the Greek "iconoclasts."

TN: The play is Shakespeare's inquiry into "Wars and lechery," which of course gives him his cue equally to examine peace and love, the ideal possibilities of human contact as opposed to the worse bestial instincts that so readily dominate our behavior. The war in question has been caused by the elopement of Helen with Paris; or, in other words, either an example of pure love, or an example of unbridled lust and selfish recklessness. Is the resulting Greek invasion high-minded and principled or a bloodthirsty adventure in pursuit of spoils and bloody revenge? For Shakespeare, the two very different cultures, Greek and Trojan, don't divide at a moral fault line, with all the honor and principle on one side and all the compromise and pragmatism on the other. In both camps there are those who uphold the highest principles and those who cynically see how the world actually is, most particularly the world-weary Pandarus and the obsessed satirist Thersites.

At the level of both design and interpretation, did you seek a sharp distinction between Greeks and Trojans? It's sometimes said that the Trojans embody an older code of honor and chivalry, the Greeks a more "modern," political, even Machiavellian stance, but it's not quite that simple, is it?

MB: Both Greeks and Trojans were revealed as venal, self-seeking, and flawed, but there was something peculiarly chilling about Colin Hurley's utterly plausible Ulysses, and we felt an instinctive warmth toward the Trojans who were at least a family, albeit dysfunctional. The Greeks were wealthier, better dressed, and more urbane.

TN: I wanted to make the maximum distinction between Greek and Trojans and so, choosing my casting from a large semipermanent multiracial ensemble, I had all of the Trojan parts played by artists of color, making the Trojan world an African civilization, in strong contrast to the Greek invaders who were all Caucasian, and as if from another hemisphere.

The Trojan world in my production was heavy with hieratic ritual; the Greek world, less obviously religiously coherent and more individually anarchic, giving rise to Ulysses' plea for order, as he reminds his colleagues:

> Take but degree away, untune that string
> And, hark, what discord follows . . .

Unquestionably, the impression was given in this production that the Trojan culture was the more ancient and mystical, and that the Greeks were a more recent power with colonial ambitions, but with high intellectual and moral standards:

> For beauty, wit,
> High birth, vigour of bone, desert in service,
> Love, friendship, charity, are subjects all
> To envious and calumniating time.

Ulysses is as educated and sensitive a spokesman as any to be found in the Shakespeare canon but, unquestionably, he is a rationalist.

There are several scenes of watching and overhearing (the return of the Trojan soldiers near the beginning, Troilus in the Greek camp near the end): how did you handle these?

MB: One convention that we enjoyed, especially when emotions ran high, was to make the overhearer "invisible" to those overheard, and let him be unrealistically close enough to smell them and stab them. It helped to dramatize and externalize the violent impulse, pent up in the verse.

TN: The pivotal scene for me, with respect to these two cultures (placed pivotally in the play by Shakespeare), was the "tent scene," Hector and his fellow Trojans being welcomed—Troilus included—by the Greek generals into their camp: as potent as the famous Christmas Day impromptu football match between a group of German and British soldiers, an exchange of friendship and admiration amongst men who know that tomorrow they are committed to killing each other: "Tomorrow do I meet thee, fell as death: / Tonight all friends."

In my production, these two very distinct cultures, unfamiliar with each other's ways, finally found themselves dancing and even embracing together, a brief peace process seeming to render the continuation of the war unnecessary.

In a *coup de théâtre* of genius, Shakespeare uses that same brief truce to allow Troilus to roam around the Greek camp in search of Cressida, only to witness the love of his life giving in to the seduction of Diomedes, a scene of almost unbearable pain and cruelty. The device of overhearing a crucial conversation is one that Shakespeare has used a number of times before, in plays such as *Two Gentlemen of Verona*, *Love's Labour's Lost*, *Twelfth Night*, and *Much Ado About Nothing*, and will go on to use to equally devastating effect in *Othello* and in the sleepwalking scene in *Macbeth*. But no overhearing scene is quite so distressing as this, when the young and idealistic Troilus is witness to everything that gives meaning to his life crumble and turn to ash. We in the audience experience the pain of this overhearing with him.

Troilus has to believe in his own romantic passion for Cressida, but do the audience?

MB: We are not asked to "believe in" Troilus' passion in the same way we are perhaps invited to with Romeo, but to feel no sympathy with Troilus' love for Cressida and sit in cool judgment on his passion, is to sit with Ulysses' reductive smugness, and be content with an evening that proves you right. It also makes the fatal mistake of reading the end of the play and Cressida's betrayal into Act 1.

6. William Houston as Troilus and Jayne Ashbourne as Cressida in Michael Boyd's 1998 RSC production.

Cressida is bartered by the Trojans and bullied by the Greeks: how did you avoid making her into, above all else, a *victim*?

MB: Shakespeare avoids that sentimentalism by making Cressida a survivor, who is aware of her own erotic authority and sexual needs, as well as her capacity for love.

TN: It was essential in my production that it should not be in any sense in Cressida's *character* or nature to be disloyal or superficial or opportunistic:

> Prince Troilus, I have loved you night and day
> For many weary months.

She is so clearly enraptured by the idea of becoming the wife of Troilus; she is so clearly a victim of war, as she is forcibly uprooted from Troy to become a humiliated fantasy plaything for an array of sex-starved Greek generals, and isolated and desperate as she is, her actions are all too understandable in giving in to her would-be protector, Diomedes. Her great declaration of fidelity, climaxing in "As false as Cressid," had to be, for us, a huge *unconscious* irony. Shakespeare seems to be proclaiming her human limitations, she is flawed; but the great humanist is reminding us that we all are . . . it happens.

The play at this exact point abandons the ideal of noble or honorable behavior (apart from Hector allowing Achilles to escape), and the bestial nature of human beings in conflict becomes the dominant theme. Hector is greedily distracted in pursuit of a magnificent armor; Achilles slaughters the unarmed hero with the aid of a pack of Myrmidons, and not in the long-heralded test of single combat; Hector's body is dragged disgustingly around the walls of Troy; Troilus becomes a killing machine. Thersites' vision of a bestial world is fulfilled, and a pox-ridden Pandarus bequeaths venereal disease to his audience, to succeeding generations, and unmistakably to Shakespeare's London, as he taunts "the brethren and sisters of the hold-door trade."

How do you see the roles of the other women in the play?

MB: We noticed that Troy was a much more feminine world. We found that only Cressida's voice had strength enough to survive the relentless logic of war and manipulative power politics, and that even her hideously compromised voice was more vivid than that of Helen. The clearest marker of Shakespeare's pessimism is how little space he can bring himself to give to Cassandra.

How did you and your actors approach the roles of Pandarus in the love plot and Thersites in the war plot?

MB: Roy Hanlon as Pandarus brought all the warmth and vulnerability of an aging wild-man, and had the great gift of being able to genuinely move us as well as clearly manipulate us into being moved. A ruthless, sentimental old queen, who finally bares his rotten teeth in the face of despair. Lloyd Hutchinson was part ravaged war correspondent, and part self-loathing stand-up. Ferocious, funny, and bleak, he hacked away at all the bad faith around him in search of something true.

For actors as well as audiences, the language of this play is some of the toughest, most crabbed, in Shakespeare. Did you have any

7. Sophie Okonedo as Cressida in Trevor Nunn's 1999 National Theatre production in London.

special techniques for dealing with this? And any special insight into why Shakespeare wrote this particular way in that particular language?

MB: The language, like the action of the play, depicts the hopeless car crash between one failing code of behavior and its discreditable successor. The rhetorics of both courtly romanticism and political expedience are found to be strained and empty. A new language, reminiscent of *King Lear* and Ted Hughes, is forged in the violence of Shakespeare's raging disappointment.

TN: My approach to solving the language, which admittedly is more difficult to unlock than most, was to organize a text workshop for a full week before rehearsals of the play itself began. The actors and I were able to remind ourselves of first principles, but then chart in what ways Shakespeare increasingly manipulates and improvises around these principles in plays leading up to the writing of *Troilus*. We discovered that, repeatedly, he is creating more naturalistic conversational effects, moving between verse and prose in ways that he clearly no longer wishes to be distinct, and therefore we found it vital to relax many of the "rules" of pentameter verse-speaking. If, for example, Shakespeare is insisting that his sense is governed by the punctuation and not by the line ending, we do him a crippling disservice to insist on marking the line ending, and thus interrupting the sense. We discovered we had to break the rules, but to *know* that we were breaking them and why. The pentameter pulse must be felt and breathed by the actors, but not marked. I did cut in areas like the big debating scenes, but each cut in pursuit of maintaining dramatic tension was an agonizing decision, in the knowledge that some richness of thought or layer of argument would be lost.

And do you think that some of the long speeches in the scenes of debate and argument need heavy cutting for a modern audience?

MB: We pruned, for instance, Nestor, when we thought that Shakespeare's satirical intentions had sufficiently made their point. We gave a lot of space, however, to the steady progress of the boa constrictor of Ulysses' rhetoric.

The ending is abrupt, somehow incomplete, isn't it? And with some differences between the early Quarto and Folio texts. How did your production end?

MB: Pandarus' epilogue remains a very powerful and satisfactory final note, spilling the play's diseases into the laps of the audience. We interpreted Troilus' final call for a revenge attack as consciously reckless and therefore suicidal. His self-destruction was our climactic action, though we left the final word with Pandarus.

TN: The published play ends unsatisfactorily for performance, and since so many questions surround the veracity of the text, I took it upon myself to edit and transpose, and in imitation of Henryson's "The Testament of Cresseid," I provided a final scene of Pandarus wandering the battlefield bartering a ruined and broken Cressida for sex—a pimp and a whore brought to desperation by war. The extraordinary articulacy of Ulysses, defining Hellenic ideals in philosophical debate with his colleague generals, the purity and high-mindedness of the Trojan debate over the future of Helen and the emergence of Hector as the embodiment of honor, are all now memories that have faded into a backdrop of savage irony as the realities of all-consuming war fill the foreground, men revealed as bloodlusting animals disconnected from their capacity to reason. Of course it is a "problem play" if an audience or a readership doesn't want to believe in that grim conclusion, but increasingly in our world four hundred years later, it is the conclusion we know in so many cases to be the truth.

SHAKESPEARE'S CAREER
IN THE THEATER

BEGINNINGS

William Shakespeare was an extraordinarily intelligent man who was born and died in an ordinary market town in the English Midlands. He lived an uneventful life in an eventful age. Born in April 1564, he was the eldest son of John Shakespeare, a glove maker who was prominent on the town council until he fell into financial difficulties. Young William was educated at the local grammar in Stratford-upon-Avon, Warwickshire, where he gained a thorough grounding in the Latin language, the art of rhetoric, and classical poetry. He married Ann Hathaway and had three children (Susanna, then the twins Hamnet and Judith) before his twenty-first birthday: an exceptionally young age for the period. We do not know how he supported his family in the mid-1580s.

Like many clever country boys, he moved to the city in order to make his way in the world. Like many creative people, he found a career in the entertainment business. Public playhouses and professional full-time acting companies reliant on the market for their income were born in Shakespeare's childhood. When he arrived in London as a man, sometime in the late 1580s, a new phenomenon was in the making: the actor who is so successful that he becomes a "star." The word did not exist in its modern sense, but the pattern is recognizable: audiences went to the theater not so much to see a particular show as to witness the comedian Richard Tarlton or the dramatic actor Edward Alleyn.

Shakespeare was an actor before he was a writer. It appears not to have been long before he realized that he was never going to grow into a great comedian like Tarlton or a great tragedian like Alleyn. Instead, he found a role within his company as the man who patched up old plays, breathing new life, new dramatic twists, into tired repertory pieces. He paid close attention to the work of the university-educated dramatists who were writing history plays and tragedies for the public stage in a style more ambitious, sweeping, and poetically grand than anything that had been seen before. But he may also have noted that what his friend and rival Ben Jonson would call "Marlowe's mighty line" sometimes faltered in the mode of comedy. Going to university, as Christopher Marlowe did, was all well and good for honing the arts of rhetorical elaboration and classical allusion, but it could lead to a loss of the common touch. To stay close to a large segment of the potential audience for public theater, it was necessary to write for clowns as well as kings and to intersperse the flights of poetry with the humor of the tavern, the privy, and the brothel: Shakespeare was the first to establish himself early in his career as an equal master of tragedy, comedy, and history. He realized that theater could be the medium to make the national past available to a wider audience than the elite who could afford to read large history books: his signature early works include not only the classical tragedy *Titus Andronicus* but also the sequence of English historical plays on the Wars of the Roses.

He also invented a new role for himself, that of in-house company dramatist. Where his peers and predecessors had to sell their plays to the theater managers on a poorly paid piecework basis, Shakespeare took a percentage of the box-office income. The Lord Chamberlain's Men constituted themselves in 1594 as a joint stock company, with the profits being distributed among the core actors who had invested as sharers. Shakespeare acted himself—he appears in the cast lists of some of Ben Jonson's plays as well as the list of actors' names at the beginning of his own collected works—but his principal duty was to write two or three plays a year for the company. By holding shares, he was effectively earning himself a royalty on his work, something no author had ever done before in England. When the Lord Chamberlain's Men collected their fee for performance at court in the Christmas season of 1594, three of them went along to the Treasurer of the Chamber: not just Richard Burbage the tragedian and Will Kempe the clown, but also Shakespeare the scriptwriter. That was something new.

The next four years were the golden period in Shakespeare's

career, though overshadowed by the death of his only son Hamnet, aged eleven, in 1596. In his early thirties and in full command of both his poetic and his theatrical medium, he perfected his art of comedy, while also developing his tragic and historical writing in new ways. In 1598, Francis Meres, a Cambridge University graduate with his finger on the pulse of the London literary world, praised Shakespeare for his excellence across the genres:

> As Plautus and Seneca are accounted the best for comedy and tragedy among the Latins, so Shakespeare among the English is the most excellent in both kinds for the stage; for comedy, witness his *Gentlemen of Verona*, his *Errors*, his *Love Labours Lost*, his *Love Labours Won*, his *Midsummer Night Dream* and his *Merchant of Venice*: for tragedy his *Richard the 2*, *Richard the 3*, *Henry the 4*, *King John*, *Titus Andronicus* and his *Romeo and Juliet*.

For Meres, as for the many writers who praised the "honey-flowing vein" of *Venus and Adonis* and *Lucrece*, narrative poems written when the theaters were closed due to plague in 1593–94, Shakespeare was marked above all by his linguistic skill, by the gift of turning elegant poetic phrases.

PLAYHOUSES

Elizabethan playhouses were "thrust" or "one-room" theaters. To understand Shakespeare's original theatrical life, we have to forget about the indoor theater of later times, with its proscenium arch and curtain that would be opened at the beginning and closed at the end of each act. In the proscenium arch theater, stage and auditorium are effectively two separate rooms: the audience looks from one world into another as if through the imaginary "fourth wall" framed by the proscenium. The picture-frame stage, together with the elaborate scenic effects and backdrops beyond it, created the illusion of a self-contained world—especially once nineteenth-century developments in the control of artificial lighting meant that the auditorium could be darkened and the spectators made to focus on the lighted stage. Shakespeare, by contrast, wrote for a bare platform stage with a standing audience gathered around it in a courtyard in full daylight. The audience were always conscious of themselves and their fellow spectators, and they shared the same "room" as the actors. A sense of immediate presence and the creation of rapport with the audience were all-important. The actor could not afford to imagine he was in a closed world, with silent witnesses dutifully observing him from the darkness.

Shakespeare's theatrical career began at the Rose Theatre in Southwark. The stage was wide and shallow, trapezoid in shape, like a lozenge. This design had a great deal of potential for the theatrical equivalent of cinematic split-screen effects, whereby one group of characters would enter at the door at one end of the tiring-house wall at the back of the stage and another group through the door at the other end, thus creating two rival tableaux. Many of the battle-heavy and faction-filled plays that premiered at the Rose have scenes of just this sort.

At the rear of the Rose stage, there were three capacious exits, each over ten feet wide. Unfortunately, the very limited excavation of a fragmentary portion of the original Globe site, in 1989, revealed nothing about the stage. The first Globe was built in 1599 with similar proportions to those of another theater, the Fortune, albeit that the former was polygonal and looked circular, whereas the latter was rectangular. The building contract for the Fortune survives and allows us to infer that the stage of the Globe was probably substantially wider than it was deep (perhaps forty-three feet wide and twenty-seven feet deep). It may well have been tapered at the front, like that of the Rose.

The capacity of the Globe was said to have been enormous, perhaps in excess of three thousand. It has been conjectured that about eight hundred people may have stood in the yard, with two thousand or more in the three layers of covered galleries. The other "public" playhouses were also of large capacity, whereas the indoor Blackfriars theater that Shakespeare's company began using in 1608—the former refectory of a monastery—had overall internal dimensions of a mere forty-six by sixty feet. It would have made for a much more intimate theatrical experience and had a much smaller capacity, probably of about six hundred people. Since they paid at least six-pence a head, the Blackfriars attracted a more select or "private" audience. The atmosphere would have been closer to that of an indoor performance before the court in the Whitehall Palace or at Richmond. That Shakespeare always wrote for indoor production at court as well as outdoor performance in the public theater should make us cautious about inferring, as some scholars have, that the opportunity provided by the intimacy of the Blackfriars led to a sig-nificant change toward a "chamber" style in his last plays—which, besides, were performed at both the Globe and the Blackfriars. After the occupation of the Blackfriars a five-act structure seems to have become more important to Shakespeare. That was because of artifi-cial lighting: there were musical interludes between the acts, while the candles were trimmed and replaced. Again, though, something similar must have been necessary for indoor court performances throughout his career.

Front of house there were the "gatherers" who collected the money from audience members: a penny to stand in the open-air yard, another penny for a place in the covered galleries, sixpence for the prominent "lord's rooms" to the side of the stage. In the indoor "private" theaters, gallants from the audience who fancied making themselves part of the spectacle sat on stools on the edge of the stage itself. Scholars debate as to how widespread this practice was in the public theaters such as the Globe. Once the audience were in place and the money counted, the gatherers were available to be extras on stage. That is one reason why battles and crowd scenes often come later rather than early in Shakespeare's plays. There was no formal prohibition upon performance by women, and there certainly were women among the gatherers, so it is not beyond the bounds of possi-bility that female crowd members were played by females.

The play began at two o'clock in the afternoon and the theater had to be cleared by five. After the main show, there would be a jig—which consisted not only of dancing, but also of knockabout comedy (it is the origin of the farcical "afterpiece" in the eighteenth-century theater). So the time available for a Shakespeare play was about two and a half hours, somewhere between the "two hours' traffic" men-tioned in the prologue to *Romeo and Juliet* and the "three hours' spectacle" referred to in the preface to the 1647 Folio of Beaumont and Fletcher's plays. The prologue to a play by Thomas Middleton refers to a thousand lines as "one hour's words," so the likelihood is that about two and a half thousand, or a maximum of three thousand lines, made up the performed text. This is indeed the length of most of Shakespeare's comedies, whereas many of his tragedies and histories are much longer, raising the possibility that he wrote full scripts, possibly with eventual publication in mind, in the full knowledge that the stage version would be heavily cut. The short Quarto texts published in his lifetime—they used to be called "Bad" Quartos—provide fascinating evidence as to the kind of cutting that probably took place. So, for instance, the First Quarto of *Hamlet* neatly merges two occasions when Hamlet is overheard, the "Fishmonger" and the "nunnery" scenes.

The social composition of the audience was mixed. The poet Sir John Davies wrote of "A thousand townsmen, gentlemen and whores, / Porters and servingmen" who would "together throng" at the public playhouses. Though moralists associated female playgoing with adultery and the sex trade, many perfectly respectable citizens' wives were regular attendees. Some, no doubt, resembled the modern groupie: a story attested in two different sources has one citizen's wife making a post-show assignation with Richard Burbage and ending up in bed with Shakespeare—supposedly eliciting from the latter the quip that William the Conqueror was before Richard III. Defenders of theater liked to say that by witnessing the comeuppance of villains on the stage, audience members would repent of their own wrongdoings, but the reality is that most people went to the theater then, as they do now, for entertainment more than moral edification. Besides, it would be foolish to suppose that audiences behaved in a homogeneous way: a pamphlet of the 1630s tells of how two men went to see *Pericles* and one of them laughed while the other wept. Bishop John Hall complained that people went to church for the same reasons that they went to the theater: "for company, for custom, for recreation . . . to feed his eyes or his ears . . . or perhaps for sleep."

Men-about-town and clever young lawyers went to be seen as much as to see. In the modern popular imagination, shaped not least by *Shakespeare in Love* and the opening sequence of Laurence Olivier's *Henry V* film, the penny-paying groundlings stand in the yard hurling abuse or encouragement and hazelnuts or orange peel at the actors, while the sophisticates in the covered galleries appreciate Shakespeare's soaring poetry. The reality was probably the other way around. A "groundling" was a kind of fish, so the nickname suggests the penny audience standing below the level of the stage and gazing in silent open-mouthed wonder at the spectacle unfolding above them. The more difficult audience members, who kept up a running commentary of clever remarks on the performance and who occasionally got into quarrels with players, were the gallants. Like Hollywood movies in modern times, Elizabethan and Jacobean plays exercised a powerful influence on the fashion and behavior of the young. John Marston mocks the lawyers who would open their lips, perhaps to court a girl, and out would "flow / Naught but pure Juliet and Romeo."

THE ENSEMBLE AT WORK

In the absence of typewriters and photocopying machines, reading aloud would have been the means by which the company got to know a new play. The tradition of the playwright reading his complete script to the assembled company endured for generations. A copy would then have been taken to the Master of the Revels for licensing. The theater book-holder or prompter would then have copied the parts for distribution to the actors. A partbook consisted of the character's lines, with each speech preceded by the last three or four words of the speech before, the so-called "cue." These would have been taken away and studied or "conned." During this period of learning the parts, an actor might have had some one-to-one instruction, perhaps from the dramatist, perhaps from a senior actor who had played the same part before, and, in the case of an apprentice, from his master. A high percentage of Desdemona's lines occur in dialogue with Othello, of Lady Macbeth's with Macbeth, Cleopatra's with Antony, and Volumnia's with Coriolanus. The roles would almost certainly have been taken by the apprentice of the lead actor, usually Burbage, who delivers the majority of the cues. Given that

8. Hypothetical reconstruction of the interior of an Elizabethan playhouse during a performance.

apprentices lodged with their masters, there would have been ample opportunity for personal instruction, which may be what made it possible for young men to play such demanding parts.

After the parts were learned, there may have been no more than a single rehearsal before the first performance. With six different plays to be put on every week, there was no time for more. Actors, then, would go into a show with a very limited sense of the whole. The notion of a collective rehearsal process that is itself a process of discovery for the actors is wholly modern and would have been incomprehensible to Shakespeare and his original ensemble. Given the number of parts an actor had to hold in his memory, the forgetting of lines was probably more frequent than in the modern theater. The book-holder was on hand to prompt.

Backstage personnel included the property man, the tire-man who oversaw the costumes, call boys, attendants, and the musicians, who might play at various times from the main stage, the rooms above, and within the tiring-house. Scriptwriters sometimes made a nuisance of themselves backstage. There was often tension between the acting companies and the freelance playwrights from whom they purchased scripts: it was a smart move on the part of Shakespeare and the Lord Chamberlain's Men to bring the writing process in-house.

Scenery was limited, though sometimes set pieces were brought on (a bank of flowers, a bed, the mouth of hell). The trapdoor from below, the gallery stage above, and the curtained discovery space at the back allowed for an array of special effects: the rising of ghosts and apparitions, the descent of gods, dialogue between a character at a window and another at ground level, the revelation of a statue or a pair of lovers playing at chess. Ingenious use could be made of props, as with the ass's head in *A Midsummer Night's Dream*. In a theater that does not clutter the stage with the material paraphernalia of everyday life, those objects that are deployed may take on powerful symbolic weight, as when Shylock bears his weighing scales in one hand and knife in the other, thus becoming a parody of the figure of Justice who traditionally bears a sword and a balance. Among the more significant items in the property cupboard of Shakespeare's company, there would have been a throne (the "chair of state"), joint stools, books, bottles, coins, purses, letters (which are brought on stage, read, or referred to on about eighty occasions in the complete works), maps, gloves, a set of stocks (in which Kent is put in *King Lear*), rings, rapiers, daggers, broadswords, staves, pistols, masks and vizards, heads and skulls, torches and tapers and lanterns which served to signal night scenes on the daylit stage, a buck's head, an ass's head, animal costumes. Live animals also put in appearances, most notably the dog Crab in *The Two Gentlemen of Verona* and possibly a young polar bear in *The Winter's Tale*.

The costumes were the most important visual dimension of the play. Playwrights were paid between £2 and £6 per script, whereas Alleyn was not averse to paying £20 for "a black velvet cloak with sleeves embroidered all with silver and gold." No matter the period of the play, actors always wore contemporary costume. The excitement for the audience came not from any impression of historical accuracy, but from the richness of the attire and perhaps the transgressive thrill of the knowledge that here were commoners like themselves strutting in the costumes of courtiers in effective defiance of the strict sumptuary laws whereby in real life people had to wear the clothes that befitted their social station.

To an even greater degree than props, costumes could carry symbolic importance. Racial characteristics could be suggested: a breastplate and helmet for a Roman soldier, a turban for a Turk, long robes for exotic characters such as Moors, a gabardine for a Jew. The figure of Time, as in *The Winter's Tale*, would be equipped with hourglass, scythe, and wings; Rumour, who speaks the prologue of *2 Henry IV*, wore a costume adorned with a thousand tongues. The wardrobe in the tiring-house of the Globe would have contained much of the same stock as that of rival manager Philip Henslowe at the Rose: green gowns for outlaws and foresters, black for melancholy men such as Jaques and people in mourning such as the Countess in *All's Well That Ends Well* (at the beginning of *Hamlet*, the prince is still in mourning black when everyone else is in festive garb for the wedding of the new king), a gown and hood for a friar (or a feigned friar like the duke in *Measure for Measure*), blue coats and tawny to distinguish the followers of rival factions, a leather apron and ruler for a carpenter (as in the opening scene of *Julius Caesar*—and in *A Midsummer Night's Dream*, where this is the only sign that Peter Quince is a carpenter), a cockle hat with staff and a pair of sandals for a pilgrim or palmer (the disguise assumed by Helen in *All's Well*), bodices and kirtles with farthingales beneath for the boys who are to be dressed as girls. A gender switch such as that of Rosalind or Jessica seems to have taken between fifty and eighty lines of dialogue—Viola does not resume her "maiden weeds," but remains in her boy's costume to the end of *Twelfth Night* because a change would have slowed down the action at just the moment it was speeding to a climax. Henslowe's inventory also included "a robe for to go invisible": Oberon, Puck, and Ariel must have had something similar.

As the costumes appealed to the eyes, so there was music for the ears. Comedies included many songs. Desdemona's willow song, perhaps a late addition to the text, is a rare and thus exceptionally poignant example from tragedy. Trumpets and tuckets sounded for ceremonial entrances, drums denoted an army on the march. Background music could create atmosphere, as at the beginning of *Twelfth Night*, during the lovers' dialogue near the end of *The Mer-*

chant of Venice, when the statue seemingly comes to life in *The Winter's Tale*, and for the revival of *Pericles* and of *Lear* (in the Quarto text, but not the Folio). The haunting sound of the hautboy suggested a realm beyond the human, as when the god Hercules is imagined deserting Mark Antony. Dances symbolized the harmony of the end of a comedy—though in Shakespeare's world of mingled joy and sorrow, someone is usually left out of the circle.

The most important resource was, of course, the actors themselves. They needed many skills: in the words of one contemporary commentator, "dancing, activity, music, song, elocution, ability of body, memory, skill of weapon, pregnancy of wit." Their bodies were as significant as their voices. Hamlet tells the player to "suit the action to the word, the word to the action": moments of strong emotion, known as "passions," relied on a repertoire of dramatic gestures as well as a modulation of the voice. When Titus Andronicus has had his hand chopped off, he asks "How can I grace my talk, / Wanting a hand to give it action?" A pen portrait of "The Character of an Excellent Actor" by the dramatist John Webster is almost certainly based on his impression of Shakespeare's leading man, Richard Burbage: "By a full and significant action of body, he charms our attention: sit in a full theater, and you will think you see so many lines drawn from the circumference of so many ears, whiles the actor is the centre. . . ."

Though Burbage was admired above all others, praise was also heaped upon the apprentice players whose alto voices fitted them for the parts of women. A spectator at Oxford in 1610 records how the audience were reduced to tears by the pathos of Desdemona's death. The puritans who fumed about the biblical prohibition upon cross-dressing and the encouragement to sodomy constituted by the sight of an adult male kissing a teenage boy on stage were a small minority. Little is known, however, about the characteristics of the leading apprentices in Shakespeare's company. It may perhaps be inferred that one was a lot taller than the other, since Shakespeare often wrote for a pair of female friends, one tall and fair, the other short and dark (Helena and Hermia, Rosalind and Celia, Beatrice and Hero).

We know little about Shakespeare's own acting roles—an early allusion indicates that he often took royal parts, and a venerable tradition gives him old Adam in *As You Like It* and the ghost of old King Hamlet. Save for Burbage's lead roles and the generic part of the clown, all such castings are mere speculation. We do not even know for sure whether the original Falstaff was Will Kempe or another actor who specialized in comic roles, Thomas Pope.

Kempe left the company in early 1599. Tradition has it that he fell out with Shakespeare over the matter of excessive improvisation. He was replaced by Robert Armin, who was less of a clown and more of a cerebral wit: this explains the difference between such parts as Lancelet Gobbo and Dogberry, which were written for Kempe, and the more verbally sophisticated Feste and Lear's Fool, which were written for Armin.

One thing that is clear from surviving "plots" or storyboards of plays from the period is that a degree of doubling was necessary. *2 Henry VI* has over sixty speaking parts, but more than half of the characters only appear in a single scene and most scenes have only six to eight speakers. At a stretch, the play could be performed by thirteen actors. When Thomas Platter saw *Julius Caesar* at the Globe in 1599, he noted that there were about fifteen. Why doesn't Paris go to the Capulet ball in *Romeo and Juliet?* Perhaps because he was doubled with Mercutio, who does. In *The Winter's Tale*, Mamillius might have come back as Perdita and Antigonus been doubled by Camillo, making the partnership with Paulina at the end a very neat touch. Titania and Oberon are often played by the same pair as Hippolyta and Theseus, suggesting a symbolic matching of the rulers of the worlds of night and day, but it is questionable whether there would have been time for the necessary costume changes. As so often, one is left in a realm of tantalizing speculation.

THE KING'S MAN

On Queen Elizabeth's death in 1603, the new king, James I, who had held the Scottish throne as James VI since he had been an infant, immediately took the Lord Chamberlain's Men under his direct patronage. Henceforth they would be the King's Men, and for the rest of Shakespeare's career they were favored with far more court performances than any of their rivals. There even seem to have been rumors early in the reign that Shakespeare and Burbage were being considered for knighthoods, an unprecedented honor for mere actors—and one that in the event was not accorded to a member of the profession for nearly three hundred years, when the title was bestowed upon Henry Irving, the leading Shakespearean actor of Queen Victoria's reign.

Shakespeare's productivity rate slowed in the Jacobean years, not because of age or some personal trauma, but because there were frequent outbreaks of plague, causing the theaters to be closed for long periods. The King's Men were forced to spend many months on the road. Between November 1603 and 1608, they were to be found at various towns in the south and Midlands, though Shakespeare probably did not tour with them by this time. He had bought a large house back home in Stratford and was accumulating other property. He may indeed have stopped acting soon after the new king took the throne. With the London theaters closed so much of the time and a large repertoire on the stocks, Shakespeare seems to have focused his energies on writing a few long and complex tragedies that could have been played on demand at court: *Othello*, *King Lear*, *Antony and Cleopatra*, *Coriolanus*, and *Cymbeline* are among his longest and poetically grandest plays. *Macbeth* only survives in a shorter text, which shows signs of adaptation after Shakespeare's death. The bitterly satirical *Timon of Athens*, apparently a collaboration with Thomas Middleton that may have failed on the stage, also belongs to this period. In comedy, too, he wrote longer and morally darker works than in the Elizabethan period, pushing at the very bounds of the form in *Measure for Measure* and *All's Well That Ends Well*.

From 1608 onward, when the King's Men began occupying the indoor Blackfriars playhouse (as a winter house, meaning that they only used the outdoor Globe in summer?), Shakespeare turned to a more romantic style. His company had a great success with a revived and altered version of an old pastoral play called *Mucedorus*. It even featured a bear. The younger dramatist John Fletcher, meanwhile, sometimes working in collaboration with Francis Beaumont, was pioneering a new style of tragicomedy, a mix of romance and royalism laced with intrigue and pastoral excursions. Shakespeare experimented with this idiom in *Cymbeline* and it was presumably with his blessing that Fletcher eventually took over as the King's Men's company dramatist. The two writers apparently collaborated on three plays in the years 1612–14: a lost romance called *Cardenio* (based on the love-madness of a character in Cervantes' *Don Quixote*), *Henry VIII* (originally staged with the title *All Is True*), and *The Two Noble Kinsmen*, a dramatization of Chaucer's "Knight's Tale." These were written after Shakespeare's two final solo-authored plays, *The Winter's Tale*, a self-consciously old-fashioned work dramatizing the pastoral romance of his old enemy Robert Greene, and *The Tempest*, which at one and the same time drew together multiple theatrical traditions, diverse reading, and contemporary interest in the fate of a ship that had been wrecked on the way to the New World.

The collaborations with Fletcher suggest that Shakespeare's career ended with a slow fade rather than the sudden retirement supposed by the nineteenth-century Romantic critics who read Prospero's epilogue to *The Tempest* as Shakespeare's personal farewell to his art. In the last few years of his life Shakespeare certainly spent more of his time in Stratford-upon-Avon, where he became further involved in property dealing and litigation. But his London life also continued. In 1613 he made his first major London property purchase: a freehold house in the Blackfriars district, close to his company's indoor theater. *The Two Noble Kinsmen* may have been written as late as 1614, and Shakespeare was in London on business a little over a year before he died of an unknown cause at home in Stratford-upon-Avon in 1616, probably on his fifty-second birthday.

About half the sum of his works were published in his lifetime, in texts of variable quality. A few years after his death, his fellow actors began putting together an authorized edition of his complete *Comedies, Histories and Tragedies*. It appeared in 1623, in large "Folio" format. This collection of thirty-six plays gave Shakespeare his immortality. In the words of his fellow dramatist Ben Jonson, who contributed two poems of praise at the start of the Folio, the body of his work made him "a monument without a tomb":

> And art alive still while thy book doth live
> And we have wits to read and praise to give . . .
> He was not of an age, but for all time!

SHAKESPEARE'S WORKS:
A CHRONOLOGY

1589–91	*? Arden of Faversham* (possible part authorship)
1589–92	*The Taming of the Shrew*
1589–92	*? Edward the Third* (possible part authorship)
1591	*The Second Part of Henry the Sixth*, originally called *The First Part of the Contention betwixt the Two Famous Houses of York and Lancaster* (element of coauthorship possible)
1591	*The Third Part of Henry the Sixth*, originally called *The True Tragedy of Richard Duke of York* (element of co-authorship probable)
1591–92	*The Two Gentlemen of Verona*
1591–92; perhaps revised 1594	*The Lamentable Tragedy of Titus Andronicus* (probably cowritten with, or revising an earlier version by, George Peele)
1592	*The First Part of Henry the Sixth*, probably with Thomas Nashe and others
1592/94	*King Richard the Third*
1593	*Venus and Adonis* (poem)
1593–94	*The Rape of Lucrece* (poem)
1593–1608	*Sonnets* (154 poems, published 1609 with *A Lover's Complaint*, a poem of disputed authorship)
1592–94/ 1600–03	*Sir Thomas More* (a single scene for a play originally by Anthony Munday, with other revisions by Henry Chettle, Thomas Dekker, and Thomas Heywood)
1594	*The Comedy of Errors*
1595	*Love's Labour's Lost*

1595–97	*Love's Labour's Won* (a lost play, unless the original title for another comedy)
1595–96	*A Midsummer Night's Dream*
1595–96	*The Tragedy of Romeo and Juliet*
1595–96	*King Richard the Second*
1595–97	*The Life and Death of King John* (possibly earlier)
1596–97	*The Merchant of Venice*
1596–97	*The First Part of Henry the Fourth*
1597–98	*The Second Part of Henry the Fourth*
1598	*Much Ado About Nothing*
1598–99	*The Passionate Pilgrim* (20 poems, some not by Shakespeare)
1599	*The Life of Henry the Fifth*
1599	"To the Queen" (epilogue for a court performance)
1599	*As You Like It*
1599	*The Tragedy of Julius Caesar*
1600–01	*The Tragedy of Hamlet, Prince of Denmark* (perhaps revising an earlier version)
1600–01	*The Merry Wives of Windsor* (perhaps revising version of 1597–99)
1601	"Let the Bird of Loudest Lay" (poem, known since 1807 as "The Phoenix and Turtle" [turtledove])
1601	*Twelfth Night, or What You Will*
1601–02	*The Tragedy of Troilus and Cressida*
1604	*The Tragedy of Othello, the Moor of Venice*
1604	*Measure for Measure*
1605	*All's Well That Ends Well*
1605	*The Life of Timon of Athens*, with Thomas Middleton
1605–06	*The Tragedy of King Lear*
1605–08	? contribution to *The Four Plays in One* (lost, except for *A Yorkshire Tragedy*, mostly by Thomas Middleton)

1606	*The Tragedy of Macbeth* (surviving text has additional scenes by Thomas Middleton)
1606–07	*The Tragedy of Antony and Cleopatra*
1608	*The Tragedy of Coriolanus*
1608	*Pericles, Prince of Tyre*, with George Wilkins
1610	*The Tragedy of Cymbeline*
1611	*The Winter's Tale*
1611	*The Tempest*
1612–13	*Cardenio*, with John Fletcher (survives only in later adaptation called *Double Falsehood* by Lewis Theobald)
1613	*Henry VIII (All Is True)*, with John Fletcher
1613–14	*The Two Noble Kinsmen*, with John Fletcher

THE HISTORY BEHIND THE TRAGEDIES: A CHRONOLOGY

Era/Date	Event	Location	Play
Greek myth	Trojan War	Troy	*Troilus and Cressida*
Greek myth	Theseus king of Athens	Athens	*The Two Noble Kinsmen*
c. tenth–ninth century BC?	Leir king of Britain (legendary)	Britain	*King Lear*
535–510 BC	Tarquin II king of Rome	Rome	*The Rape of Lucrece*
493 BC	Caius Martius captures Corioli	Italy	*Coriolanus*
431–404 BC	Peloponnesian War	Greece	*Timon of Athens*
17 Mar 45 BC	Battle of Munda: Caesar's victory over Pompey's sons	Munda, Spain	*Julius Caesar*
Oct 45 BC	Caesar returns to Rome in triumph	Rome	*Julius Caesar*
15 Mar 44 BC	Assassination of Caesar	Rome	*Julius Caesar*
27 Nov 43 BC	Formation of Second Triumvirate	Rome	*Julius Caesar*
Oct 42 BC	Battle of Philippi	Philippi, Macedonia	*Julius Caesar*
Winter 41–40 BC	Antony visits Cleopatra	Egypt	*Antony and Cleopatra*
Oct 40 BC	Pact of Brundisium; marriage of Antony and Octavia	Italy	*Antony and Cleopatra*
39 BC	Pact of Misenum between Pompey and the triumvirs	Campania, Italy	*Antony and Cleopatra*

Era/Date	Event	Location	Play
39–38 BC	Ventidius defeats the Parthians in a series of engagements	Syria	*Antony and Cleopatra*
34 BC	Cleopatra and her children proclaimed rulers of the eastern Mediterranean	Alexandria	*Antony and Cleopatra*
2 Sep 31 BC	Battle of Actium	On the coast of western Greece	*Antony and Cleopatra*
Aug 30 BC	Death of Antony	Alexandria	*Antony and Cleopatra*
12 Aug 30 BC	Death of Cleopatra	Alexandria	*Antony and Cleopatra*
Early first century AD	Cunobelinus/ Cymbeline rules Britain (and dies before AD 43)	Britain	*Cymbeline*
During the reign of a fictional (late?) Roman emperor		Rome	*Titus Andronicus*
c. ninth–tenth century AD	Existence of legendary Amleth?	Denmark	*Hamlet*
15 Aug 1040	Death of Duncan I of Scotland	Bothnguane, Scotland	*Macbeth*
1053	Malcolm invades Scotland	Scotland	*Macbeth*
15 Aug 1057	Death of Macbeth	Lumphanan, Scotland	*Macbeth*
7 Oct 1571	Naval battle of Lepanto between Christians and Turks	The Mediterranean, off the coast of Greece	A context for *Othello*

FURTHER READING AND VIEWING

CRITICAL APPROACHES

Adamson, Jane, *Troilus and Cressida*, Harvester New Critical Introductions to Shakespeare Series (1987). Useful guide to text, characters, and context.

Bowen, Barbara E., *Gender in the Theater of War: Shakespeare's Troilus and Cressida* (1993). Feminist account of play's politics and gender.

Bradshaw, Graham, *Shakespeare's Scepticism* (1987). Highly intelligent, acute critical reading.

Charnes, Linda, "'So Unsecret to Ourselves': Notorious Identity and the Material Subject in Shakespeare's *Troilus and Cressida*," *Shakespeare Quarterly* 40 (1989), pp. 413–40. Dense investigation of questions of identity.

Colie, Rosalie L., "Forms and Their Meanings: 'Monumental Mock'ry,'" in *Shakespeare's Living Art* (1974), pp. 317–49. Lucid and compelling.

Elton, W. R. *Shakespeare's Troilus and Cressida and the Inns of Court Revels* (2000). Fascinating, detailed study which argues that the play was written for an audience of law students and lawyers.

Girard, René, "The Politics of Desire in *Troilus and Cressida*," in *Shakespeare and the Question of Theory*, ed. Patricia Parker and Geoffrey Hartman (1985), pp. 188–209. Critically sophisticated.

Grady, Hugh, *Shakespeare's Universal Wolf: Studies in Early Modern Reification* (1996). Striking mix of historical and Marxist thinking.

Greene, Gayle, "Shakespeare's Cressida: 'A Kind of Self,'" in *The Woman's Part: Feminist Criticism of Shakespeare*, ed. Carolyn Ruth Swift Lenz, Gayle Greene, and Carol Thomas Neely (1983), pp. 133–49. Good example of a feminist approach.

Martin, Priscilla, ed., *Shakespeare: Troilus and Cressida: A Casebook* (1976). Selection of important early criticism and influential twentieth-century criticism up to 1975.

Rossiter, A. P., *Angel with Horns and Other Shakespeare Lectures* (1961). One of the first modern readings of the play.

Vaughan, Virginia Mason, "Daughters of the Game: *Troilus and Cressida* and the Sexual Discourse of Sixteenth-Century England," *Women's Studies*

International Forum, No. 3 (1990), pp. 209–20. Historical placing of attitudes to women and sex.

THE PLAY IN PERFORMANCE

Apfelbaum, Roger, *Shakespeare's Troilus and Cressida: Textual Problems and Performance Solutions* (2004). Detailed exploration of stage history.

Jackson, Russell, and Robert Smallwood, eds., *Players of Shakespeare 3* (1993). Simon Russell Beale discusses playing Thersites in Sam Mendes' RSC production.

Loggins, Vernon P. *The Life of Our Design: Organization and Related Strategies in Troilus and Cressida* (1992). Detailed discussion of the play's structure and problems/possibilities in performance.

McCandless, David, *Gender and Performance in Shakespeare's Problem Comedies* (1997). Marries theory and performance: chapter 3 on *Troilus and Cressida*.

Shirley, Frances A., ed., *Troilus and Cressida*, Shakespeare in Production Series (2005). Introduction to the play's history with annotated play text including stage directions of important productions.

AVAILABLE ON DVD

Troilus and Cressida, directed by Jonathan Miller (1981, DVD 2006). Part of the BBC Shakespeare. Strong performances from Anton Lesser, Suzanne Burden, Charles Gray, and Benjamin Whitrow.

REFERENCES

1. Mark van Doren, *Shakespeare* (1939), p. 202.
2. W. R. Elton, *Shakespeare's Troilus and Cressida and the Inns of Court Revels* (2000), p. 7.
3. Rosalie Colie, *Shakespeare's Living Art* (1974), pp. 320–21.
4. Alvin Kernan, "The Satiric Character of Thersites" (1959), in Priscilla Martin, ed., *Troilus and Cressida: A Casebook* (1976), p. 98.
5. A. P. Rossiter, *Angel with Horns and Other Shakespeare Lectures* (1961), pp. 133–34.
6. Jan Kott, *Shakespeare Our Contemporary* (1965), p. 65.
7. Northrop Frye, *The Myth of Deliverance: Reflections on Shakespeare's Problem Comedies* (1983), p. 63.
8. Frank Kermode, *Shakespeare's Language* (2000), p. 134.
9. Gayle Greene, "Shakespeare's Cressida: 'A Kind of Self,'" in Carolyn Ruth Swift Lenz, Gayle Greene, and Carol Thomas Neely, eds., *The Woman's Part: Feminist Criticism of Shakespeare* (1983), pp. 133–49 (pp. 136–37).
10. Elizabeth Freund, "'Ariachne's Broken Woof': The Rhetoric of Citation in *Troilus and Cressida*," in Patricia Parker and Geoffrey Hartman, *Shakespeare and the Question of Theory* (1985), pp. 19–36 (p. 21).
11. R. A. Foakes, *Shakespeare, the Dark Comedies to the Last Plays: From Satire to Celebration* (1971), pp. 44–45.
12. Bruce R. Smith, *Homosexual Desire in Shakespeare's England* (1991), p. 198.
13. G. Wilson Knight, *The Wheel of Fire* (1930), pp. 47, 62.
14. Kott, *Shakespeare Our Contemporary*, p. 64.
15. Smith, *Homosexual Desire in Shakespeare's England*, p. 59.
16. Hugh Grady, *Shakespeare's Universal Wolf: Studies in Early Modern Reification* (1996), p. 59.
17. Qa (1609), title page.
18. Qb, (1609), p. 2.
19. John Dryden, *Troilus and Cressida; or, Truth Found Too Late* (1679), Prologue.
20. *Troilus and Cressida* (1852), p. 7.
21. *Birmingham Gazette*, 13 May 1913.
22. *Birmingham Gazette*, 13 May 1913.

23. *Morning Post,* 14 May 1913.
24. *Evening Standard,* 3 June 1907.
25. *Morning Post,* 8 November 1923.
26. Frances A. Shirley, *Troilus and Cressida* (2005), p. 18.
27. *Stratford-on-Avon Herald,* 24 April 1936.
28. Harold N. Hillebrand, ed., *Troilus and Cressida* (1953), p. 512.
29. *The Times,* London, quoted in Wilhelm Hortmann, *Shakespeare on the German Stage: The Twentieth Century* (1998), p. 108.
30. *Birmingham Post,* 25 April 1936.
31. *The Times,* London, 25 April 1936.
32. *Birmingham Mail,* 25 April 1936.
33. *The Times,* London, 24 September 1938.
34. *Birmingham Gazette,* 9 July 1948.
35. *Birmingham Mail,* 3 July 1948.
36. *Financial Times,* 14 July 1954.
37. *Daily Mail,* 14 July 1954.
38. *Daily Express,* 4 April 1956.
39. Shirley, *Troilus and Cressida,* p. 33.
40. *Daily Express,* 27 July 1960.
41. *Star Ledger,* 19 April 2001.
42. John Pettigrew and Jamie Portman, *Stratford: The First Thirty Years* (1985), Vol. 1, p. 168.
43. *Daily Telegraph,* 19 June 1976.
44. *The Times,* London, 19 June 1976.
45. Henry Fenwick, *The BBC TV Shakespeare: Troilus and Cressida* (1981), p. 27.
46. Wilhelm Hortmann, "The Scenography of Recent German Productions," in *Foreign Shakespeare* (1993), pp. 241–42.
47. *Sunday Telegraph,* 21 March 1999.
48. *Independent on Sunday,* 21 March 1999.
49. John Golder and Richard Madelaine, eds., *O Brave New World* (2001), p. 263.
50. *Guardian,* 16 August 2006.
51. *Sunday Times,* London, 16 February 2003.
52. *Birmingham Mail,* 14 July 1954.
53. Shirley, *Troilus and Cressida,* p. 82.
54. *Telegraph,* 30 May 2008.
55. *Guardian,* 29 May 2008.
56. Quoted in Fenwick, *Troilus and Cressida,* p. 24.
57. *The Times,* London, 24 July 2009.

58. W. H. W., *Birmingham Mail*, 27 July 1960.

59. J. C. Trewin, *Birmingham Post*, 27 July 1960.

60. Edmund Gardner, *Stratford-upon-Avon Herald*, 29 July 1960.

61. *Sunday Times*, London, 31 July 1960.

62. John Barton, "Company Notes," RSC theater program, 1968.

63. Benedict Nightingale, *New Statesman*, 16 August 1968.

64. Irving Wardle, *The Times*, London, 9 August 1968.

65. Nightingale, *New Statesman*, 16 August 1968.

66. B. A. Young, *Financial Times*, 9 August 1968.

67. Herbert Kretzmer, *Daily Express*, 9 August 1968.

68. Barton, "Company notes."

69. Robert Cushman, *Observer*, 22 August 1976.

70. Michael Billington, *Guardian*, 19 August 1976.

71. Billington, *Guardian*, 19 August 1976.

72. B. A. Young, *Financial Times*, 18 August 1976.

73. Roger Warren, *Shakespeare Survey*, 30 (1977), p. 174.

74. J. W. Lambert, *Sunday Times*, 22 August 1976.

75. Warren, *Shakespeare Survey*, 30, p. 176.

76. Irving Wardle, *The Times*, London, 8 July 1981.

77. *Shakespeare Survey*, 35 (1982), p. 149.

78. Michael Billington, *Guardian*, 9 July 1981.

79. Nicholas Shrimpton, *Shakespeare Survey*, 39 (1986), p. 203.

80. John Peter, *Sunday Times*, London, 30 June 1985.

81. Irving Wardle, *The Times*, London, 27 June 1985.

82. Peter Holland, *Shakespeare Survey*, 44 (1992), p. 175.

83. Paul Taylor, *Independent*, 30 June 1990.

84. Robert Smallwood, *Shakespeare Quarterly*, 42 (1991), p. 357.

85. Smallwood, *Shakespeare Quarterly*, 42, p. 357.

86. Holland, *Shakespeare Survey*, 44, p. 175.

87. Simon Russell Beale, *Players of Shakespeare* 3, p. 160.

88. Charles Spencer, *Daily Telegraph*, 28 April 1990.

89. Russell Jackson, *Shakespeare Quarterly*, 48 (1997), p. 212.

90. Ian Judge, *Troilus and Cressida* RSC Programme Notes, 1976.

91. Michael Billington, *Guardian*, 25 July 1996.

92. Charles Spencer, *Daily Telegraph*, 9 November 1998.

93. Paul Taylor, *Independent*, 7 November 1998.

94. Joyce McMillan, *Scotsman*, 16 August 2006.

95. Edmund Gardner, *Stratford-upon-Avon Herald*, 29 July 1960.

96. Nightingale, *New Statesman*, 16 August 1968.

97. W. A. Darlington, *Daily Telegraph*, 9 August 1968.

98. Warren, *Shakespeare Survey*, 30, p. 175.

99. *Daily Mail*, 8 July 1981.

100. Carol Royle, in an interview with Linda Christmas, *Guardian*, July 1981.

101. Juliet Stevenson in Carol Rutter, *Clamorous Voices* (1988), p. xviii.

102. Nicholas Shrimpton, *Shakespeare Survey*, 39 (1987), p. 203.

103. Roger Warren, *Shakespeare Quarterly*, 37 (1986), p. 117.

104. Benedict Nightingale, *Guardian*, 28 April 1990.

105. Martin Hoyle, *The Times*, London, 28 April 1990.

106. Nicholas de Jongh, *Evening Standard*, 25 July 1996.

107. *Daily Telegraph*, 26 July 1996.

108. Spencer, *Daily Telegraph*, 9 November 1998.

109. Alistair MacAulay, *Financial Times*, 10 November 1998.

ACKNOWLEDGMENTS AND PICTURE CREDITS

Preparation of "*Troilus and Cressida* in Performance" was assisted by a generous grant from the CAPITAL Centre (Creativity and Performance in Teaching and Learning) of the University of Warwick for research in the RSC archive at the Shakespeare Birthplace Trust.

Thanks as always to our indefatigable and eagle-eyed copy editor Tracey Day and to Ray Addicott for overseeing the production process with rigor and calmness.

The second half of the introduction ("The Critics Debate") draws extensively on a longer overview of the play's critical history prepared for us by Sarah Carter.

Picture research by Michelle Morton. Grateful acknowledgment is made to the Shakespeare Birthplace Trust for assistance with picture research (special thanks to Helen Hargest) and reproduction fees.

Images of RSC productions are supplied by the Shakespeare Centre Library and Archive, Stratford-upon-Avon. This Library, maintained by the Shakespeare Birthplace Trust, holds the most important collection of Shakespeare material in the UK, including the Royal Shakespeare Company's official archive. It is open to the public free of charge.

For more information see www.shakespeare.org.uk.

1. Directed by Anthony Quayle (1948) Angus McBean © Royal Shakespeare Company
2. Directed by John Barton (1976) Joe Cocks Studio Collection © Shakespeare Birthplace Trust
3. Directed by Sam Mendes (1990) Joe Cocks Studio Collection © Shakespeare Birthplace Trust

4. Directed by Peter Hall and John Barton (1960) Angus McBean © Royal Shakespeare Company

5. Directed by Howard Davies (1985) Joe Cocks Studio Collection © Shakespeare Birthplace Trust

6. Directed by Michael Boyd (1998) Joe Cocks Studio Collection © Shakespeare Birthplace Trust

7. Directed by Trevor Nunn (1999) © Donald Cooper/photostage .co.uk

8. Reconstructed Elizabethan Playhouse © Charcoalblue

MODERN LIBRARY IS ONLINE AT
WWW.MODERNLIBRARY.COM

MODERN LIBRARY ONLINE IS YOUR GUIDE TO CLASSIC LITERATURE ON THE WEB

THE MODERN LIBRARY E-NEWSLETTER

Our free e-mail newsletter is sent to subscribers, and features sample chapters, interviews with and essays by our authors, upcoming books, special promotions, announcements, and news. To subscribe to the Modern Library e-newsletter, visit **www.modernlibrary.com**

THE MODERN LIBRARY WEBSITE

Check out the Modern Library website at
www.modernlibrary.com for:

- The Modern Library e-newsletter
- A list of our current and upcoming titles and series
- Reading Group Guides and exclusive author spotlights
- Special features with information on the classics and other paperback series
- Excerpts from new releases and other titles
- A list of our e-books and information on where to buy them
- The Modern Library Editorial Board's 100 Best Novels and 100 Best Nonfiction Books of the Twentieth Century written in the English language
- News and announcements

Questions? E-mail us at **modernlibrary@randomhouse.com**.
For questions about examination or desk copies, please visit
the Random House Academic Resources site at
www.randomhouse.com/academic